A Musical Season

Andrew Porter

A Musical Season

A Critic from Abroad in America

The Viking Press
New York

Contents

A Musical Season

The Mérimée Perspective

The dramatic force of Bizet's *Carmen*, an *opéra comique* done very often, and seldom very well, is most potently released in a small theater, by a cast of actors who share the language of the audience. In most large opera houses the casts are international, yet *Carmen* cannot be denied to them, any more than *Don Giovanni*, *Fidelio*, and many another work more striking in smaller space—for then most big cities would have no *Carmen*, and most big companies would run short of the popular repertory they need to keep going at all. However, since these major companies command the major interpreters, they can start with a different advantage, and by it overcome the space handicap and the language barrier, both of which reduce the impact of a piece that was meant, above all things, to be emotionally direct. These familiar reflections are fresh-prompted by the Metropolitan's new presentation of *Carmen*, which is boldly and intelligently addressed to just such problems. Other, special problems were involved, too. The basic cast had been determined, if unwittingly, by Sir Rudolf Bing, who had engaged Marilyn Horne, James McCracken, and Tom

Krause for a revival of *Tannhäuser*. Goeran Gentele, preferring to open his new regime with a new show, switched them to *Carmen*. Before his death he had plotted the production that has now been executed in detail by Bodo Igesz. Mr Gentele's aim was not a "spectacular" such as Karajan mounted in Salzburg (where the heroine summoned a corps de ballet to support her intimate dance in Act II); visually this *Carmen* is sober: no horses, no bulls, not even a donkey. Three things make it unusual—things that have been tried before, but never all at once in a large-scale presentation. Guiraud's intrusive recitatives have been scrapped in favor of the spoken dialogue of the original. A dozen or more passages of music that were cut before the first performance of 1875 have been reinstated. And an attempt has been made to re-establish the "Mérimée perspective," which places Don José Lizarrabengoa, rather than the titular heroine, at the center of the drama.

The curtain rises in mid-prelude, and as the Fate motif surges from the pit José is revealed on the darkened stage, staring with wild surmise into the blackness; then he disappears amid the bright bustle of the opening chorus. At the final curtain he is again alone, with Carmen's corpse, on an empty stage: no crowd, no Escamillo, just a single row of heads high above, peering over the rim of the bull ring. He is brought into similar prominence during several moments that traditionally "belong" to Carmen. The Habanera is almost a duet, with José's line in dumb show. It contradicts the text ("Si tu ne m'aimes pas, je t'aime"—but this José is visibly panting with love), contradicts the direction that José should remain indifferent to the song, and the implication that it is his very indifference which piques Carmen's interest. The snatch of dialogue before the flower is thrown ("What are you doing there?" "Making a chain for my firing-pin" "Firing-pin indeed! . . . Firer of my soul") is not restored; at the Fate motif the lights dim to a glow around

Carmen, another round José. Something is lost by this handling of the Habanera; instead, we learn that José was lost from the moment he set eyes on his *démon*.

At the close of the act José positively insures Carmen's escape, barring the way to her pursuers. The spoken dialogue reminds us that he has fled Navarre and joined the Army because in quarrel he killed a man; indeed, the text has been rewritten to make this more evident than in Meilhac's and Halévy's original. (In Mérimée's tale, he also kills Carmen's husband, and the lieutenant.) The man's violence is stressed. He handles Carmen roughly. In the duel he goes for the elegant *torero* like a maddened, blundering bull (their duet, though shortened, still contains some of the weakest music in the opera, but is very well staged). Mr McCracken is good at this. In *Otello* he has often conveyed the sense of violence scarce-checked, smoldering beneath a heavy surface until suddenly it breaks through. Verdi spoke slightingly of *Carmen*, but his Othello borrowed features of Don José; the same singers—Zenatello, Martinelli, in our day Jon Vickers and Mr McCracken—have often excelled in both roles. Mr McCracken's José was forceful and passionate—a powerful interpretation, powerfully sung. The timbre was fiery, the phrasing hammered to keenness. Connoisseurs at the old Opéra-Comique used to classify their favorites by the execution of the Flower Song's peroration: *en tête* or *en poitrine* (most favored of all were tenors who commanded both methods, and used the *bis* to demonstrate it). Mr McCracken sang the pianissimo phrase *en tête*; his head-voice sounded unnatural, but no more so than Bizet's rum cadence, which must be meant to tell of all reason gone. On the first night he failed us only at the end; the final outburst lacked power.

What of Carmen? In neither appearance nor temperament is Miss Horne completely suited to the role; nor, for that matter, in timbre: Carmen's voice needs a dusky glint, a dark sudden flash, and these were lacking. Yet beyond expectation Miss Horne succeeded: by a direct, fearless, forthright portrayal that was uncommonly well sung. The card scene was especially striking, delivered, as Bizet directed, *simplement et très également*, with delicate attention to the detailed dynamics. The Habanera was held too strictly in time; we missed those seductive little pushes and pauses of rhythm that give it life. In the Séguedille, however, there were some bewitching little flicks and flourishes. The Gypsy Song combined grace with exuberance. Miss Horne resisted any temptation to wow us with trombone tones from the chest (except once, when closing the second strophe of the Habanera). Her French was boldly handled, though somewhat broad. In spoken dialogue she was disconcertingly apt to suggest a big jolly girl, as refreshingly harmless underneath as any Micaëla. She won many laughs.

Micaëla was Adriana Maliponte, conventional, unremarkable, but not colorless. Mr Krause played a slim, spry Escamillo. He looked good, but his singing was monotonous and imprecise, and his French barely intelligible; the role needs a more swiftly focused voice, of bright, forward, thrusting quality. Among the minor parts Raymond Gibbs's cheerful, dapper young Moralès and Donald Gramm's bluff Zuniga were outstanding. The choruses were confident, and the urchins quite excellent.

In the pit, Leonard Bernstein began ill, as if illustrating Inghelbrecht's discourse on "How Not to Conduct *Carmen*": all battery and brass, where what matters is that we should hear vigorous string articulation. But thereafter he led a colorful, nicely judged account of the score, marked by some intense solo playing, strong in atmosphere and picturesque detail. Lazy, seductive tempi were well set for Carmen's solos. The Quintet and the refrain of the Card Trio were robbed of vivacity, however, by breakneck tempi that gave their phrases no chance to tell.

The line of the Gentele-Igesz production was clear. It was set in plain off-white scenery, by Josef Svoboda, of strong general effect but unpleasing shape and proportion. Mr Svoboda is a fluent, versatile designer, much in demand. He knows every trick of the trade, and technically he can be fascinating; but the cut of his sets is often awkward and crude. Act I here is a courtyard, gated from the largely invisible square and containing both guardhouse and the entrance to the cigar factory: an ingenious but unconvincing solution to the tricky problems of crowd/solo alternation. "Sur la place chacun passe," sing the soldiers, staring out front, but in the square just about no one comes, no one goes; Seville lacks civilians. The inn of Act II is roofed by a lattice roll decked with fairy lights. In Act III we shift to abstract geometry: a parabolic funnel-gorge, and the Bayreuth inclined circle. Act IV, though clumsy to look at, cunningly combines enough space for promenade and *corrida* processions with the suggestion of a menacing corner in which Carmen is trapped. The opening of this scene needs more lively action; the crowd strolls with the regularity of a German interval audience. David Walker's Goya-based costumes are nicely detailed.

Textual matters may be dull things to discuss, but the edition chosen does much to determine the character of a *Carmen* presentation, and the textual history of the piece is as intricate as those of *Boris Godunov* and *Don Carlos*. Of the two textual decisions mentioned above, one—the use of spoken dialogue—is unquestionably right, the other controversial. Yet a question about the former had remained, until the Metropolitan Opera dared at last to solve it. Guiraud's recitatives are skillful and tasteful, but they at once eliminate detail about the characters and the action, and weaken the dramatic tensions of a carefully balanced score. Most people agreed on that, yet feared that, in a big international house, French spoken by non-French artists might prove weaker still. Not so: Guiraud's recitatives can now go the way of Costa's for *Fidelio*. Even in French of variable quality, the gain was evident.

Boris Goldovsky's New England Opera Theatre, in 1949, was the first company to produce *Carmen* with some passages previously unheard, unpublished, rediscovered in Bizet's autograph. Other houses followed suit, and then in 1965 Fritz Oeser published an *"Ur-Carmen"* containing still more music, reconstructed from the original orchestral parts. Scholarly battle had already been joined on whether the additional music (whose quality is not in question) had been struck out against Bizet's will (some of it? all of it?), or whether the vocal score published in his lifetime represented his final thoughts on a more concise, more dramatically effective version. The opera was first prepared in a disturbed and difficult atmosphere; the performers, and particularly the chorus, found it difficult (most of the cuts concern the chorus). We know that Bizet resisted changes "ferociously." But each must decide for himself which passages, if any, the composer lost reluctantly, and which losses are pure dramatic gain.

I heard the première of Dr Oeser's *"Ur-Carmen"* in Bremen (in German, only one long interval—and sets, incidentally, by Mr Svoboda). It moved swiftly and well; Bizet's first conception was plainly "viable." But further hearings in less intimate surroundings have made me increasingly doubtful whether it is suited to general use. The Metropolitan gives us Oeser pretty well whole. Carmen's mocking reprise of José's "Je souffre de partir . . . ," embellished with parody sighs from the violins, is pure gain. The full restatement of the Fate motif in Act I can be defended in this particular production. The expanded "Smoke" chorus, the lengthier quarrel—each episode in itself can be welcomed, but cumulatively they make the act seem very long: a matter not of time (for in minutes the sum of the new passages is small) but of dramatic pace. It is easy to imagine the composer himself tightening his action by these little cuts. Even easier in the finale of Act IV. The alternatives here are numerous, and the version chosen by the Metropolitan Opera is disastrously less effective than the familiar ring of fanfares cutting into José's "Eh bien! damnée!"

September 30, 1972

Fritz Oeser's edition of Carmen *is published by Alkor-Edition, Cassel; its failings were pointed out by Winton Dean in a long review in* The Musical Times *for November 1965 (Volume 106, No. 1473), and again in his articles "The Corruption of* Carmen; *or the Perils of Pseudo-Musicology" in* Musical Newsletter *for October 1973 (Volume 3, No. 4), and "Whose* Carmen?" *in the* Times Literary Supplement, *August 24, 1973. The Metropolitan Opera performance has been recorded by Deutsche Grammophon (2740 101).*

Matters of Sound and Style

The musical public becomes ever more keenly tuned to the sounds and performance styles of past centuries. Crumhorns and chitarroni, regals and racketts play to us at the turn of a switch. Urged to it by a few critics and conductors who care, our singers have begun to grace the plain printed notes on a page of Handel, Mozart, or Donizetti, our orchestras to build eighteenth-century music on a foundation of harpsichord. Musicology has become music—and the process continues. To listeners a decade or two hence, our Mozart performances at modern pitch, on modern instruments, may sound as anachronistic as to us do the Handel-Harty *Water Music* and Stokowski's orchestral Bach. Even the styles of the recent past are now studied with increasing attention; the music of Wagner, Mahler, and Elgar we want to hear as our grandfathers heard it, played with a fullness of string portamento inapt to Stravinsky's. The music of any age speaks most directly, most freshly to modern ears in the tones and idioms of its composer—or at least in as close an approximation to them as halls and instruments allow.

To this new, aurally educated public, Pierre Boulez sounds a thoroughly old-fashioned conductor—in his own way, a man like Furtwängler (who would deploy all the Berlin Philharmonic strings in Handel's D-minor Concerto Grosso) or Beecham (who decked *Messiah* in the grandeur and glitter of a Strauss-sized orchestra), unconcerned with, perhaps even contemptuous of, historical niceties. Furtwängler was a romantic, and Mr Boulez is a "modern" (Beecham defies ready classification)—but to be "modern" today when directing the music of yesterday is to be old-fashioned. With his other orchestra, the BBC Symphony, Mr Boulez has devoted a large part of his programs to "modern classics" that need a large contemporary orchestra, from *The Rite of Spring* onward. The circumstances of the Philharmonic subscription series here compel him to range more widely; at the first two Thursday concerts he brought us Haydn and Mozart, Mahler, Wagner, Ravel, and Stravinsky. All but the Ravel and the Stravinsky were, strictly speaking, unstylish. But not unimpressive. Like Furtwängler, like Beecham, Mr Boulez is a musician worth hearing whatever he does. He has a composer's ear for structure. He laid out the large, elaborate score of Mahler's Sixth Symphony like a blueprint. He clearly enjoyed, and let us enjoy, the way each piece of music had been made. The unstylishness of Haydn's "Hornsignal" Symphony and of Mozart's Sinfonia Concertante with violin and viola was largely a matter of orchestral balance: an intolerable deal of string tone to so little wind (and no harpsichord in the Haydn, though Edward Downes's program-note rightly called for it). The textures became clogged and the details blurred; fewer strings, even in the large Philharmonic Hall, would have sounded fresher. The oboes in the Mozart slow movement played with an unclassically wide vibrato. In Wagner (excerpts from *Die Meistersinger*), the unstylishness was a matter of tempo and phrasing. Just as *Parsifal* emerges

from Mr Boulez's hands lean, clean, and lucid (refreshing
when first heard but thereafter, it seems increasingly,
deficient in warmth, weight, and full-hearted eloquence), so
his Mastersingers were mustered in chipper fashion, their
portly dignity quite gone. Mr Boulez was happier with the
lithe apprentices. Wagner's music sounds most solid, its
timbre most cohesive, when the orchestra is seated in
nineteenth-century fashion: first violins to the left, seconds
to the right, and a big central foundation of double basses.
Mr Boulez favors the modern plan: all the violins on his left,
basses in a file way off on the other side. Cohesiveness of
timbre is not his aim. He might not deem "weighty" a term
of praise.

To the Mahler symphony the Philharmonic violins
brought a splendidly athletic line (though insufficient
portamento) and a tone not voluptuous, never cloying, yet
shining, forward, and firm, which to a newcomer proved the
most individual characteristic of the orchestra. Mr Boulez
does not get string tone like this from the BBC. He gripped
our attention through the long work (eighty-one and a half
minutes in this performance) not by picturesque detail, or
by beauty of sound, but by "logic": the symphony seemed
uncommonly well fashioned. That was not enough—not for
a piece that left its composer (after a rehearsal for the first
performance) "sobbing, wringing his hands, unable to
control himself." But "emotional" is another epithet Mr
Boulez would possibly despise. In Ravel's Left-Hand Piano
Concerto (with Leon Fleisher as soloist) and Stravinsky's
Symphonies of Wind Instruments and Four Studies, emotion plays no part. They were admirably done.

Questions of historical style were raised, too, by the
Donizetti revivals of the New York City Opera—*Lucia
di Lammermoor* and *Maria Stuarda*—despite their welcome

completeness of text and authentic approach to decoration in repeats. The conductor, Charles Wilson, dispatched them, except in episodes of high sentiment, with brisk metric efficiency. He showed small understanding of music that needs to be molded round a singer's inflections. Tito Capobianco, the producer, allowed Elizabeth and Leicester to loll about on the floor of the throne room, and sprawl on the steps of a Coronation chair that had somehow found its way from the Abbey to the Palace. At "Son tue cifre?" Edgardo drew a specimen signature from his cuff to verify Lucia's on the contract—a suspicious bank clerk, rather than a hero about to launch the tremendous *Maledizione.* Stylistic absurdities! But Beverly Sills commands secrets of the style. Like the old singers, she showed that with just two poignant, exquisitely uttered notes (an unwritten but musically essential bridge between phrases of Lucia's "Spargi," and Mary Stuart's "Ah! sì" in recitative reply to Talbot) she could hold a house spellbound and produce a dramatic effect no one could guess at from perusal of the printed page. Donizetti's music, like Mozart's, and Mahler's, yields its full eloquence when historical understanding and historical imagination are brought to its execution.

The City Opera's new *Don Giovanni* is a coarse, insensitive, sorry affair. Frank Corsaro, the producer, evidently dislikes soliloquies: Elvira sings "Ah, chi mi dice mai," Musetta-like, to a street crowd; Ottavio addresses "Dalla sua pace" to a friar, who grants him absolution during the closing bars; Anna's "Non mi dir" becomes the *Briefarie* of old German productions. Giovanni himself sports a trio of shameless house-doxies in fairly constant attendance. Zerlina's "Batti, batti" is an eating scene. Amid the antics, we could take pleasure in a forthright, dashing Giovanni, easily and truly sung, from Robert Hale; in pretty tone from both Veronica Tyler's and Patricia Wise's Zerlina; and in an Elvira, Patricia Brooks, who achieved Mozartian pathos despite being presented as a figure of fun—a comedy Fricka, she pursues Giovanni in a sedan chair borne by panting attendants, and belabors with her parasol a Zerlina who has literally been tumbled in the hay. What larks! Bruno Maderna, the conductor, treated the dramatic score as a light, shapely, graceful divertimento. Performances are given alternately in Italian and a poor English translation; in such circumstances, nothing about language is proved.

At the Metropolitan Opera, however, there has been a "real" performance of Mozart's opera, conducted by Peter Maag (his house début) with an intensity and passion that did not preclude grace. The production—Herbert Graf's, cared for by Patrick Tavernia—is firm, traditional, and apt; though old, it remains fresh. Ruggero Raimondi's confident, vividly inflected Giovanni, Elizabeth Vaughan's poised yet poignant Elvira, and Theodor Uppman's brilliantly various Masetto were outstanding. Though the scale was big and the orchestra large, the style was neither modern nor old-fashioned; it simply seemed right.

October 7, 1972

An Anatomy
of Biography

Shostakovich's Fifteenth Symphony, introduced to New York by the Philadelphia Orchestra at the first of its Philharmonic Hall concerts this season, is a strong, strange, impressive, and disturbing composition. Written in the summer of 1971, it was first played in Moscow, conducted by the composer's son Maxim. Official Soviet opinion was approving: Tikhon Khrennikov, the chairman of the Soviet Composers' Union, declared the new work to be "filled with optimism, affirmation of life, and trust in man's inexhaustible strength." To me, it sounds like the statement of an artist disillusioned, apprehensive, and uncertain—as never before—whether his art has any role to play in the struggle for human freedom. In fourteen earlier symphonies Shostakovich did not leave questions unanswered (private doubts found their public expression in his chamber music, in movements like the finale of the Eleventh String Quartet). There were many big, brave statements, symphonic last movements that were indeed ringing with "optimism, affirmation of life." Sometimes they even broke into words—those choral cries of "Lenin!" "Fight!" and

"October!" at the close of No. 2 (*To October: Symphonic Dedication*), and the popular jubilation that ends No. 3 (*May Day*). The Eleventh Symphony (*The Year 1905*), of 1957, and the Twelfth (*The Year 1917*), of 1961, both celebrated the triumphs of Revolution. But then the Thirteenth, of 1962, dealt with its miseries; in it Shostakovich set poems by Yevtushenko (including *Babi Yar*) fiercely critical of the Stalin epoch, and, by implication, of Stalinist spirit that survived. Still, there was affirmation at the end, although the message—from Yevtushenko's *Careers*, praising the free spirit of great men who proclaimed the truth as they saw it—was new: "Genius will conquer, regardless of the charges brought against it." This Thirteenth Symphony did not find favor in Russia. No. 14, composed in 1969, dedicated to Benjamin Britten, is a chamber symphony, and a song cycle that (like Britten's *Serenade* and *Nocturne*) sets an anthology of poems by various hands. Their subject is death. No public issues are involved. But with No. 15, Shostakovich has returned to "ideology." His noble Fifth Symphony was subtitled "A Soviet Artist's Reply to Just Criticism"; his latest might be deemed, among other things, A Just Criticism of a Soviet Artist's Art.

It starts brightly: two tings on a little bell, and a perky flute theme over chords strummed lightly by pizzicato strings. For thirty-eight bars the flute gambols on its way; it seems to be making a merry, mocking allusion to those long, low, slowly wandering themes that begin so many of Shostakovich's larger works (and subsequent events suggest that the allusion is deliberate). A quickstep rhythm begins to form, and suddenly, as "second subject," the trumpet breaks into four bars of the quickstep from the *William Tell* Overture. To American audiences, it may recall the Lone Ranger; to any audience, the dapper, jaunty little tune must bring first a smile, and then questions. What is it doing here? What does it mean? Would it be too fanciful to suggest that, whereas William Tell was an active fighter for freedom, a musician—Shostakovich now feels—has the power to make only small, ineffectual gestures? Perhaps unconsciously, the composer has altered two of Rossini's notes, trivializing the tune. The call to arms sounds as if from a toy trumpet, and the spirit of Till Eulenspiegel seems not far away—not in any specific references to Strauss's score but more generally, in nimble, jesting turns of phrase for solo instruments. Till defied Authority, and was destroyed by it. Such fancy can find support in the somber events of the last movement.

The Adagio begins with a brass chorale, a soft-swelling surge of indeterminate outline, which acts as refrain to a lyrical twelve-note theme of very definite shape. The solo cello, unaccompanied, sings it warmly; the solo violin responds later with a similar but less intricate melody. There follows a funeral march—and the earlier lyricism turns to ice when the celesta, in a quiet solo that steals into a hushed hall, spells out the cello's theme in inversion: sad, soft-falling transformation of what had been ardent and aspirant. Another twelve-note melody and its inversion start the Scherzo; soloists leap and strain as if to free themselves from a harmonic prison of open fifths and fourths. And then, heralding the Finale, we hear the Annunciation of Death motif to which, in *Die Walküre*, Brünnhilde, messenger of doom, appears to Siegmund, and which sounds again, in *Götterdämmerung*, after Siegfried has been struck by Hagen's spear. The solemn, familiar brass chords effect a different kind of shock from that created by the Rossini tune—but again we ask what the composer can mean by his quotation. (And again, the original is not cited *notatim*; Shostakovich has altered the rhythm and relative pitch of the fatal drumbeats.) In *Götterdämmerung* the sequence is resolved into the soft, ecstatic radiance of Siegfried's greeting to Brünnhilde, present in mystical vision to his dying eyes. Shostakovich, however, has nothing to offer but a meaningless, meandering, almost automatic though agreeable little tune. When the movement reaches its climax there seems to be a distorted, despairing reference to the heroics of the *Leningrad* Symphony. The close is a tocking and chocking of percussion (side drum, castanets, wood block, pattering tomtom); for page after page the strings, unchanging, have held to a far-flung open fifth of A and E—a hollow chord made major at the last by the tapping of the xylophone and the ting of the little bell.

Shostakovich's symphonies are the public biography of a great musician in his relation to Soviet art. In this latest chapter, even while he seems now to say that the struggle for artistic freedom has been in vain, he in effect continues it, still fearless and independent. There remains a heroic vigor of mind in this new questioning of his old heroic affirmations. His musical invention is as vigorous and fertile as ever. The forms of the movements and the form of the whole are masterly. This late style embraces both the delicate "chamber" textures of No. 14 and the earlier easy handling of large forces on a large scale. The symphony lasts something over forty minutes. The orchestra is standard (double woodwind), augmented only by piccolo and much percussion. Britten's music seems to have left some influence (even more marked than in the Fourteenth Symphony) on the limpid instrumental textures, on the use of twelve-note melodies within a basically diatonic context, and on the nature of motivic interrelationships that reveal themselves more clearly at each hearing.

The Philadelphia Orchestra has long been associated with Shostakovich's symphonies (it gave the American premières, also, of Nos. 1, 4, 6, 13, and 14), and its conductor, Eugene Ormandy, has an instinctive understanding of his music. The performance was supremely eloquent precisely because it was so beautifully played—

generously, amply, with superb yet never showy technique. The solo cellist, Samuel Mayes, and the solo flutist, Murray W. Panitz, deserve special mention. As broadcast, that Moscow première was less impressive, less exciting.

Of some tales by E. T. A. Hoffmann, two Frenchmen, Jules Barbier and Michel Carré, made first a *drame fantastique* and, thirty years later, an opera libretto. The tales were unrelated. The authors tried to link them by providing a pattern, superimposing a theme: four separate heroines became four aspects of predatory Woman, whose wiles, if unchecked, could distract Hoffmann from his true poetic vocation. They provided an Evil Genius, who turned up in each episode. Their work was not tidy: the Evil Genius in effect *saves* the hero from entanglement with four fatal women, and thus furthers the design of his Good Genius, Nicklausse, whom later revisers identified with his Muse. It would be silly, though not impossible, to essay a Jungian interpretation concerned with Dark Shadows and the Anima—but *Les Contes d'Hoffmann* is not *The Ring*. Offenbach, when he set the libretto to music, made no attempt to resolve the inconsistencies and contradictions of the piece. There is a sort of loosely unifying theme, which need not be examined too closely. There is a fine chance for a theatrical display of the Daemonic, the Supernatural, and the extravagantly Romantic—in three well-contrasted central scenes calling for different kinds of magical trick-effect in each (in fact, both play and libretto are more conventionally "Hoffmannesque" than Hoffmann's original tales). There is some pretty music. And the three (in some editions, four) heroines allow either a single versatile soprano to show diverse aspects of her voice and personality, or scope for starry casting (when the Metropolitan Opera first mounted *Hoffmann*, in 1913, the audience could enjoy Frieda Hempel,

Olive Fremstad, and Lucrezia Bori on the same evening). Although the score is not one of Offenbach's most attractive or diverting, these assets have been enough to keep *Les Contes d'Hoffmann* in the international repertory. Moreover, since there is no definitive edition, no *"Ur-Hoffmann,"* any passions for tinkering or rectification can freely be indulged. Surviving only as an untidy patchwork, the opera has long been fair game for any itchy-fingered editor. So the tale of the *Tales* is tangled. In brief, Offenbach died while the opera was in rehearsal, and Ernest Guiraud (New Orleans' most famous musical son, whose compositions are heard the world over, almost whenever *Hoffmann* and *Carmen* are performed) completed the piece for its Opéra-Comique première, in 1881. He dropped the Giulietta act, but in order to use the Barcarolle he shifted Antonia from Munich to Venice. Giulietta returned in 1893, but in the wrong sequence—before Antonia. Then, in Vienna, Mahler scrapped Prologue and Epilogue. In Berlin, in 1905, Hans Gregor opened the Komische Oper with a new, fuller *Hoffmann*, including both Coppélius's "Spectacle" and Dapertutto's "Diamond" arias (which Gregor had discovered among such Paris material as escaped the 1887 fire at the Opéra-Comique; the authenticity of the "Diamond" aria has since been questioned); as a result of this production Choudens and Peters published the score of *Hoffmann* that has been the basis of most later performances. In recent years, however, Walter Felsenstein at the Komische Oper, and Edmund Tracey and Colin Graham for Sadler's Wells at the London Coliseum, have produced new editions fresh-based on Offenbach's original ideas.

No similar freshness marks the text used for the New York City Opera's new production of *Hoffmann*. The edition, thoroughly corrupt, combines the worst of all worlds. Offenbach's numbers are linked by long pages of undistinguished, tedious recitative (by Guiraud and others), which, through anticipation and reiteration of the composer's melodies, weakens the effect of his music when at last it is heard. The show, though given by an English-speaking cast to an English-speaking audience, is in French (the words of the chorus and of the hero are hard to distinguish), which destroys its vivacity. The Antonia and Giulietta acts are still reversed. The Epilogue is omitted (against the wishes of the company's director, Julius Rudel, and in deference to the producer's and bass's wishes—according to Mr Rudel's own statement), so whatever slight coherence the drama had is destroyed. Nor was there very much, on the first night, for eye or ear to enjoy. Ming Cho Lee's décor, shopwindow rococo, looks flimsy and fussy. There was an awful lot of primping and posturing in Tito Capobianco's production. The magic was paltry. The shade of Antonia's mother appeared in full view of all but those in the orchestra stalls—a far too human figure calling through cupped hands from the pit. Good singing might have redeemed much, but Beverly Sills, the multiple heroine, was in poor voice: her Olympia lacked sweetness and purity of tone, her Giulietta was edgy, and only a phrase or two of Antonia's Dove Song had the right gentle charm. Michele Molese, as Hoffmann, sounded strained, ill at ease. Norman Treigle played the villain roles with a relish that would have been more effective had it been less thickly spread. There was little sparkle or lightness in Mr Rudel's accompaniment.

October 14, 1972

Shostakovich's Fifteenth Symphony has been recorded by the Philadelphia Orchestra, under Ormandy, on RCA ARD1 0014 (also available as a cartridge, ARS1 0014, and a casette, ARK1 0014). A performance by the original interpreters, the Moscow Radio Symphony Orchestra conducted by Maxim Shostakovich, is recorded on Melodiya-

Angel SR 40213. A study score of the work is published by Leeds Music.

Beverly Sills, Norman Treigle, and Julius Rudel as conductor take part in the ABC recording of Hoffmann *(ATS 20014; cassette D 52014), which uses an edition similar to that of the City Opera. Joan Sutherland is the heroine of a London recording (13106; cassette 2D 31217) with spoken dialogue.*

Dance of Plastic Circumstance

City Center has launched the fall dance season with six weeks of the Joffrey Ballet at the titular theater, and at the ANTA Theatre, nearby, a six-week stretch of contemporary dance called a "Marathon"—and thus miscalled, unless the management is thinking, maybe, of a spectator in constant attendance. An Athenian ran the historic course himself from beginning to end, but eighteen troupes and some eminent solo artists are performing at ANTA in relays, two or three on each bill. The Joffrey season could more aptly be termed a "Marathon," for here a single company has been set a course tracing the development of ballet Romantic, Classical, and Modern, and involving the styles of Bournonville, of Fokin, Massine, and Balanchine, of Kurt Jooss, of Jerome Robbins, John Butler, and Alvin Ailey, and many others. Meanwhile, ballets deftly made for the dancers by their own versatile, eclectic house choreographer, Gerald Arpino, offer progress reports on the diverse styles captured to date, and in doing so help to formulate an individual company manner. Robert Joffrey is a collector; a glance at the repertory makes that clear. His tastes range widely, and his eye is good. His new acquisitions this season are Massine's *Le Beau Danube*, Jerome Robbins' *Interplay* (Mr Robbins' second ballet, made in 1945 for Billy Rose, since done by several companies), and Benjamin Harkarvy's *Grand Pas espagnol* (created for the Netherlands Dance Theatre in 1963, later taken up by the Harkness Ballet). The collector of ballets from both the far and the near past can acquire only copies—though copies made by a creator may on occasion surpass the original when the materials, the living dancers who are the choreographer's medium, are of superior quality, or when the artist has refined his earlier ideas. But some copies are faded, and others are crude; some are executed in material that cannot reproduce the fine shades of the original. The Joffrey *Petrushka*, for example, is a daub: a performance clumsily lit, coarsely produced, with an overanimated crowd, and soloists whose brash inflections are very different from those to be discerned in copies based more closely on Fokin's 1911 original.

To put it another way, no single company can be first rate in as many styles as the Joffrey Ballet is called on to deploy. In Fokin, the performers looked unconvincing, and only a little less so in Massine (and that despite the fact that Mr Massine himself mounted this revival of *Le Beau Danube*). But in their own works, those made for them by Mr Arpino, they looked splendid. The simple rule—that dancers shine most brightly in dances that have been composed "on" them, or at least "on" the company they belong to—is generally true. In Mr Arpino's *Trinity*, the Joffrey dancers display their immediately attractive virtues of speed, exuberance, buoyancy, and naturalness. Legs and arms fly high, and a certain untidiness around wrists and ankles is of small account, irrelevant to the exhilarating effect of the whole. *Trinity* wears well; the score, by Alan Raph and Lee Holdridge, is a masterly blend of simplicity and cunning. In the performance of Mr Arpino's *Kettentanz* we perceive the same merits: zest, zip, and also (notably in Gay Wallstrom's undulant solo) an easy, unmannered lyricism that is fresh and appealing. The company shows to advantage in the high dramatics of Mr Ailey's tragedy after Lorca, *Feast of Ashes*, while Mr Butler's *After Eden*, once a Harkness ballet, was so tenderly and so subtly danced by Starr Danias and Dennis Wayne that it seemed as if the piece had indeed been written for them. (These two works gave substance to fare containing many soufflés.) But *Petrushka* and, for that matter, *Le Beau Danube* were written for executants whose norm was a striving for the classical ideal. Behind the distortions of the former (a "burlesque ballet in one act and four scenes") and the merry "character" inflections of the other, we should sense at least the possibility of a Petipa back and of a Petersburg line flowing through arms and shoulders. Few of the Joffrey dancers command a pure classical style. In many of their offerings it does not matter very much. Verve, velocity, and high kicks carry them through a very acceptable presentation of Ruthanna Boris's Gottschalk extravaganza *Cakewalk* (devised for the New York City Ballet). Their *Interplay* is buoyant enough to make one overlook some faults of placing. Eliot Feld's *Meadowlark* and Mr Arpino's own *Confetti*, however, contain classical sequences (some reminiscent of Bournonville, others of Ashton) in which charm, freshness, and gaiety are not quite enough to atone for untidy hands, imperfect beats, or smudged finishes to a sequence.

Are we expecting too much of the company? We are—but not more than Mr Joffrey himself expects of it when setting it to so many different tasks. Carping is in order when classical standards implicit in the choreography of a piece are not maintained; plausible approximations can be enjoyed, but must be noted for what they are. Equally in order is generous praise for a troupe so spirited, adventurous, and accomplished. The dancers may not be noble, but they are captivating. Audiences have been warmly enthusiastic—and even, through excess of zeal, uncouth. Four fouettés on end have been enough to elicit shouts of delight that drown the rest of the feat. Many a dancer has had the start of her solo ruined by applause banging on from the preceding variation. It matters most in the divertissement episodes that Mr Arpino likes to compose in continuous sequence, one invention piled on another to generate a cumulative excitement that applause can only shatter. Perhaps a request in the program booklet, that the audience should follow with ears as well as eyes, and give its appreciation audible form only at a "natural break," might help to deter the wreckers. The booklet should also catalogue the exhibits in Mr Joffrey's choice collection more amply, and provide at least date of original, provenance, date of copy, and precise identification of the music.

The ANTA season was opened by the company of José Limón. His new *Carlota* is a powerful piece. The imagery—Mr. Limón in his fierce, fine-mettled Spanish vein —is familiar: the proud male violence couched in forms like those of High Mannerism, where limbs grow long and hands seem huge; the passions of a woman racked, or rapt in delusory dreams of bliss; the formal chivalric pavanes broken by rough patterns of brutality. They are applied here to a vision of the aged, widowed Carlota, reliving brief imperial splendors, recalling Maximilian's fall, stricken by his execution. The ballet opens with screams, such as are silently but unmistakably uttered by much of Mr Limón's movement, now actually sounding from a dark stage. Then the work is danced in silence—but, strangely, an implicit music seems often to emerge: the lilt of a waltz, the rude blare of a patriotic march, a funeral lament. A composer might even feel inspired to make music for this autonomous dance-drama, rather as a choreographer is impelled to find movement to match his hearing of a score. Mr Limón has always constructed securely. His command of form is especially apparent in this work, where the dance dictates its own patterns in time. There were strong performances from Carla Maxwell in the title role, Peter Sparling as an elegant, gallant Maximilian, and Edward DeSoto as a seedy, formidable Benito Juárez. Charles D. Tomlinson's costumes were once again a perfect caparison, in form and color, for Mr Limón's ideas. In all that I saw it do this season, the Limón company was confident and gleaming.

Any general reflections on shadows cast or mantles passed by the Graham or Weidman-Humphrey schools can wait until more of the "Marathon" has been run. Among the independents taking part, Lotte Goslar and her Pantomime Circus have been outstanding. Miss Goslar is an endearing, indomitable dumpling, surrounded by a troupe of tragical-comical clowns in assorted sizes. Her new offering was an episode from *Circus Scene*, a work in progress. The scenario was written for her by Brecht: the clown is trapped in the lion's cage during a sequence at once poetic, alarming, and entertaining. Some of her other sketches were very simple, not always disarmingly so. A short solo for Ray Collins struck exactly the note of those Brecht ballads that lay horror bare by straightforward statement in artless metres.

The songs of the humpback whale, published on disc in 1970, have moved listeners to many moods, the commonest, perhaps, being awe at these mysterious, lyrical melodies of the deep. The timbre of whale song often suggests a cello. George Crumb in his *Vox Balaenae*, introduced to New York by the Aeolian Chamber Players at their Town Hall concert last week, has achieved a closer simulation, using a trio of flute, cello, and piano, each electrically amplified. Much sonic experiment must have preceded the composition. Among other new devices, the piano strings are stroked by "a five-eighths-inch chisel with smooth cutting edge" (which, as the composer rightly observes, "will produce a very delicate sound"); the cello mews softly in small reiterated cries ("sea-gull effect") while the player's fingers slide the length of the string; the flutist sounds the opening theme by at once playing on, and, an octave lower, gently singing into, his instrument. All three players wear black half masks—or should do so, though on this occasion the spectacled pianist had to remove his in order to see. This was not just a stunt; the depersonalization enhanced the spell. And the work—a theme with five variations and epilogue—was not merely a collection of cunning sound-inventions but, rather, a quiet, beautiful, many-hued composition that stole into stillness, grew, developed, then faded at last beneath a scarce-moving sea ripple. The players—Erich Graf, Jerry Grossman, and Walter Ponce—were poetic virtuosos. *Vox Balaenae* was the central work in a civilized and thoroughly enjoyable program, which also included Mario Davidovsky's elegant, interesting *Synchronisms II*.

Last week, in describing Ernest Guiraud as "New Orleans' most famous musical son," I may have slighted the shade of Louis Moreau Gottschalk, born there eight years before Guiraud. At any rate, his name has been before me ever since: at the Joffrey Ballet's *Cakewalk*; in Brooklyn's Greenwood Cemetery, where he lies now and was visited on Saturday by the Friends of Central and Prospect Parks; then at Saturday midnight, when sixteen pianists assembled at eight Steinways, in Philharmonic Hall, to give a Monster Concert in the Gottschalk tradition. It included the *Hexameron* put together by Liszt. That walk through Greenwood had passed the Steinway mausoleum, and the grave of Liszt's friend Lola Montez. The omens were good; the concert was but a diverting curiosity, no more. Pianos are subject to a law of diminishing returns. An opera overture transcribed for two coruscant hands can astound us; strummed out by thirty-two, in strict tempo, it sounds too easy, pointless after the first surprise effect of the timbre has passed. The pianists, led by Eugene List, were teachers and graduates from the Eastman School, at Rochester. In the Pixis variation of the *Hexameron* Barry Snyder was brilliant, but some of the ensemble efforts sounded underrehearsed. Yet Gottschalk, with his *La Gallina* and *Ojos Criollos*, stole the evening. Only a very severe taste could resist his buoyant, catchy tunes. And he really knew the medium: no diminishing returns here—the more the merrier!

October 21, 1972

Mario Davidovsky's Synchronisms I, II, *and* III, *for instruments and electronic sounds, are recorded on CRI SD 204.*

Clowns, Craftsmen, Creators

Tim Burton's *Six Solos in the Form of a Pair*, created last week in the Kitchen of the Mercer Arts Center, pays punning titular homage to Erik Satie (composer of *Trois Morceaux en forme de poire*), and at first it seemed that we might be in for a modern version of one of Satie's *rudes saloperies*. Within his instrument, the pianist, Don Gillespie, suspended a series of "stimulators"—small battery-powered agitated rods, which teased and tickled the strings until they sang out with sounds suggesting a frenzied aeolian harp. Against this background, he then began, at the keyboard, to play a brief sequence based on dominants of G major but never resolved to the home chord. Satie's *Vexations* is a single short progression reiterated without changes for some twenty-four hours; Mr Burton's somewhat similar piece allows for variations of texture, dynamics, and rhythm, and it lasted for about an hour and a half, continuing as accompaniment and "pair" to the five subsequent solos. The first of these was a song, *Free Offer Inside*, sung by Judy Sherman in bright, precise tones. The text had been assembled from the covers of matchbooks ("50¢ can get you $50,000!"); "Close cover before striking" was its refrain. *Solo Melancholia* for clarinet mused attractively in the chalumeau reaches of the instrument, while *Festoons* for flute was a gentle piece made largely of small repeated musical cells, somewhat Oriental in effect. Both these solos were exceptionally well played by, respectively, Jan Coward and Rhys Chatham. A theatrical element entered with *Potpourri* for percussion: on a *batterie de cuisine* ranged gamelanwise, Mike Levenson beat out some lively, ingenious, and surprisingly musical episodes. Mr Burton himself closed the evening with clowning, cymbal crashes, and a final wry allegory of a musician whose symbols refused to obey his will. The evening could have been just boring, or silly, but was neither. Though the materials were simple, and the structures even simpler, there was enough incident to please the ear and sustain the attention. Mr Burton has a musical mind whose workings were agreeable, and sometimes astonishing, to follow, and he had gathered a first rate team of interpreters.

This was one aspect of contemporary music-making. The first of the "Prospective Encounters" (silly title), presented by the New York Philharmonic in the Loeb Student Center of New York University, with Pierre Boulez as conductor and compère, revealed others. Jacob Druckman's *Incenters*, composed four years ago, and recorded by Nonesuch, has its starting point in a basic idea as simple as any of Mr Burton's—three brass players as instigators of musical actions that disturb "the equilibrium established by the other instruments," and prod their patterns into new shapes—which is worked out with much industry, application, and technical skill. The detailed facture lent itself to the sectional analysis that is usually a feature of Mr Boulez' instructive concerts; after conducting the piece once through, he brought on the composer to dissect a few episodes, and provided him with live-music examples. Demonstration done, he invited questions from the floor, and hinted that we might like to ask Mr Druckman what his music meant, as opposed to how it had been constructed. No one did ask that. *Incenters* was played again, and, as before, it sounded not specially interesting, but thoroughly made, like many other works of its kind.

Inspiration is something more easily sensed than described. Peter Maxwell Davies' *Eight Songs for a Mad King*, the other piece on the Prospective Encounters bill, sounds inspired. (It was composed in 1969, and has also been published on record.) The sources of Mr Davies' inspiration were manifold: images of the sad, mad George III pattering in purple dressing gown and ermine nightcap among his caged bullfinches, striving to teach them his music, or "trying to sing with them, in that ravaged voice made almost inhuman by day-long soliloquies"; the tunes of the little organ, still surviving, which he would play for the birds' instruction; his recorded utterances and actions; and Randolph Stow's finely wrought poems, which evoke all these things and incorporate some of the King's own words. The idea took dramatic form: a monologue for the King, in costume; flutist, clarinettist, violinist, and cellist within the cages among which he wanders—his finches as accompaniment, singing to him, provoking his delight, or wrath; the percussionist as his keeper, who finally whips him, howling, from the stage. When it came to finding notes to express the idea, there was another form of inspiration, too: the talents of the remarkable players, Mr Davies' own Fires of London, for whom he was writing—above all the vivid clarinet virtuosity of Alan Hacker, and the gentle intensity of the cellist Jennifer Ward Clarke. As protagonist he had Roy Hart, an actor who has trained his voice to compass many octaves, and croak in chords. The *Mad King* is an exceedingly complicated piece from every point of view: in its

networks of historical allusion, paralleled by musical references ("Comfort ye," from *Messiah*, is quoted directly, and
then parodied as a foxtrot, while "if not the notes at least
aspects of the styles of many composers are referred to, from
Handel to Birtwistle"); in its kaleidoscopic flicker of
emotions; in the interplay of verbal and visual imagery; and
in the subtly intricate writing for instruments and voice. Yet
it is a composition easy to understand, and ever arresting.
The impact is direct, and sometimes painful—as it was
meant to be. Mr Boulez did well to present it without
preamble. But afterward, when questions were concerned
mainly with details of execution, and the nature of the
King's malady, some discussion of Mr Davies' highly
unconventional methods of composition would have been
welcome. The performance, clear and careful from a
musical point of view, lacked the flare of passion and
wildness that inflames the composer's own direction of his
piece, and the Philharmonic production was untheatrical:
baldly lit and insensitively "acted" by the instrumentalists,
well though they played. In the central role, however, Julius
Eastman was impressive; he combined dignity with pathos,
and coped brilliantly with an extravagantly fantastic vocal
line.

When question time comes at Mr Boulez' "informal"
concerts, I find him more formidable than friendly;
I'm scared to ask anything, fearing a verbal rap from that
keen, dry Gallic mind. Alan Rich's touch, during question
time after the first of the Composers' Forum recitals in the
Donnell Library Auditorium, last Saturday, was much
lighter. He kept things flowing—it was more of a conversation, less of a class—and elicited some good observations.
The composers represented were John Heiss (born 1938)
and James Dashow (born 1944), both Princeton-trained. In

his brief Quartet for flute, clarinet, cello, and piano, of 1971,
and his early, even briefer Four Short Pieces for Piano, Mr
Heiss appeared to be what is unfavorably termed an
"academic" composer—which is to say a diligent and able
craftsman whose products are decently, irreproachably
made by approved modern methods, but a creator with
nothing urgent or compelling to say. The music revealed no
personality. His own instrument is the flute, and his Four
Movements for Three Flutes (1969) proved a little more
interesting, by reason of some mildly adventurous use of
unconventional playing techniques.

Mr Dashow has a more picturesque turn of mind. His
Burst! (1971) sets a passage from Jack Kerouac's novel
Desolation Angels for soprano accompanied by an eventful
electronic tape. The piece has abundant energy. It sounds
at once spontaneous in invention—Mr Kerouac's words
inspired the electronic composition, which was in turn
crowned by the vocal line—yet precisely ordered. Tape and
voice formed a musical ensemble; it was not just a song
against a background of sound effects. Mr Dashow's *Ashbery
Setting* (1971-1972) has a text drawn from John Ashbery's
poem *Clepsydra*, from the *Rivers and Mountains* collection,
again set for soprano, but now with flute and piano
accompaniment. This seems to be a poetic and beautiful
composition; the trouble was that it was sung blandly,
monotonously. We needed Cathy Berberian as soloist.
Charlotte Regni has a gentle voice whose timbre was pure
and true through an exceptionally wide range, but she
made nothing of the words. Her eyes, unchanging in
expression, remained glued to the score; we heard a
sounding of the notes rather than a performance; the
relation of the music to the text went unperceived. Although
the vocal setting "strives to maintain the natural accents of
the spoken words as they would be read," it would be too
much to ask that *all* the lines should be audible, in music

that leaps so freely; the words should at least have been printed on the program sheets. It was not enough just having Mr Ashbery read us, in advance, the relevant excerpts of his poem; he did so in a gray undertone, communicating as little of their sense as did the singer. Yet both of Mr Dashow's compositions prompted a wish to hear them again. The wish can be gratified, for scores and tapes of the Composers' Forum recitals are made available in the Library of Performing Arts at Lincoln Center.

October 28, 1972

Jacob Druckman's Incenters *is recorded on Nonesuch H 71221. Peter Maxwell Davies'* Eight Songs for a Mad King *is recorded on Nonesuch H 71285 with Julius Eastman as the protagonist and the Fires of London conducted by the composer.*

The Cumulative Flute

Many long studies have been made of *The Magic Flute*; dozens of books have been written about it; and whenever the opera is in question, two ghosts still rise. One, Karl Gieseke's, claims part authorship of Schikaneder's libretto, and the other poses the problem of whether, or why, there was a change in the direction of the plot after work on the piece had begun. Despite strong scholarly exorcisms, neither ghost will be laid—and it is easy to discover why, for the sources of the libretto are manifold, and the accounts of its creation confused and contradictory. I have been spending some time with Lulu (who is a prince), the *strahlende Fee* Perifirime, and their magic flute; with Sethos and Daluca among the Pyramids; and with the actors, authors, and gossips who, rather too long after 1791, set down their fallible recollections of how the opera had come into being. One witness, Kaspar the Fagottist, I have not yet traced; he was the hero of *Die Zauberzither*, a comedy by Joachim Perinet and Wenzel Müller, which was put on shortly before *Die Zauberflöte* and was so successful that—according to one account—Schikaneder and Mozart decided to change the plot of their piece, lest it be deemed a plagiarism. But even without Kaspar's testimony at first hand, I have come to a conclusion—a lifelike, untidy conclusion, probably unacceptable to the neat-minded scholars who try to label each contradictory account as either fact or fabrication. It is that *all* the memoirs are true at least in part, and that by superimposing them we achieve a most plausible account of a show which in its final form incorporated all sorts of suggestions from all sorts of people. Anyone who has been concerned with the making of a musical comedy will recognize the procedure. By this reckoning, Gieseke does not deserve the drubbings he has had from the Viennese theater historians (it has even been doubted whether in 1791 he was a Mason, although his certificate attesting to the fact survives in Trinity College, Dublin). He may well have lent a hand in the shaping of the plot; what more likely, since he was a librettist in Schikaneder's troupe, besides playing a bit part (first slave) in the première? All we need assume is that the old boy exaggerated his contribution—after all, he had been living in Ireland—when chatting to his Viennese cronies about the past.

Die Zauberflöte opens much as does *Lulu, oder die Zauberflöte*, a tale in the *Dschinnistan* collection assembled by Wieland. A radiant supernatural being (Perifirime/the Queen of Night) sends a handsome young prince (Lulu/Tamino) on a rescue expedition against an evil sorcerer, arming him with a magic flute whose music can awaken or calm any passion, as desired. Otto Jahn provides a summary of the *Dschinnistan* tale in his Mozart biography; though not quite accurate, it is all that most later commentators seem to have read. But in any case the authors of *Die Zauberflöte* soon dropped *Dschinnistan* and headed instead for the Abbé Terrasson's *Sethos . . . Ouvrage dans lequel on trouve la description des Initiations aux Mystères Égyptiens*, an allegory of Masonic ritual trials; their Tamino begins to take on the features of Prince Sethos, and their Queen of Night those of Queen Daluca. The two sources became confluent (Three Ladies are found in *Sethos*, Three Boys in another *Dschinnistan* tale). On the Masonic level, Light finally conquers Darkness; on the romantic level, the boy, as in *Dschinnistan*, wins his girl, while from the blending of popular fairy tale and lofty allegory there resulted an opera that has never ceased to fascinate, delight, and occasionally exasperate its listeners— an opera that has inspired almost as much speculation, and occasional nonsense, as the *Ring* itself.

That there was a change of plot, early on, seems to me quite clear—though this has often been denied. In no other way can it convincingly be explained why the noble Sarastro should employ the wicked Monostatos to guard Pamina. Besides, the authors left a loose end: in the second scene, Pamina refers to Sarastro as someone who will put Papageno to death with limitless tortures should he be caught; this is not the Sarastro she addresses in the finale of the act. On the other hand, it seems to me equally clear that Mozart and Schikaneder made a dramatic virtue of the change—or, as Ignaz von Seyfried put it, in one of the more controversial of the memoirs mentioned above, the reshaping proved to be "for the happiness and health of the whole work, since without it it would have been difficult for Mozart to bequeath to us, as his swan song, so marvellous a model of poesy and romanticism." In the third scene, after the change of plan, when Tamino discovers that nothing is quite what he and we have been told it is ("So everything is then a sham!"), the hero takes his first steps toward maturity, and the opera moves to sublimity. Tamino had been dazzled by the glittering apparatus of the Queen, her pyrotechnics of stage management and of vocal prowess. In his cry of "O ew'ge Nacht! Wann wirst du schwinden?" he seems now to echo the Queen's first utterance (there are several uses of leitmotiv in the score); in his C-major flute solo we can hear an attempt to dissipate the darkness.

Does any of this matter? It does when after a performance we try to decide why we have been stirred, or disappointed; when the lighting plot has failed to reflect the intensities of illumination, picturesque and symbolic at once, so clearly indicated by Mozart's music (and, for that matter, often enough specified in the stage directions); when we have been bored by a ponderously solemn presentation that ignored the playful aspects of the piece, or been left unsatisfied by a reading that sounded no depths; when a producer has attempted a controversial, particularized interpretation (as Michael Geliot did for the Welsh National Opera, setting the work in the South American jungle, with the Queen as a star-circled Madonna, her Three Ladies as three nuns, and Sarastro as the Inca); and above all when, by so sensitive and admirably balanced an account of the work as that offered by the Metropolitan Opera last week, we marvel afresh, as if for the first time, at Mozart's compound of gaiety, seriousness, and spiritual beauty.

Günther Rennert has produced *Die Zauberflöte* many times. His New York version, first done in 1967 (Bodo Igesz is currently listed as its stage director), still has the essential quality of the others by him that I have seen: directness, naturalness. There was no overemphasis on pomp at the expense of the pleasantries, or the other way round, but a supple response to all the diverse elements—a theater man's understanding of the kind of piece it is coupled with a poet's feeling for its sense. Mozart brings out the best in Mr Rennert. Peter Maag had not conducted the opera before in New York. Appreciation of his performance can begin with that third scene already mentioned. The dialogue between Tamino and the Old Priest is marked by many changes of tempo. Mr Maag observed them to perfection. In the declamation of the free recitative, his Tamino, Stuart Burrows, was ardent and impetuous, and his Priest, Donald Gramm, measured and grave. Their conversation flowed. It had character, and variety. As if through Tamino's ears the listener heard each calm statement, then followed Tamino's mind as it leapt in wild exclamation or surmise. Yet the piece was shaped as a single musical number. The sotto-voce offstage pronouncements later in the scene ("Bald, bald, Jüngling, oder nie!") gave further proof of careful, detailed preparation; the placing, the acoustics, the balance, and the pure intonation of the chords conspired to create an extraordinary atmosphere of mystery and awe. (The choral singing throughout the evening was excellent.) Many other points about Mr Maag's interpretation deserve notice; a few must suffice. Of the Queen's second air he conducted the fiercest, most fiery account I have ever heard—and in Edda Moser he had a brilliant, powerful, fearless, and accurate Queen. In the last trial scene, his handling made me aware, for the first time, of a beautiful detail: the strings softly prolonging the chords on "Nacht" when the voices and other instruments have ceased. His shaping of the march through fire and through water was exquisite. Ensemble, it must be said, became once or twice less than precise, yet this seemed to happen not through any carelessness but, rather, because both singers and conductor were caring so much to give the phrases full expression. Once or twice, Mr Maag set an unwontedly fleet, though never uncomfortable, tempo. Most delicately he shaped the close of each number. (But what is his justification for slackening speed at Papageno's entry in the trio of Act I?)

The singers were lyrical, and they sang exceptionally well in tune; during ensembles, the movement of their carefully molded lines was a delight to follow. Mr Burrows' Tamino is polished yet unaffected, at once firm and graceful. The timbre of Adriana Maliponte's Pamina was often uncannily, almost disconcertingly, like that of a clarinet: pure, steady, and precisely focused—a clarinet superlatively well played, with a complete command of line and phrase. As Sarastro, that fine young bass Hans Sotin made his Metropolitan début; his tone is so beautiful and his line so smooth that, the better to enjoy them, we could have accepted slower tempi for his airs. He has a noble presence. Theodor Uppman's bright young Papageno might by some be judged a shade overactive, but I found him captivating, both in the playing of the part and in the well-shaded, unroutined phrasing. Paul Franke, as Monostatos, and Betsy Norden, as Papagena, were good—but unexceptional in an otherwise outstanding cast. The Three Ladies were charmers. The Three Boys, played by boys, sang truly, though their German sounded like a lesson learned, not a language understood.

Chagall's décor is pretty, as *Zauberflöte* décor should be, but also aptly solemn in the ritual scenes. There is fancy in it, and we sense a happy, enthusiastic response to Schikaneder's detailed specifications. The sets, however, may disturb anyone who puzzles over the significance of the painter's familiar, favorite images, recurrent in scrim and sky, instead of regarding them as so much shape and color.

When just about everything is right, a critic may venture a suggestion or two without being thought curmudgeonly. The dialogue between Tamino and the Old Priest would be more eloquent still if the appoggiatura convention were more stylishly observed. The trials by fire and water produce too little effect of physical danger (it might help to observe the stage direction that Tamino is skimpily clad, and barefoot). The light that bursts out at the C-major "Triumph" chorus, once the elements have been successfully braved, should be maintained until the final chord,

even if this delays the scene change by a few seconds. For
the rest, Beckmesser's slate is bare. The great opera was by
all concerned uncommonly well performed.

The New York City Opera has put on a very decent
repertory *Carmen*. José Varona's sets are traditional, and
agreeably so; they recall those of the original Opéra-Comique production. His costuming breaks unconvincingly
with convention when Carmen dons breeches to go a-smug-
gling. Ann Howard, at her New York début, did not repeat
her London success in the title role—she makes more of
English words than of the French—but was more than
acceptable. Julius Rudel conducted with vigor, though he
was sometimes brisk to the point of discourtesy. Harry
Theyard's Don José was remarkable. Mr Theyard can act.
He sings French as if he could speak the language; the
words were vivid. His timbre, though it might be called
tight, was forward and "typically French" in a way that
suits the music and is seldom heard-today. José's character
and its development were consistently and cogently portrayed. The edition included both the discredited Guiraud
recitatives and some of the "new" passages.

Two other operatic events were more notable for enterprise in the choice of program than for much merit in
the execution. It is hard to discern why Verdi thought he
had done well in *Attila*—much of it recalls Donizetti below
his best; there is a curious and rather taking soprano air
with mock-Meyerbeer accompaniment—but it is a piece
rare enough to be worth crossing a river to hear. A
performance by the Opera Theater of New Jersey, in New-
ark's handsome neo-Roman Symphony Hall, was sketch-
ily sung, heedlessly acted, and enthusiastically received.

The principal roles were taken by Leyla Gencer (who did at least make something of that air) and Jerome Hines.

Thomas Scherman celebrated the twenty-fifth anniversary of his Little Orchestra Society with a Richard Strauss evening in Philharmonic Hall—excerpts from four operas he had introduced (or in the case of *Die Aegyptische Helena*, reintroduced after a long absence) to New York. The items were not snippets, but whole scenes—of *Die Frau ohne Schatten*, the greater part of Act III. The singers had got their roles by heart, which was laudable, and allowed for some simple action on the platform. *Die Frau* came off best: William Lewis was a capable Emperor, and Doris Jung a reliable Dyer's Wife; Margaret Tynes had some touching moments as the Empress, and the solo cellist was eloquent. The offstage choir was secure. But the other soloists, and the orchestra under Mr Scherman, were not up to the music.

November 4, 1972

A good starting point for anyone wishing to explore the sources of The Magic Flute *is Peter Branscombe's paper* "Die Zauberflöte: *some textual and interpretative problems" in* Proceedings of the Royal Musical Association *92 (1965–66); but investigators should also plunge into* Dschinnistan *and* Sethos *for themselves. The relevant passages of memoirs by Seyfried, Cornet, and Castelli are reprinted in O. E. Deutsch's* Mozart: Die Dokumente seines Leben (*also available in English translation, as* Mozart: A Documentary Biography).

The Sound of Music

I am not altogether happy with the sound of Philharmonic Hall. Finding words that convey just why is hard. The science of acoustics is not a precise one (if it were, there would be fewer disappointing modern concert halls). Instruments can measure to a decibel of intensity and a microsecond of decay the sound-properties of a place at any frequency, at any dynamic level, in any location, but what they tell us may bear little relation to the effect of music in performance. A listener's reactions are more complicated, and more subjective. Sitting in different seats from night to night, hearing different orchestras under different conductors, he distills his impressions from a host of variables. Though he, too, has measuring instruments of uncommon range and sensitivity (according to the acoustician Llewelyn S. Lloyd, "the loudest sound our ears can bear to hear has an intensity ten million times that of the faintest sound the most acute ear can detect"), he formulates the result of his "readings" imprecisely, often in terms of visual or tactile metaphor. One hall is "bright" and another "murky," one "warm" and another "cold." And sight, I believe, can affect what we think about sound in subtle ways often unconsidered. When I first entered Philharmonic Hall, eight years ago, large areas of it were painted navy blue, a color that always seems to "suck up the sound." Wooden walls, such as it has now, lead us to expect "warmth." When the lighting is reduced to a dim religious gloom, a corresponding "brightness" seems to go from the music (quite apart from the fact that it then becomes difficult to follow miniature scores, or the printed texts of vocal pieces). The effect is very noticeable when, as sometimes happens, the man at the switchboard, late on cue, dims just after the music has begun. And, in fact, I think the acoustics of Philharmonic Hall could be "improved" by stepping up somewhat the level of illumination during performances. The scientists' meters would register no change, but the listener might well "hear" a difference. So unscientific are a musician's reactions that old halls can even seem to acquire a sonic "patina," as if years of fine performances within them had tempered and tuned their structures to respond to the sound of music. I feel this in Carnegie Hall, in Vienna's Musikvereinsaal, in Boston's Symphony Hall and Philadelphia's Academy of Music. When so much is "in the imagination" (not a bad place for artistic experience to be), it is hazardous to generalize, and surprising that there should be any consensus of acoustic judgment. Yet to a limited extent there is. Many of the admired older halls are rectangular, fairly broad in relation to their length, with flat floors, coffered ceilings, a balcony opposite the platform, and, often, shallow balconies continued down the long sides. This seems to be a good formula for good sound. Many large modern halls built in a fan or funnel shape, with the platform at the narrow end, and surfaces to reflect and project the sound, have run into troubles—particularly when, as in Philharmonic Hall and London's Queen Elizabeth Hall, they are also long and relatively narrow.

Successful halls—such as Berlin's Philharmonie, where the orchestra is out in the open, surrounded by auditors—tend to be successful from the start. Yet the troubles can be lessened, sometimes even cured. The Royal Albert Hall, notorious a whole century for its acoustics, has now been improved out of recognition by the clusters of flying saucers suspended from the ceiling. London's Royal Festival Hall has been made rather more tolerable by a system of electrically aided resonance. The modifications to Philharmonic Hall have been many; the latest round has involved replacing the lower section of the organ shutters by an unbroken wooden background to the platform, and providing a resonant floor beneath all the players. The best sound I have heard there this season was at a Philadelphia Orchestra rehearsal of Shostakovich's Fifteenth Symphony under Eugene Ormandy—the hall empty and well lit, the tone of both solo instruments and the ensemble marvelously warm, full, and immediate. One might have been in the Amsterdam Concertgebouw, a place that seems to resonate like the body of a violin. That evening, in a crowded hall, the sound was still excellent but a shade less bewitching. (I did not mind, for at the rehearsal I had been too much captivated by sheer timbre to follow the sense of the symphony.) The worst sound I have heard there this season was at a Philharmonic concert, under Pierre Boulez, which opened with Schütz's *Fili mi, Absalon* and ended with Berlioz' Te Deum. The Schütz, a *symphonia sacra* for solo bass, four trombones, and continuo, sounded . . . well, "murky"—blurred, indistinct in line and attack. The Te Deum is one of Berlioz' massive pieces (he wanted close on a thousand performers), calculated to make a great effect in a huge, resonant space. (When Berlioz arrived in Rome he "rushed directly to St Peter's. Immense! sublime! overpowering! . . . As I thought of the glorious role my cherished art must play there, my heart began to beat with excite-

ment." Anticlimax followed—the music he heard in St
Peter's was wretched—but his own Requiem and Te Deum,
which he called "architectural" works, must have been
inspired by those first impressions.)

In New York, the Cathedral of St John the Divine is the
place for Berlioz' Te Deum. There the composer's spatial
effects could be achieved: organ at one end and orchestra at
the other, so that "Pope and Emperor speak in dialogue
from opposite ends of the nave"; twin choirs ranged with
the orchestra; and somewhere in the midst of it all a vast
chorus of choirboys (Berlioz asked for six hundred). Such
things are not possible in Philharmonic Hall, but, now that
electronic instruments have become so good, the organ
could at least have kept a due pontifical distance. Instead,
the regular instrument was used, and singers and players
were clustered near it—"huddled" is perhaps the word,
since the architects of the place provided surprisingly little
platform space to such a deal of auditorium. And so the
result was not massive but a little mean. The music did not
surge into grandeur or, during the gently devotional "Te
ergo," lap the spaces above us with mystic radiance. The
inventions sounded commonplace, their scoring more odd
than inspired—the old charges against Berlioz, which a
noble performance swiftly disproves. "One will either miss
the drift of the whole," said the composer, "or be crushed by
a tremendous emotion." I wasn't crushed.

Of course, a hall cannot be condemned because it does
not adequately hold Berlioz' Te Deum; it can be said only
to have shown its limitations in a special case. Moreover, we
must take into account that Mr Boulez is not exactly a man
given to purveying "a tremendous emotion." How much
was it his fault, how much the hall's, that Bartók's *Cantata
Profana*, in the same program, lost its rich impressionist
colors, or that at a later concert Skryabin's *Poem of Ecstasy*
was scarcely voluptuous or luscious in tone? Do Karl

Richter and the Munich Bach Choir and Orchestra really give so lackluster a reading of Bach's St Matthew Passion as I heard in Philharmonic Hall one Sunday afternoon: sober, respectable, carefully rehearsed, marked by all the virtues we dub "Kapellmeisterly"—and uninspiring? Why did Szymanowski's Second Violin Concerto, so richly wrought, so delicately jeweled, sound drab, even with that violinist of glowing tone, Henryk Szeryng, as soloist (this at a Philharmonic concert conducted by Stanislaw Skrowaczewski)? My general impression of the hall's acoustics, based on these and several other performances, is that resonance has now been achieved, but not yet "presence." Too often, the sound does not seem to "speak" to a listener, hold his attention. I have heard most of the Philharmonic concerts from seat X 123, which is midway in the orchestra, off the left-hand aisle. Everything has been clear; little has been compelling. At the Philadelphians' concerts, I have been rather closer, in N 123, which has been rather better. At Mr Skrowaczewski's concert, I was near the front—too near to hear a true orchestral balance.

Elsewhere, there have been some exquisite sounds. Musica Sacra, under Richard Westenburg, filled the Central Presbyterian Church with beautifully articulated Bach. The small choir of twenty-two voices and the small orchestra achieved a blaze of splendor in Cantata No. 11 (the Ascension Oratorio) and the Magnificat. The latter was done in its original, lengthier version, which includes Christmas interpolations; one of these, the cradlesong "Virga Jesse," a soprano-bass duet at once gentle and elaborate, was sung chorally, in tender tones and with perfectly balanced, pearly runs in which the singers breathed and phrased as one. Ornamentation and rhythmic interpretation of the printed notes were handled with a scholarly (and artistic) care that put the Munich group to shame. A program note rightly drew attention to "the proper acoustical framework" for Bach's music provided by the church.

Three Americans took the first three places in the Leeds International Piano Competition this year—Murray Perahia, Craig Sheppard, and Eugene Indjic. In the semifinals, each played a Mozart concerto ("Alone of the three," reports an English colleague, "Perahia had the real Mozartian limpidity, but he almost overdid the half-shades, applying exquisite pianissimo like a thin coat of varnish"), and then another concerto in the finals. Mr Sheppard and Mr Indjic chose Rakhmaninov's Third, Mr Perahia Chopin's E minor. The judges have awarded first prize not to a hard hitter, or to a conventionally "big" pianist, but to a poet. Fresh from his win, Mr Perahia, at Hunter College, played Mozart's E-flat Concerto, K. 271, and then Mendelssohn's Second, accompanied by an anonymous orchestra under Alexander Schneider. His tone was consistently and enchantingly beautiful. His modeling of line was delicate, loving, almost without affectation (not quite, for occasionally a phrase would melt into an almost inaudible final note). All in all, his playing showed a rare technical and interpretative finesse, and grace that did not preclude energy.

By chance, the same Mozart concerto turned up on the bill of the Philadelphia Orchestra's second New York concert, and was there given a capable but far more conventional performance, with Philippe Entremont as soloist and Riccardo Muti as conductor. Mr Muti has won golden opinions for his work in the opera houses of Europe. On the concert platform, his Mozart—he began the evening with the C-major Symphony, K. 338—was disappointing: plump, bland, smooth-jowled. And in his account of Prokofiev's Third Symphony—a fiery work drawn from the opera *The Fiery Angel*—there was a similar lack of keen-edged attack and rhythmic muscle.

November 11, 1972

Two acousticians' defense of the "traditional" shape for concert halls can be found in T. Somerville's and C. L. S. Gilford's "Tonal Quality in Concert Halls" in The Musical Times, *September 1963 (Volume 104, No. 1447). In his international survey of concert halls,* Music, Acoustics, and Architecture, *L. L. Beranek concluded that halls of traditional design provided the most acceptable sound, though he claimed that their sound quality could be synthesized in modern halls by the correct provision of reflecting surfaces.*

Westerlies

Internationally, the San Francisco Opera has the reputation of being America's first: the big company that most successfully combines excellent casts, enterprise in the choice of repertory, and a serious approach to dramatic presentation. A three-day visit to San Francisco, providing performances of Meyerbeer's *L'Africaine*, of *Götterdämmerung*, and of Gottfried von Einem's *The Visit of the Old Lady*, suggested that the reputation was not undeserved. During its previous five seasons, the company put on fifty operas; only nine productions were repeated, none more than once. This year, in a fiftieth-anniversary season, there are new productions of *Norma*, *Lucia di Lammermoor*, *L'Africaine*, *Tosca*, and *The Visit of the Old Lady*; three *Ring* cycles; and revivals of *Le nozze di Figaro* and *Aida*.

L'Africaine, Meyerbeer's last opera, is his best—and that despite a long, difficult gestation (the composer worked at it, on and off, from 1837 until his death in 1864), what might be called a posthumous birth, and the lack of any definitive edition. The outline of Scribe's action is clear: a hero is loved by two women, the fair and the dark; his life is saved once by the former, thrice by the latter; and with somewhat disconcerting versatility he is prepared to sing love duets with either. The plot unfolds amid scenes of spectacle: a Grand Council, a Brahman royal wedding, a shipwreck in which a huge vessel grinds onto a reef and is boarded by a Malagasy horde. The details are a mess. Originally Scribe's action was set in Seville, at sea, and "au centre de l'Afrique, près des sources du Niger." A reworking transferred the terminal localities to Lisbon and Calcutta: the hero became Vasco da Gama, and the dark heroine not an African but an Indian maid; the opera was renamed for the Portuguese explorer. Meyerbeer died, entrusting his score to François Joseph Fétis, director of the Brussels Conservatoire. Fétis took long leave. He came to Paris, was installed in the Opera, and sifted through the manifold alternatives Meyerbeer had left, in order to devise a performing version for the première, in 1865. Since the work had long been promised as *L'Africaine*, and Fétis wished to retain the title, he compromised between continents by setting Acts IV and V "on an isle off the east coast of Africa"—in effect, Madagascar. Sélika, the Hindu heroine, could then still be considered an African, and people could make what they would of the Brahman rites that remained (the librettist had already confounded geography by having the manchineel, a West Indian tree whose blossoms—for operatic purposes—breathe ecstasy, and death, play a determinant role in the action). The singers then took a part in the shaping. Jean-Baptiste Faure, the baritone, seized an opportunity while Fétis was ill to give himself the last word, and transfer to the close of the opera (which should end with Sélika's Liebestod) a *cavatine* from Act III. Meyerbeer established the final version of his scores during rehearsal, and made cuts *in situ*. Fétis arranged a complete runthrough of *L'Africaine* without scenery and without intervals; the music lasted four and a half hours. He cut about an hour of it, and

later published some of the cut passages, together with
alternative versions of a few numbers, as *L'Africaine—Part II*.
Even so, the first performance ran for nearly six hours; the
scenery was elaborate, and required a long while for its
setting. In San Francisco, there was still more surgery; less
than three hours of music was performed. Given that the
evening had to be shortened (for there even the *Ring* operas
are cut), the abridgment was sensitively done. Nevertheless,
it seemed a pity, when so much trouble had been taken to
mount *L'Africaine* in style, that it was not presented at
greater length: could the performance not have started an
hour earlier, as that of *Götterdämmerung* did? Yet besides
abridgment there was also some amplification: a fifth-act
aria for Inès, the other heroine, "O toi que j'adore," rejected
by Fétis, was reinstated.

L'Africaine is a grand piece. It was grandly done. Wolfram
Skalicki, the designer, provided a front curtain suggesting
that of the Paris Opera and scenery that, without being
heavily realistic, evoked Manueline splendors in the first
two acts, provided a handsome ship for the third, and raised
an exotic Eden for the fourth and fifth. Amrei Skalicki's
costumes were of 1865, not Vasco's day; they were dashing
and colorful. Lofti Mansouri massed his crowds and moved
his principals with a sure hand. Jean Perisson's handling of
the score was masterly: bold, free, delicately nuanced,
responsive to all the choice, curious instrumental inventions
with which the composer delighted to surprise his audiences. This was the best big Meyerbeer presentation I have
seen: less ponderous than La Scala's *Les Huguenots*, more
muscular than Florence's *Robert le diable*—a keen-minded
endeavor by all concerned to recapture not only the
magnificent sweep but also the energy of Meyerbeer's
conception. It was well sung. Shirley Verrett, as the titular
heroine, lacked only the calm majesty implied in much of
the vocal writing. She electrifies whatever she touches; the

result was exciting, but constantly tense both in timbre and in musical manner. Better that, however, than dullness. Miss Verrett looked gleaming. Her tones flashed and glittered. She was splendid. So was Evelyn Mandac as the fair Inès, her rival. This young Philippine soprano, known at the Seattle and Santa Fe Operas, is ready for the world's stages. She is beautiful. Her voice is pure and steady, truly focused, smoothly and surely projected. The timbre has character. And her phrasing is most musical, supple, and inventive. Miss Mandac's bewitching execution of Inès's opening *romance*, "Adieu, mon beau rivage," was one of the two great pieces of singing during the show. The other was Placido Domingo's account of Vasco's *grand air* "O paradis," high point of his noble performance. He provided a few minutes during which all the listeners' senses seemed to be flooded with rapture in the glorious sound of the tenor's tones, and his magisterial use of them. Such an experience may not be "what opera is all about," but is certainly one of the things that a composer like Meyerbeer counted on. Norman Mittelmann's Nélusko was big, powerful, and impressive. Simon Estes as Don Pedro, the bass, was a shade too jaunty, not quite grand enough. Small roles were strongly cast (Allan Monk's High Priest deserves mention), and Byron Dean Ryan's choruses sang bravely.

The old question—can Meyerbeer stand revival?—has in the last decade been answered. He has been revived with success: *Les Huguenots* at La Scala, *Robert* in Florence, *Le Prophète* in Zurich, *L'Africaine* in Munich, Naples, Florence, and now, most splendidly, San Francisco. The operas have proved to be not merely historically interesting monsters. By mid-nineteenth-century critics they were overrated: if Mozart was Music's Raphael, they said, then her Michelangelo was . . . not Beethoven, but Meyerbeer! The composers who learned from him exposed his weaknesses. Verdi's *Don Carlos* is an opera cast in Meyerbeer mold but infused with warmth and human feeling; the Nile duet of *Aida* is like a recomposition of Sélika's and Vasco's in Act IV of *L'Africaine*, brought to life by a directness of emotional expression that Meyerbeer could never achieve. Wagner's epigram "Effects without causes" stuck, and set the tone for the Meyerbeer assessments in our histories. Performance alone can reveal his strengths. In vocal score, the music often looks dry. In recorded excerpt, deprived of context, his airs are apt to limp. But in the theater his operas can be overwhelming. He was a *génie composé*, superlatively well trained, encyclopedic in his knowledge of what other men had written, single-minded in his striving to enlarge on and surpass their achievements. He exploited all the resources of his carefully picked singers, and devised new feats of prowess for them. He was master of both the grand climax and the dying fall, a constructor with an unerring eye for the shape of a scene, of an act. He was not very good at inventing tuneful cabalettas, but expert at concealing this weakness by extended, cumulative passages that produce an effect of power through sheer scale. (When one of his weak scenes is abridged, what remains seems weaker still.) Fétis tells us that he was also a fluent, fertile improviser; the meticulous musical calculation began later, once rehearsals had started. This helps to explain why *L'Africaine* seems the least labored, by far the freshest and most spontaneous, of his scores. It is also a compendium of his most attractive rhythmical, melodic, and textural mannerisms, painstakingly mastered in the earlier operas, now effortlessly deployed. Plainly, it was not just the roster of great singers (Ponselle, Rethberg, Martinelli, Gigli, De Luca) that kept *L'Africaine* on the boards of the Metropolitan from 1923 to 1933. The work, too, has notable merits.

$\mathcal{S}$ an Francisco's *Götterdämmerung* can be considered later, along with the Metropolitan Opera's productions of *Die Walküre* and *Siegfried*, involving the same trio of principals: Birgit Nilsson, Jess Thomas, and Thomas Stewart. The new piece, *The Visit of the Old Lady*, must claim my space. Gottfried von Einem, born in 1918, is perhaps the most successful of living opera composers: not in terms of critical acclaim, or, for that matter, of popular reputation, but simply because his works are played so often, particularly in German-speaking houses. With *Dantons Tod*, first done at the 1947 Salzburg Festival, Einem hit a jackpot. *Der Prozess* (Salzburg, 1953) did pretty well. His latest opera, *Der Besuch der alten Dame*, had its première at the Vienna Festival last year, and was quickly booked by companies the world over. Büchner, Kafka, Dürrenmatt—the composer chooses his subject matter with cunning (as librettist-collaborator on these pieces he worked with, respectively, Boris Blacher, Caspar Neher, and Dürrenmatt himself). The popularity in the straight theater of *Der Besuch der alten Dame* (the play that the Lunts brought to New York as *The Visit*) had prepared the way for that of the musical version. Regular opera companies, performing throughout the year, need new, well-made works that audiences will attend; Einem's fit the bill. They are not very ambitious, not particularly difficult to perform or listen to. His easy, eclectic style puts no obstacles in the way of an audience that has hurdled *Wozzeck*. He can slip into a fluent melodious vein recalling now Puccini, now Richard Strauss, and has also learned newer tricks of his trade. A cunning theater man, he aptly paces his score to the dramatic motion of a scene. He is good at proportions, contrasts of texture, control of climax. He puts his accents in the right place. His roles, large and small, are "rewarding" to their interpreters: gratefully written for the voice, and effective to enact. It is all supremely efficient. Is it enough? Not for anyone who prefers a flawed, even failed attempt at a masterpiece to flawless mediocrity—but excellent fodder for a working troupe, and for conventional audiences lured to a new opera and then surprised to find that "modern music" can be so undemanding.

Mediocrity is an unkind but not unjust word. *The Visit of the Old Lady* (San Francisco gave the work in Norman Tucker's English translation) is not so much a music-drama as a drama set to music of mostly middling quality. The score has little intrinsic life. Except at the close, it adds almost nothing to the play; that may have been Einem's intention. Dürrenmatt, declaring that *The Visit* was "an action and not an allegory," advised producers and directors to "follow the flights of my fancy and let the deeper meanings take care of themselves." He did not want interpretation: "If the foreground I have provided be correctly played, the background will emerge of its own accord." But it is music's nature to communicate "deeper meanings," and if a composer is not to be in some sense an interpreter he might as well leave a text to speak for itself, undecked, and more directly.

Dürrenmatt's "action" concerns the return of the Old Lady to the hamlet of Güllen where at the age of seventeen she was seduced, discarded by her lover—who, his eye on a richer match, bought false witnesses to her promiscuity—and abandoned to a career of prostitution, from which she has emerged as the richest woman in the world (her name, Claire Zachanassian, "is a contraction of Zacharoff, Onassis, and Gulbenkian"). Güllen is poverty-stricken; Mme Zachanassian, we suddenly learn much later, has bought it up, street by street, factory by factory, and deliberately ruined it. She offers the Gülleners wealth untold—on one condition: that they kill her seducer, Alfred Ill. On behalf of the citizens, the Mayor refuses the monstrous proposal, and the first-act curtain falls on the Old Lady's line: "I'll wait."

Acts II and III trace the yielding to temptation; the close is
Ill's ritual murder. *The Visit* is a hard, glittering piece of
work, a study in the corrupting power of capitalism as
impassioned as *The Ring*, but cast in the form of a folk play
(Dürrenmatt asked producers to treat him "as a kind of
conscious Nestroy"). The form owes something to Lenz (*Die
Soldaten*), Büchner, and Wedekind (*Frühlings Erwachen*), and
the short scenes lend themselves to musical setting. On the
other hand, the recurrent device of sudden, chilling revela-
tions that cut into episodes humorous, even tender, in tone
makes an operatic difficulty. If the libretto has been read in
advance, the *coups de théâtre* lose the force of surprise; if not,
then important statements are likely to be missed.

A comparison suggests itself with Hans Werner Henze's
Der junge Lord, based on a tale by Wilhelm Hauff but
probably owing something to Dürrenmatt's *The Visit*. In
both operas a wealthy, malicious visitor exposes the shallow
foundations, and effects the collapse, of *Kleinstadt* morality.
Henze's music is so rich, many-leveled, expansive, emotional, dramatic in its large-scale developments, and intensely alive, that it seems almost to shape, rather than
serve, Ingeborg Bachmann's libretto. Einem's score is slim-
mer, less adventurous, less interesting, and far more modest.
He eschews some "cues for music" suggested in the play—
the town band, the children's choir of greeting to the Old
Lady—perhaps because they had already figured in the
similar arrival scene of *Der junge Lord*. At the end, he
replaces Dürrenmatt's long "Greek tragedy" chorus by a
brief triumphal dance for all the populace, accompanied by
fierce, increasingly frenzied wordless cries. This is a master-
stroke—and almost the only moment where the music
comes powerfully into its own, expressing something un-
achievable by spoken words. At the last, the composer is
indeed an interpreter. Two other crucial scenes in Act III
are disappointing. Ill becomes a tragic hero when he accepts

his destiny but insists that the Gülleners also take responsi-
bility for theirs; he will not make things easy for them by
killing himself. Heaven knows how his long speech could be
aptly musicked; at any rate, Einem's recourse to a Straussian arioso, echoing Barak's gentle goodness in *Die Frau ohne
Schatten*, seems an inadequate and slightly sentimental
response to the situation. Soon afterward, there is a curious
episode, almost a tender love duet, between Claire and Ill.
The tone is elusive; it has eluded the composer, who sets
their conversation to phrases of a somewhat featureless
lyricism.

There were two first-rate performances, keenly acted and
vividly sung—from Raymond Wolansky as Ill and Richard
Cassilly as the Mayor. Most of the small parts were trimly
taken. But Regina Resnik could not manage the title role
(created in Vienna by the lustrous Christa Ludwig). Every
word of hers was clear, and that was good. The impersonation of "a Society Lady with a rare grace, despite the
grotesquerie," was splendid; she had humor and dignity—
an aged, implacable Medea with a certain charm. But she
simply did not have the voice to fill the music; she strained,
struggled, and yowled the high notes. From Robert Darling
there were settings more elaborate than the simple indications of locality prescribed by the playwright. Scene changes
were covered by brief interludes, but the music of these
(admired in Vienna) was covered in turn by the use of a
very noisy steam curtain. Francis Ford Coppola's production was deft, and Maurice Peress's conducting precise. The
singing of the Old Lady herself apart, the opera was ably
performed. But by the end, Einem's score—unlike Berg's for
Wozzeck, Henze's for *Der Prinz von Homburg*, or Zimmermann's for *Die Soldaten*—scarcely seemed to justify the
mustering of all the vast, expensive operatic apparatus
around a play; a small theater troupe could as effectively
have communicated the same experience. Essentially, *Der*

Besuch der alten Dame is a *Gebrauchsoper*, something to keep the opera machines running between masterpieces. As such, it functions admirably.

November 18, 1972

*John Roberts, of the University of California, Berkeley, directed me to Georges Servières's important article "Les Transformations et tribulations de l'*Africaine," *in* Rivista musicale italiana, *Volume 34* (*1927*).

Northwest Passage

A chain of opera companies spans the West Coast from San Diego to Seattle, and over the border to Vancouver. Seattle is a place where "Opera Lives." Buttons and bumpers proclaim it. The management of the Seattle Opera points with pride to figures that show a higher proportion of opera-attending populace than can be found in any other American city. As a rule, each production is given seven times: four times in the original language, with international artists; thrice in English, with the resident company. The Opera House is a handsome, comfortable, friendly building that seats just over three thousand people; it dates from the 1962 World's Fair. On my visit, earlier this month, I found work in progress on the company's long-term plan of staging *The Ring* and preparing audiences for it, a *Manon Lescaut* in design, and a *Faust* in dress rehearsal. Though reviewing a show on the basis of a rehearsal is inadmissible, the merits of the Marguerite can fairly be noted. Margarita Kyriaki, Greek-born, Graz-based, singing for the first time in America, has a supple, well-schooled soprano. Its timbre is darkly lustrous, well knit, lyrical, distinctive. She phrases in long, shapely spans. She should also be very good in roles like Amelia in *Boccanegra*, Desdemona, and Eva in *Die Meistersinger*.

In Vancouver, there was Donizetti's *Lucrezia Borgia*, with Joan Sutherland as heroine. Miss Sutherland chose Seattle for her first Lakmé and first *Hoffmann* heroines in French, Vancouver for her first Norma, and now the Borgia—a role that suits her very well. Among Donizetti's middle operas, *Lucrezia Borgia* ranks high. It dates from 1833, the year of *Il furioso*, *Parisina*, and *Torquato Tasso*—fine and unusual pieces all. The libretto, by Felice Romani after Victor Hugo, has some unusual features. For one, there is no love interest: Gennaro, the tenor, feels a distinct attraction toward the beautiful woman who wakes him with a kiss (on the hand) in the Prologue, but embarks on no love duet—which is just as well, since he learns in the last few moments of the opera that she is, in fact, his mother. For another, there are no big, set spectacles, no processions or dances or elaborate crowd scenes—just an offstage *festa* as backdrop to the action of the Prologue, and a brief party in Act II. The women of the chorus are scarcely used. In this concentration on the principals, varied by male-voice choruses, *Lucrezia* recalls another opera based on Hugo. Verdi, when he turned *Le Roi s'amuse* into *Rigoletto*, may have remembered the parallel between the two dramas drawn by the playwright in his preface to *Lucrèce Borgia* and repeated by Romani in his foreword to the libretto. In one play of this "bilogy," said Hugo, we find "physical deformity sanctified by paternal emotion"; in the other, "moral deformity purified by maternal emotion." "Purified" is rather strong. Lucrezia is not a nice woman. Though she feels warmly toward her son, once she thinks he is safely out of town she poisons off his five best friends. With unveiled menace she sings to her spouse, Alfonso d'Este, who has crossed her, "Take care, Don Alfonso, my *fourth* husband!" Donizetti makes frequent use of the friends as a male-voice quintet (stretching the term to include, along the top line, the transvestite contralto, Orsini). The predominance of low voices, both choral and solo, gives to the score of *Lucrezia* a rich tonality; the single soprano role of the heroine stands out in high relief. The forms are similarly unconventional. Only the bass, Alfonso, sings a straightforward full-scale aria with cabaletta. The soprano has a brief and beautiful *romanza*, "Come è bello," the tenor his "Di pescator" (set into a duet), the contralto a little narrative song and the famous *brindisi*, both with a refrain from the companions. All the rest is duet, trio, or ensemble, carefully and richly composed, until we reach Lucrezia's final bravura outburst, over the corpse of her son. Even this defies convention by juxtaposing slow and fast sections in a single, repeated stanza. (The number was included, we are told, only at the insistence of the first Lucrezia, against the wishes of composer and librettist; in that case, Méric-Lalande's dramatic instincts were sounder than theirs.) The surge and impetus of the score are considerable. Each scene is dynamically constructed, and the music drives forward with the action. Some of the melodies have close counterparts in Verdi's *Il trovatore*. There are impressive strokes. At the climax of the Prologue the quintet cries "È la Borgia!" in bare octaves, doubled by menacing brass, as the mask is torn from the heroine's face. (Gautier left a vivid description of Giulia Grisi's Lucrezia at this moment: "Features pale as if cut in marble, and defiant, flashing eyes.") The second verses of "Come è bello" and of "Di pescator" are not straight repeats; in the former, there are subtle variations of the vocal line; in the other, little changes of melody and harmony sensitive to the words. A brief colloquy between rival rogues, sent by Duke and by Duchess to Gennaro (the encounter suggests that of Mime and Alberich in *Siegfried*), could easily have been treated as an episode of no great musical importance; instead, Donizetti writes a flowing instrumental melody, wittily scored, dovetails into it the *parlante* exchanges, and creates a little gem of a scene.

Richard Bonynge conducted the Vancouver Symphony with spirit, with style, with appreciation of the orchestral colors and chivalrous attention to the vocal phrasing. Beverly Fyfe's chorus was well prepared. José Varona's set—a single construction, differently decked for each scene—was bold, and good to look at, Irving Guttman's production straightforward and sensible. In such a frame the singers must have found it easy to give of their best. During that tender *romanza* in her first scene, Miss Sutherland could not be acquitted of mooching along the vocal line, sounding droopy when she aimed to be delicate, but as soon as the Borgia was angered the soprano became energetic. Her rhythms were incisive, her tones flashing. Her performance was both brilliant and passionate—perhaps her most exciting achievement since the Scala Semiramide. The role of Lucrezia gives scope not only to the accuracy and agility of her voice but also to its amplitude and power. Miss Sutherland should surely be adding Abigail in *Nabucco*, Lady Macbeth, and Hélène in *Les Vêpres siciliennes* to her repertory. Huguette Tourangeau's Orsini had the right sparky quality. Her *brindisi* sounded like a madcap improvisation, and there was an astonishing moment in the second verse when, from the heart of a low note, there suddenly shone and swelled a high note two octaves above. John Alexander, the Gennaro, is a tenor who gets steadily better. The timbre may be rather plain, not individual, but his singing is at once fluent, elegant, and manly. In successive revivals of the opera, Donizetti enlarged the tenor role: for Napoleone Moriani, the *tenore della bella morte*, he devised a beautiful death, a G-major larghetto, which is the most romantically Verdian passage of the score, and this was by Mr Bonynge rightly included; for Mario, the composer added a suave cantabile air in Act II, "Anch'io provai le tenere," and a different, elegantly amorous one for Nicholas Ivanov, "T'amo, qual s'ama un angelo." The Ivanov air, the autograph of which is now in the Morgan Library, was chosen for Vancouver, and with it Mr Alexander made a great effect. Alfonso, a bass role (composed for Luciano Mariani, Bellini's Count Rodolfo in *La sonnambula*), has long been adopted by baritones; by Louis Quilico it was securely and imposingly sung. Donizetti revivals, when carelessly undertaken, with emphasis only on a prima donna, or crudely cut, ineptly staged, can be sorry, insubstantial—or, at best, one-sided—affairs. This Vancouver *Lucrezia*, however, was at all points strong. So well done, it proved to be an opera well worth doing.

November 25, 1972

Forging the Ring

The notion of staging *The Ring* at Salzburg came to Herbert von Karajan, he said, during a summer festival while he was conducting there his own spectacular production of *Boris Godunov*. An enormous stage, with superb technical equipment, unused for most of the year; a theater with uncommonly fine, warm, delicate acoustics; a small, beautiful town, where the artists could gather to rehearse intently, away from the bustle of the everyday musical round, and to which the audience could come as pilgrims with nothing but Wagner (and perhaps a concert or two) to fill their days—all things conspired to suggest that there *The Ring* he had dreamed of but had never been able in ordinary theaters to achieve might be created. And thus the idea of the Salzburg Easter Festival was born. It would be like Bayreuth but in some ways even better: present-day Bayreuth puts on a pretty hefty season; at Salzburg each year Karajan would concentrate on bringing just one opera—and perhaps a revival as well, but never a complete *Ring*—to the performance pitch he had in mind. More—preparation could be doubly thorough if during the previous fall he were to record that opera. In the Berlin studios, with the forthcoming Salzburg cast and his own orchestra, the Berlin Philharmonic, he would undertake the detailed work, the paragraph-by-paragraph polishing involved in the making of a record. Then at Salzburg, at Easter, it would all join together while Karajan the producer gave visual shape to what Karajan the conductor had achieved.

Beginning in 1967, it came to pass, and the Salzburg *Ring* was a marvelous experience. The performances had so strong a character that, despite the year that elapsed between installments and despite changes of cast in the principal roles, one entered the Festspielhaus and was caught up almost at once in the powerful, particular *Ring* world, unlike any other, that Karajan had created. Above all, it was distinguished by the most beautiful orchestral playing of our day. To the magnificent Berlin orchestra everything else was subordinate. It did not drown the singers, for Karajan held much of its playing to a chamber-musical finesse. Rather, he accompanied his instrumentalists with voices that were, in the main, far lighter and less imposing than those of the heroic singers traditionally associated with *The Ring*. Similarly, though the stage pictures (scenes by Günther Schneider-Siemssen, costumes by George Wakhevitch, both working under Karajan's spell) were large, wonderful, and impressive, they seemed to have been planned solely as illustrations to a drama that was unfolding in the pit. They glowed dim and mysterious; it was easier to read expression on the instrumentalists' faces than on those of the actors. There were high, breath-taking moments when eye, ear, and mind together were amazed: the dragon of *Das Rheingold* shaping itself from the glittering goldheap, embodiment of the evil creed Alberich has just expounded; in *Die Walküre*, Brünnhilde appearing to Sieg-mund in a *mandorla* of blue radiance, apt vision of a stern and lovely messenger from another world. Nevertheless, something was missing. In all operas, the main emphasis must be on the stage—even in Wagner's operas, I was going to add, but should perhaps say: and especially in Wagner's operas, since that idea determined the very form of his Bayreuth theater, designed expressly to focus attention on the scene. In Salzburg, the scrim between actors and audience was also symbol of a barrier that kept us from direct emotional involvement in the drama of gods and men, and distanced their passions. We watched, we heard, we marveled. The luminous texture of the sound, the grandeur, the delicacy, the clarity of instrumental and verbal detail, the long line of Karajan's reading, the wizardry of his vast, inventive stagecraft—all these brought their rewards. In many ways, this was the most nearly perfect realization of *The Ring* anyone could hope to encounter: a great conductor's vision of what it might be, shaped without impediment, with all the practical and technical circumstances right, limited only by the human failings of one or two singers taxed beyond their powers. But in one important way it was imperfect: straightforward, simple response to the singers was inhibited.

A brief assessment of the Salzburg *Ring* is the necessary prelude to any consideration of the Metropolitan Opera's *Ring* in progress, since the latter is a by-product of the Karajan presentation. It could not be the same, even if he were still here to direct it. The orchestra is no longer Karajan's own. The carefully rehearsed original casts are changed. The scenery needs drastic reduction before it can fit on the Metropolitan stage. The operas must be sandwiched into a busy repertory, and therefore the theater cannot be devoted for weeks to nothing but Wagner; orchestra, stagehands, and lighting crew have other cares, and so, for that matter, has a city audience. Given the present circumstances of New York opera, these things are inevitable, yet the basic plan remains a good one: to build, on the Salzburg foundation, a repertory *Ring* of unusual quality. Karajan produced his *Walküre* here in 1967, his *Rheingold* in 1968. This year, but without him, the cycle is resumed; *Siegfried* has been added and *Die Walküre* revived. Erich Leinsdorf is the conductor and Wolfgang Weber the stage director. Both operas contain individual performances of great merit.

For several years, Birgit Nilsson has not sung Brünnhilde in either Bayreuth or Covent Garden—and in Salzburg never. Though we can admire, in the work of her younger colleagues, the fresh tones and naturalness of Catarina Ligendza and the passion of Berit Lindholm, Miss Nilsson remains unmatched for the heroic, goddesslike vigor of her voice, effortlessly powerful, brilliant and burnished, untiring, unforced. She sounds the subtleties of the role, vividly declaims and inflects the words. A stern critic may note that once or twice she was not perfectly in tune (decisively, almost defiantly so, for Miss Nilsson always hits and sustains her notes dead-center, even when they may be not quite the right ones), that some episodes of the *Siegfried* love duet call ideally for a more tender tone, and that several phrases (for example, "Der diese Liebe mir in's Herz gehaucht," in the last act of *Die Walküre*) would be more eloquent still if sung with an ampler use of portamento—but then must add that these things hardly mattered and that it was glorious to hear her Brünnhilde once again. Jess Thomas, the Siegfried, and Thomas Stewart, the Wanderer, are both singers of uncommon intelligence and imagination. Each was cogent, each in his best voice. Mr Thomas was far more lyrical, freer, and fuller of tone, and Mr Stewart far more steady and commanding, than in much of their recent work. The Volsung twins in *Die Walküre* were Gwyneth Jones and Jon Vickers. I have heard them often, in various productions of the opera, but never in better form. Gone was the unruliness that sometimes ruins Miss Jones's singing; beautifully handled the warm, full, lustrous voice, reflection of a warm, spontaneous personality. Again, more portamento would have been welcome, and also a clearer utterance of the words; again, it hardly mattered when the general effect was so radiant. This Sieglinde was Miss Jones's Metropolitan début, and a successful one. Mr Vickers did not croon; he sang Siegmund's music freely, fully, easily, with the poetic intensity and incisive utterance of the words for which he is famous. Miss Jones and Mr Vickers made a lyrical, ardent pair. Wotan in this opera was Theo Adam. In an age that lacks true *Heldenbaritone*, Mr Adam approaches most often to the weight and grandeur of delivery that are needed, and on this occasion he, too, reached peak form. Gerhard Stolze's Mime and Gustav Neidlinger's Alberich (the latter a local début) are justly celebrated. John Macurdy was a ringing, decisive Hunding, who bore himself bravely and sang out in a dark, impressive voice of impeccable focus. Mignon Dunn's Fricka and Lili Chookasian's Erda were weaker.

When several of the world's regular Wagner singers are heard performing at their very best, their conductor must obviously share in the praise. Mr Leinsdorf's readings also had the virtue of being energetic. There were dramatic moments: the chords that accompany the emergence of Erda, for example, were timed with real theatrical flair. But in general his conduct of the score was choppy. Tempi did not grow one from another or relate to the basic movement of an act, even of a scene. The string tone was shallow, and the brass tone mat, with mean, tinny sound from the solo trumpet. The aim seemed to be to get everything done with as fast as possible. There was no weight, no breadth. Moment after great moment passed by signaled with just a spurt of emphasis but never any attempt to let the music breathe or to let us appreciate the full sense of a chord shift or color change. Wotan was urged to gabble his narration as

if it were *secco* recitative; did Mr Leinsdorf fear that his
listeners might grow bored? (But the passage becomes
boring only when they are not invited to follow, word for
word, thought by thought, the progress of the god's brooding.) The noble rhetoric of his "Wunschmaid war'st du mir"
was reduced to a scramble. Though the stopwatch is not a
precise critical instrument, it can confirm impressions of
undue haste or of dawdling, and if there were some squalid
little race in which conductors vied to see who could
dispatch *The Ring* most quickly, Mr Leinsdorf would now
probably hold two lap records. The first *Walküre* in Bayreuth, under Richter, in 1876, lasted three hours and
thirty-nine minutes, and the very fastest in the annals,
Otmar Suitner's, of 1966, three hours and twenty-seven. Mr
Leinsdorf last week managed it in three hours and nineteen.
For the first two acts of *Siegfried*, Lorin Maazel holds the
Bayreuth record, set in 1968, at two hours and twenty-two
minutes (Richter had taken two hours and forty); Mr
Leinsdorf has now clipped nearly two minutes off that time.
(His Act III timing is irrelevant, since there was a rude cut
in the encounter between the Wanderer and his grandson.)
In defense of this racer, it can be said that the singers
seemed to thrive at his speeds (though the music did not)
and on occasion took in a single breath phrases for which
they generally require two.

The Karajan-Weber production is hard to appraise.
Besides being technically less accomplished than in its
Salzburg incarnation, it now inevitably gives the impression
of being a series of illustrations to a "text"—Karajan's—
that is no longer there. On the other hand, as "house *Rings*"
go, it must be among the best: large, handsome, and for the
most part uneccentric. The light levels are higher than they
were in Salzburg, which is good (how important it is to be
able to "read the libretto from the singers' lips"), though
some scenes could be brighter still. The murmuring forest

needs a sunnier dapple; Brünnhilde should wake to greet a more glorious radiance—sense, sound, and the shine of Miss Nilsson's voice all demand it. In general, not much impression remains of a single directing personality with convictions about what *The Ring* should express. The work can mean many things. It was first plotted as a political allegory, influenced by Bakunin and proclaiming that wealth and power should not be left in private hands (as Wieland Wagner put it, too bluntly: "Walhalla is Wall Street"), and this, of course, it remains. But then it also became an allegory of how man learned to know and command both himself and the natural world around him. The forging scene is an epitome of the elements harnessed to man's use. On a deeper level, the forces influencing human action, which at the start are externalized in gods, are by the end analyzed as aspects of man's psyche. (It was in this sense that Wieland planned his 1965 production.) On a simpler but not insignificant level, it is a rousing old tale with interesting characters acting hugely amid highly picturesque scenery, and a feast of splendid music. If Karajan cannot be brought back, then, given the shifting casts, the short rehearsal time, and the fact that no other great producer with a mind of his own will want to work to Karajan's visions, the Metropolitan should probably be content to offer a large, impressive frame in which the world's seasoned Wagnerians can be seen and heard to best advantage, both individually and in mutual reaction. To this end, a more realistic enactment of emotions is needed. Brünnhilde should really look at Siegmund during the Annunciation of Death, meet his eyes not only on arrival but also while he fires her heart with new, strange feelings. (Looking is very important in *Die Walküre*; there is scarcely a page of the libretto in which eyes and glances are not mentioned—another reason for insisting on adequate light.) Brünnhilde and Siegfried should sing their love duet side by side, as lovers might, and address one another, not hold forth independently.

To judge only—and therefore on inadequate evidence—by the final *Götterdämmerung*, the San Francisco *Ring* produced by Paul Hager, designed by Wolfram Skalicki, has a more distinctive character. It favors a straightforward, direct presentation of emotions. Bernard Shaw's dictum—that if a passage of Wagner's is rendered as faithfully as possible it simply cannot take on the wrong expression—can be extended to the staging of his operas. Miss Nilsson was superb. Mr Thomas was reliable; the interpretation was well studied and keenly presented, but his tone flowed less lyrically than in New York. Mr Stewart's Gunther was first-rate; so were Clifford Grant's bold, clever, powerful Hagen and Margarita Lilova's shining Waltraute. Mr Suitner, conducting, was fast but not flip. With unusual candor, the program revealed that he used Gotthold Lessing's reduced orchestration, often heard but seldom remarked. The whole performance generated that special excitement which so often marks the final night of a *Ring* series.

December 2, 1972

Jon Vickers is the Siegmund, Jess Thomas the Siegfried, and Thomas Stewart the Wotan and Wanderer of Karajan's Walküre *and* Siegfried *recordings (Deutsche Grammophon 2713002 and 2713003). Erich Leinsdorf has recorded* Die Walküre *with Birgit Nilsson as Brünnhilde and Jon Vickers as Siegmund (RCA).*

Terpsichore's Touch

Why, they ask me, do you so much enjoy living in New York? And I reply that from rooms high above the Hudson I look into light that makes each day a visual adventure, or that after years of Kensington's traffic stench and jet-loud skies New York seems the most serene of great cities to work and walk in. And if those are deemed reasons insufficient I add that the New York City Ballet also lives and works here. Imagine a world in which Mozart's music was played regularly in only one town, by an ensemble directed by its composer, while in other places it could be enjoyed only when that ensemble made one of its rare foreign tours—apart from a few performances of a few compositions (as it were, "his" *Apollo, Serenade, Night Shadow, Palais de Cristal*) scattered through the repertory of local troupes. What person to whom music matters would not wish to spend long months in that town? What person to whom ballet matters cannot wish to spend long months in New York? There are other composers than Mozart, other ballet-makers than George Balanchine. But each is central to his art.

Ballet began when Terpsichore touched Apollo's finger, as on the Sistine ceiling God touches Adam's, and inspired a pas de deux in which movement became form and bodies learned to speak and sing—a pas de deux that whenever it is re-enacted holds implicit in its plastic images all dance, past, present, and future. This symbolic moment outside time, when Terpsichore joined her sisters Polyhymnia and Calliope on equal terms, was first shaped in mortal history on June 12, 1928, on the stage of the Théâtre Sarah-Bernhardt in Paris; in cold print it is recorded just before rehearsal-figure 64 of Stravinsky's score *Apollo Musagetes*. The Stravinsky-Balanchine *Apollo* is missing on the bills of the current City Ballet season, but there are many other works of that marvelous partnership, including two new masterworks that were made for the company's Stravinsky Festival earlier this year—*Violin Concerto* and *Duo Concertant*. Balanchine had used the Violin Concerto before, for *Balustrade*, a de Basil ballet of 1941. A phrase of Edwin Denby's about that ballet lingers in my mind—"the wonderfully sensual acrobatics of the middle section" (but it was in the outer movements that he traced the start of Balanchine's "direct new classicism")—and eight minutes of it linger on film in the New York Public Library's Dance Collection at Lincoln Center. Stravinsky recalled *Balustrade* as "one of the most satisfactory visualizations of any of my works" (adding in parenthesis Hofmannsthal's remark to Strauss: "Ballet is perhaps the only form of art which permits real, intimate collaboration between two people gifted with visual imagination"). Yet a more precise bodily articulation of Stravinsky's score than the new *Violin Concerto* could not be conceived. The composer declared that by making his *Movements* visible Balanchine had advanced the acceptance of that score by at least a decade. *Violin Concerto*, like *Orpheus*, like *Agon*, seems almost to flow from a single mind, an entity called Stravinsky-Balanchine. The opening toccata is built with a double subject (two couples)—used not in the sonata-form manner of the soloist and couple in the first movement of *Brahms-Schoenberg Quartet* but in shifting relationships, like the two contrasted musical themes that either soloist or orchestra can play. The first aria is a breath-taking two-part invention for more or less equal "voices," Karin von Aroldingen and Jean-Pierre Bonnefous; the second is a lyrical cantilena in which Kay Mazzo's melody is supported, and shaped, by Peter Martins. The choreography discovers a playfulness in the music unheard in straight concert accounts. Stravinsky smiles most often when he is in performance with Balanchine; flashes of wit pass between the two men, in *Violin Concerto* as they do in *Agon*. The audience observes them; the players and dancers remain intent on their tasks, smiling no more than does a piano at some sly sally of the pianist.

The solo-instrumental part of *Violin Concerto* was admirably played by Joseph Silverstein. Musicians who plan to play Stravinsky should study Balanchine, definer of impetus, clarifier of textures, master of counterpoint and of subtle variation. "Accompanying" dance is a task some performers think beneath them, but during a Balanchine ballet one is apt to hear music more intently than in the concert hall—and, with Balanchine to inspire them, Lamar Alsop and Gordon Boelzner, violin and piano, gave, I swear, a more elegant, stylish, and cogent account of Stravinsky's Duo Concertant than did Rafael Druian and Michel Beroff at their Philharmonic Hall recital, in October. The relations between sonic and visual imagery, readily experienced, are seldom straightforward, rarely as plain as in the Bransle Simple of *Agon* (a canon for two trumpets, and for two boys). How often Balanchine's work makes me wish that I could read dance notation, and that his compositions were available in print, to be studied and savored at leisure!

In Stravinsky's career, the Duo Concertant followed directly on the Violin Concerto and continued, with chamber forces, that vein of rhythmicized lyricism. Formally, Balanchine's *Duo Concertant* is a different sort of work altogether from *Violin Concerto*: not so much a fusion with the score as a commentary on it—and perhaps also a description, unusually frank and confiding, of his way of assembling a ballet. To the first of the five movements the dancers, Miss Mazzo and Mr Martins, just listen. In the second, they try out some steps. He invites her to initiate moves to the third, follows her lead, tries her ideas, modifies them, checks her once, and, after her gentle insistence, checks her again with courteous determination to impose his own pattern. (Something similar has happened between the instrumentalists.) Music akin to that of *Violin Concerto* has led to some movements, in this different context, recalling the manner of their pas de deux in that ballet. In the final Dithyramb, it is as if some new spell had been cast. The light fades. The dancers disappear, are found again. Some phrases can take visual shape, others are left to the musicians alone. It is a small ballet that is mysterious, satisfying, and perfect.

In 1936 Balanchine produced Gluck's *Orfeo* for the Metropolitan Opera. That Opera's current *Orfeo* is a dismal affair, wretchedly danced and dully sung; I will not dwell on it. In any moment of City Ballet's *Orpheus*, a composition Stravinsky and Balanchine planned together from the start, there was a clearer, nobler appreciation of the myth, and Mr Bonnefous, with his clear, precise classicism and elegantly Attic shape, has become the interpreter of the title role the work has long needed. Melissa Hayden was an urgent Eurydice; Francisco Moncion was moving in his original role of the Dark Angel. How much passion can be compassed within a classical style! The range of ballets presented is immense. The finale of *Symphony in C* is surely the grandest thing danced since Petipa dreamed up the Kingdom of Shades scene of *La Bayadère* (and is a hundred times more interesting and distinguished in invention). *Western Symphony* shows how classicism can acquire an authentic cowboy accent not through distortion of its forms but by force, rapidity, and indolent grace of delivery; the Muses who drew Apollo's chariot can flick into high-stepping fillies hauling a buggy. I missed *Episodes*, but have seen, at last, the wonderful *Four Temperaments*, the first creation of the company (then the Ballet Society) back in 1946. Anyone accustomed to ensembles that prepare only a handful of works at a time must be astounded at the enormous repertory that City Ballet has brought to performance pitch—not only by the dancers but also, be it added, by Robert Irving's capable orchestra. Though *Agon* at one performance fell short of what memory said it was, at the next it was as outrageously audacious, and limpidly beautiful, as ever. (This is another score that sounded difficult until Balanchine made it as accessible as a Mozart divertimento.) *Brahms-Schoenberg Quartet* was also a discovery for me. It is evidently not performance-proof. One matinée it seemed just—just!—brilliantly fashioned; a few evenings before, with a single cast change and a different conductor, the andante had been the most poignantly lyrical dance I had seen in years.

A love affair of long standing—it began when City Ballet first came to Covent Garden, in 1950—has lost none of its intensity. Love need not blind one to faults. Much of the lighting has been less than expertly handled. Dreadful things have been done to *Firebird*. It is now "conceived as Chagall accompanied by music and dance"; the Bird's monstrous costume, inhibiting speed and flutter, allows scarcely more than a stately ostrich progress to the rapid, glittering music. The set for the *Swan Lake* excerpt looks mean; property swans dragged across the stage suggest a parody; the orchestra sounds thin, not sumptuous. Why do the episode? (Oh, well, it does contain some sumptuous dancing.) But nothing by, nothing wholly by, Balanchine has been disappointing. His dancers, new and old, are still superbly tuned instruments, large, lucid and pure in style, cutting the air cleanly, long-phrased in adagio, effortlessly rapid, rhythmical, buoyant.

I should have said something about Jerome Robbins' important contributions to the City Ballet repertory, and should squeeze in at least a word or two about Paul Taylor's fresh, thoroughly likable Dance Company, which has been at the Brooklyn Academy of Music, and Alvin Ailey's exhilarating, popular young Dance Theatre, at City Center. Mr Taylor's new *So Long Eden* is an innocent, carefree pas de trois in a garden not at all embattled. John Butler's new *According to Eve*, for Ailey, takes up the tale at a later chapter, in a pas de trois for Eve, Cain, and Abel. This is a pretty effective dramatic ballet; it makes, however, mainly incidental use of a score—George Crumb's *Ancient Voices of Children*—that is too positive not to resist such treatment. The Lorca texts may loosely parallel Eve's sorrows, but composer's and choreographer's images for them fit awkwardly.

Though America may lack the eighteenth-century court theaters most apt to the performance of Rameau's operas, the composer of the exotic entrées in *Les Indes*

galantes might well have enjoyed the surroundings—blended
Encyclopédiste science and marbled splendor—of the charming little Baird Auditorium in Washington's Smithsonian
Institution, where, the other day, his *La Naissance d'Osiris*
was revived. The largest tiger ever shot, the largest elephant
ever stuffed, one poised for a spring and the other trum-
peting high—Rameau could have found tense, athletic
music for these noble beasts. Lancret or Pater should have
pictured the strange dream-elegance of the scene afterward,
as the guests gathered in the long gallery to sip wine—beneath a life-size model of a blue whale played upon by
simulated submarine flicker. *La Naissance d'Osiris, ou La Fête
Pamilie*, composed to celebrate the birth of the Duke of
Berry, later Louis XVI, was first performed at Fontainebleau, in 1754, and not performed again until Alan Curtis,
of the University of California, Berkeley, prepared an
edition and got together with Shirley Wynne, of Ohio State
University, to bring it to life. Mr Curtis is a musicologist
who directs his university's Collegium Musicum, Mrs
Wynne a choreologist who directs her university's Rococo
Dance Ensemble—both happy exemplifiers of scholarly
disciplines that find fulfillment in performance, and performance practices that are illumined by scholarship. The
instruments used in their presentation were baroque, or
new-built to baroque specifications. The steps of the dance
were such as are found in eighteenth-century primers. The
costumes were designed by Louis-Simon Boquet, who
decked the first performance of the piece, at Fontainebleau.

Jean-Philippe Rameau is of all the great opera composers
the most cruelly neglected—and, for that matter, of all the
great composers the one least well served by modern
musicology. The Œuvres Complètes, begun in 1895, petered
out, leaving four full-length operas and four one-acters

untouched. (Welcome plans are afoot to make a new start.) The BBC has done some good work. The record companies have started to show interest (*Castor et Pollux* is available now, played on the right instruments). The few French revivals have generally been in faulty editions marred by tinkery. Rameau is not easily staged; all those dances pose a problem—which must be solved, for they matter. Louis de Cahusac, the librettist of *La Naissance d'Osiris*, declared (in his *La Danse ancienne et moderne*, also 1754) that in the theater movements should communicate with even more precision than the spoken or sung words: "Je dis, avec plus de précision, parce que le geste est plus précis que le discours. Il faut plusieurs mots, pour exprimer une pensée: un seul mouvement peut peindre plusieurs pensées." Moreover, the dances should be no mere *agrément isolé* but intimately bound to the main action, indissolubly one with it. Although Mrs Wynne's dances, gaily composed in the old formal language, did not really speak more clearly than words, they forwarded such slight action as *La Naissance* contains, were at one with the patterns of the music, and made a fresh, delightful effect free of museumy mustiness. Mr Curtis's little band, boasting some brilliant baroque woodwinds, revealed once again that the music of any age expresses itself most directly to modern listeners in the tones and idioms of its composer. The solo singers and the local chorus were so-so. *La Naissance* is late Rameau, without the high, sensational dramatic strokes of the *tragédies*. Pamilie's festival simply celebrates the birth of a noble heir and "la joie et le bonheur d'un Peuple aimable gouverné par la Sagesse et l'Amour" (who could foretell, in 1754, that the relations between Louis XVI and his people would one day be less than amiable?), doing so with grace, elegance, and much cunning, pretty invention. The composer himself declared that in old age, while his genius deserted him, his taste improved. His taste and skill, matched by those of the pair who directed this performance, provided an unusual and happy evening.

December 9, 1972

The recording of Rameau's Castor et Pollux *mentioned above is on Telefunken SAWT 9584-7. Rameau's* Hippolyte et Aricie *(with Janet Baker in the role of Phaedra) is recorded on Oiseau-Lyre S 286-8; the instruments are modern but the performance is moving.*

The Verdi Crusade

The works of Verdi dominate the operatic repertory as never before. During the revival and revaluation that began in the 1930s, and still continue, *Macbeth* was the first of the early, pre-*Rigoletto* operas to be esteemed highly by earnest musicians—rightly so. *Nabucco* came next. And now that they have all been heard again, everyone has his special favorites. *I due Foscari* is an intense, unusual piece, with deeper characterization than can be found in *Ernani*— though *Ernani*, stirringly sung, proves irresistible. For my money, the pair still too seldom performed are *Giovanna d'Arco*, which is swift, shapely, and uncommonly compact, and *Stiffelio*, in which the problems of a German pastor who preaches forgiveness yet cannot forgive his adulterous wife give rise to some of the composer's most interesting early inventions (well, fairly early; *Rigoletto* followed hard upon *Stiffelio*). The opera that seldom wins wholehearted approval today is *I Lombardi alla prima crociata*, Verdi's second great success. *Nabucco* was his first, and with it, his third opera, he broke all Scala records (the run of fifty-seven performances

in the autumn season of 1842 is unparalleled in that
theater's annals). *I Lombardi*, on which he collaborated with
the same librettist, Temistocle Solera, was an evident
attempt to repeat the triumph. The 1843 audiences went
wild over it; according to Verdi's early biographer Folchetto, the big chorus "O Signore, dal tetto natio" raised a
storm of approval ("move all'orgasmo il pubblico" is his
vivid phrase). Modern commentators ascribe much of the
enthusiasm to the patriotic fervor of the time. Like Boito in
his review of an 1864 revival at La Scala, they are ready to
discern "the marvellous traces, here and there, of eternal
beauty," but always there is a note of reserve. The odd thing
is that no two writers agree on which passages are splendid
and which not. I was not wholehearted about *I Lombardi*
myself until, last week, Eve Queler directed a concert
performance of the work in Carnegie Hall that swept away
all resistance to the piece and made most of the objections to
it seem trivial.

In a concert performance, of course, the problems of
staging the somewhat outrageous plot are avoided. A vision
scene in which the tenor, with attendant celestial spirits,
appears in Heaven to sing to a soprano still on earth is more
easily set in a theater of the mind than on boards and
backcloth. In a dramatic action, we might more readily
regret that Act I ends with the situation almost exactly
where it began: at the start of the act the bass, Pagano,
returns from an exile of expiation in the Holy Land,
imposed because he had tried to kill his brother; at the
close, after another bungled attempt at fratricide, he sets out
again for the Middle East and another stint of exile. But as
a musical action, the two scenes of this act magnificently
conjure up an atmosphere of violence, of communal emotions rent and distorted by personal passion, of Christian
piety and Crusader bloodlust in fierce, strange contrast.

These are the recurrent themes of the opera. They are abruptly stated in the musical confrontation of nuns' chorus, cutthroats' chorus, and Pagano's cabaletta "O speranza di vendetta," which ends the first scene. (Abruptness is a feature but not necessarily a failing of *I Lombardi*.) In *Il giuramento* (1837) Mercadante had done something similar. On one level, Solera and Verdi may simply have had recourse to an operatic device of proved effectiveness. On another, instinct, rather than any conscious planning, and sheer theatrical flair led them to shape their farrago in a way which makes excellent surreal sense, though it offends all the canons of the well-made play. Francis Toye "doubted whether the annals of opera contain a more uncouth libretto." The coincidences of the later encounters in Palestine are as great as those of *La forza del destino*, more monstrous even than the Loch Lomond meeting in the last scene of *Aroldo*—but we may recall that the program of Artaud's First Manifesto includes "a romantic melodrama in which the improbability will become an active and concrete element of poetry," and that the Conquest of Mexico epic outlined in the Second Manifesto has much in common with *I Lombardi*. All his life, Verdi looked for unusual subject matter cast in unconventional forms; in *I Lombardi* Solera provided him with a rambling, scrambling pageant that deals with the clash of cultures, the questioning of creeds, the conflict of individual emotion and national destiny, and the vision of a glorious future to be won by determination and sacrifice. No wonder his response to it was vigorous.

Solera was a feckless, colorful, attractive fellow. The son of an Italian patriot imprisoned in the Spielberg, he ran away from his Viennese school to join a circus, but was recaptured by the police in Budapest. He was composer as well as poet, and by the age of twenty-four had had two

operas performed with success at La Scala—an achievement unusual even in those days when composers began
young. For Verdi he wrote four stirring librettos, moving to
Madrid while the last of them, *Attila*, was still being
composed. From Spain, there were tales of romantic
adventures involving Queen Isabella. Later, he is reported
to have been a spy for Napoleon III, then for Cavour, to
have organized the suppression of banditry in the Basilicata,
and to have reorganized the Egyptian police. In 1861 he
was destitute, and Verdi's friend the Countess Maffei got up
a fund to establish him as an antique dealer in Florence
(Verdi was unsympathetic: "Within eight days he will be
back where he started; it's his own fault that he has not
pursued a brilliant career, and become the leading librettist
of our day"). In 1876 he landed up in England, but "the
fatal words that Dante saw written on the gates of Hell
stand now before my eyes on all the walls of London."
Within two years, he was dead. Solera's verse is usually
mocked, but I like it, enjoying the almost Byronically
chipper fashion in which he tosses grand, resonant words
about and lets them fall down pat. Toye cites a quatrain
from the chorus of incompetent cutthroats in *I Lombardi*—
"D'un sol colpo in paradiso/L'alme altrui godiam man-
dar;/Col pugnal di sangue intriso/Poi sediamo a banchet-
tar"—which he renders, not unfairly, as "With one blow we
like to send our/Fellows' souls in heaven to shine;/Then
with gore-encrusted daggers/We sit calmly down to dine."
It gets a smile; so does Verdi's dapper music to it, even from
an audience that may not be following the words in detail. I
believe that Solera and Verdi both knew exactly what they
were at, and allowed for that smile (rather as Elgar did
when composing the demon chorus of *Gerontius*—a light
moment in a work not otherwise comic). The poet who in
Nabucco paraphrased Psalm 137 as "Va, pensiero, sull'ali

dorate" and the man who set those words were not bunglers. The cutthroats were.

In her performance of *I Lombardi* Miss Queler skimped nothing and exaggerated nothing. On the rostrum, she looks like a sweet girl-graduate in her raven hair, not a fluent, fiery maestro, yet the drive of this piece, and all its variety—the blatant *banda* music to which the Crusaders advance; the serene, ecstatic choral apostrophe of the Holy City that opens Act III; the slow, strong lilt of "O Signore, dal tetto natio," the chorus of yearning for the soft Lombard plains, that chorus which, in the words of the Risorgimento poet Giuseppe Giusti, "tanti petti ha scossi e inebriati;" and the urgent swell and soaring lyrical flights of the love scenes—were by Miss Queler more vividly caught than in performances I have heard under some eminent conductors. She had an adept orchestra, led by Raymond Gniewek, the Metropolitan Opera's concertmaster (stylish soloist in that *salon* piece which introduces the celestial apparition). She had a good cast, led by Renata Scotto. Miss Scotto should not really be tackling so heavily dramatic a role as Giselda (composed for Erminia Frezzolini, a famous Lucrezia Borgia)—not if she wishes to retain the sweet, limpid timbre for which we love her. She sacrificed sweetness to power— but power she achieved. She was thrilling; she moved us all to a frenzy of excitement in the second-act finale, that startling scene in which Giselda declares that commercial interest, not morality, has prompted the invasion, and goes on to denounce "the impious holocaust of human corpses" and contradict Urban II's slogan, "Deus le veult!," which launched the First Crusade, with her own cry of "Dio nol vuole!" I have never heard Miss Scotto deploy such flashing energy of tone, rhythm, and declamation. But from the start she has been a determined artist, with ideas of her own, and good ones, about roles as diverse as Elvira, Violetta, and

Cio-Cio-San. Each year she develops. While applauding her dramatic prowess—all Giselda's music was amply and stirringly sung, with a stylish and eloquent command of portamento—I fear only lest artistic ambition lead her to punish that beautiful voice. Oronte, the Muslim prince who reaches Heaven after a deathbed baptism beside the Jordan, was done by José Carreras. He sang the part as if his life depended on it, and (despite a throat infection) in full, ardent, unforced, pliantly molded tones that were ravishing to hear. He has for some years been a promising tenor; this performance should put him in the major league. Pagano, the villain who becomes a holy hermit, was Paul Plishka, a bass whose voice has the ring, the surge, and the clean focus of a fine Verdi baritone's. So the principal roles were in good hands. The smaller parts were acceptably enough taken. The Sarah Lawrence College Chorus was spirited and accurate. All in all, an evening to remember.

L ate Verdi was also represented last week by an uncommonly fine performance: the Metropolitan Opera's revival of *Otello*. Franco Zeffirelli's production, new last season, shows a bold, imaginative, and experienced approach. Basically conventional, it is enlivened by some harmless picturesque touches (such as the unpacking of Othello's library) and by clever solutions to the tricky points of stage disposition (the garden chorus, the overhearing scene), but is flawed by some moments of silliness (would any Othello, however tidy-minded, stop while bent on murder to put away a dress that Emilia had left carelessly flung over a coffer?). The décor looks handsome, even if the turrets framing each scene join awkwardly to the raked floor, making the architecture seem unstable. Rudolph Kuntner's lighting is sensitive in the main, but the follow-spots of Act I are obtrusive; in the shaded area of Act II the sun blazes more brightly than anywhere else; and on Saturday there was some unhappy flickering, as well as a conductor's lamp that shone out into the audience's eyes more insistently than anything from the stage. Mr Zeffirelli's much criticized final scene—the bed a precipitous catafalque in a big bare room—I can only praise, since both in atmosphere and in stage plan it supported so powerful an enactment of the catastrophe.

Jon Vickers' first London Othello, earlier this year, was noble; his Othello in the new Metropolitan production (James McCracken was the protagonist last season) was superb: more controlled, more dignified, less constantly close to madness, no less passionate and intense—in voice as in demeanor. Like Tamagno, who created the role, he declaims it with heroic vigor; not just each syllable but of a word like "Gloria!" each single letter makes its effect. From Tamagno, he might well adopt a broader approach to "O! now, for ever farewell" ("Ora e per sempre addio"). Verdi's marking is *Allegro assai ritenuto,* quarter-note 88. That is just about Tamagno's basic tempo on each of the three records he made of the excerpt, but the basic tempo he freely holds up in order to stress particular words and notes, with wonderfully brilliant results. An Othello of more recent times, Martinelli, needed only one minute to record this passage, over which Tamagno took more than a minute and a half. I imagine that Mr Vickers sang it in barely a minute. But in the final "Be not afraid, though you do see me weapon'd" ("Niun mi tema") he seemed as unhurried as Tamagno himself—and he was tremendous. In London, Mr Vickers had to hold his own against a handsome, overconfident Iago (Kostas Paskalis), who swaggered as if he owned the stage—a perfectly possible way of doing the part. Here his Ancient, Louis Quilico, looked rather jolly and Falstaffian. But though this Iago may have been a shade fat he was not scant of breath, and his Creed was expounded with subtle attention to the shading of its clauses. Teresa Zylis-Gara was a lovely Desdemona whose singing combined warmth of expression with clear, full, gentle radiance of timbre. Her notes were firm and true. She moved from one to the next with beautiful control, shaped and graded the phrases, and uttered the words, with feeling. Seldom does an account of the Willow Song so touchingly combine poise and pathos.

James Levine conducted. He was alert, incisive, energetic, but gave a performance quite free from personal pushiness, from insistence that this was *his* reading. Balance was good. Instrumental colors were bright. Pacing was cogent. Transitions were deftly made. It was exciting. The love duet was charged to an unusual degree with sensuality. Miss Zylis-Gara and Mr Vickers sang and acted it with smoldering inner passion, and the sound of the solo cellos rose around them like musk. To the "Ora e per sempre," already mentioned, to the duet "Sì, pel ciel," and to the third-act finale Mr Levine could have brought greater expansiveness. The garden chorus sounded scrawny and underrehearsed, and its mandolin accompaniment crudely amplified.

A brief operatic roundup can take note of *La pietra del paragone* in Alice Tully Hall, the opening event of the Clarion Concerts season. Newell Jenkins, conducting, sometimes slogged through numbers that should sparkle. Beverly Wolff was a captivating Clarice, with plenty of character, fun, and tenderness; she has both the voice and the technique for the role. Mr Carreras was a graceful Giocondo; John Reardon, Andrew Foldi, and Justino Diaz, as

count, critic, and poet, all did well. The opera should have
been given in English, or else librettos with original and
translated texts provided; Rossini's music bubbles from
Romanelli's witty words, and both need to be followed at
once; otherwise most of the points are lost. Clayton
Garrison's "semi-production" for the concert stage was neat,
among the best of its kind I have seen. A merry evening.
Not so the Juilliard American Opera Center's *Don Pasquale*.
This *was* done in English, in Phyllis Mead's translation, and
almost every word was audible; that was one merit, at least.
But the luxus of the Juilliard Theatre had tempted Gian
Carlo Menotti to essay a bang-up staging. To move the
action to Naples in the 1920s was, well, an "idea," and
Pierluigi Samaritani had designed a once grand, now
dowdy *palazzo* apartment, a sluttish room for Norina, and
finally a *cortile* (instead of a garden) with loving realism. But
Mr Menotti's jokes more often involved the décor (a rickety
chair, a line hung with washing, etc.) than the characters of
the four principals, and were applied, not intrinsic. Pointless
business abounded. James Conlon's conducting, after a
promising overture, lacked gaiety. I heard the second cast,
which was unremarkable.

A very effective presentation of Virgil Thomson's *The
Mother of Us All*, in the auditorium of the Guggenheim
Museum, showed how with small forces—smaller than ever
the composer envisaged—and much skill the essential spirit
of an opera can on occasion be captured. The orchestra was
reduced to piano, trumpet, percussion, and organ, and the
cast to eight. Gertrude Stein's text came over with perfect
clarity. Thomson set it with a marvelous ear for rhythmic
nuance and eloquent inflection; his music is apparently
simple yet fiendishly cunning. *Mother* is a kind of masterpiece; why on earth is it not in the City Opera's repertory?
Does it shine with special brightness, is it most affecting,

when sung by clean, true young voices in a small theater? All the singers I heard must be mentioned; all were good, and a Baedeker-type star can indicate particular approval: Judith Erickson, *Kenneth F. Bell, Olivia Buckley, Jon Garrison, **Kate Hurney, Wayne Turnage, Gene West, Lynne Wickenden; musical director *Roland Gagnon.

December 16, 1973

Vanguard has recorded (in a fuller version) the Clarion Concerts performance of La pietra del paragone *(VSD 71183-5, quadraphonic VSQ 30025-7).*

Blest Pair of Sirens

Most compositions employ the mixt power of Milton's sphear-born harmonious Sisters; most music involves words—though some of the greatest does not. The lieder singer makes her (or his) effect as much through her utterance of the words as through beauty and brilliance of tone. Her matching of tune to text often determines whether a song comes to life or not. The poet's lines must suggest to her the unwritten details of rhythmic phrasing: here a sweet, lingering accent, there a sudden urgent advance. Verbal sense will indicate the vocal hues. Yet vivid declamation is not in itself enough; lieder singing, like just about every other kind of music-making, needs a command of pure line—line that is beautiful and eloquent in an "absolute" way. For particular expressive purposes that line can then be distorted, broken, or bent, but unless at the heart of a singer's interpretation there is a feeling for line she cannot wholly please us. Nor can she do so unless she brings the words to life.

Elisabeth Schwarzkopf is of all lieder singers before the public today the most accomplished. For her use of words she is famous, but any analysis of her art must begin with her control of line. This line is to be found at its purest in her account of such a song as Bach's *Bist du bei mir*. A single, quiet emotion shines through the piece; there is no dramatic content, no need to vary the vocal tints. The words must be said gently, simply, and clearly, placed without strong emphasis along a smooth melody that is almost instrumental in character. This Miss Schwarzkopf does. This she did, too, in Mozart's *Abendempfindung*, the song that opened her latest Carnegie Hall recital. The program was a progress from such tender simplicity to some of the most intricately vivid songs—Hugo Wolf's—ever written. Miss Schwarzkopf's first Wolf group closed with *Geh', Geliebter, geh' jetzt!*, from the Spanish Songbook—marvelous piece, compound of passion and *pudeur*, sensuality and shame, evoking a scene of rumpled bedclothes, dawn light piercing the shutters, stir in the streets below, and the singer's mingled guiltiness and glory in her illicit love. *Geh', Geliebter* has become one of Miss Schwarzkopf's, as it is one of Wolf's, highest achievements. Another is *Das Köhlerweib ist trunken*, which closed the second Wolf group; here, in the space of a half minute, composer and poet (Gottfried Keller), singer and pianist conspire to create a present scene (as the voice of the drunken woman carols wildly from the darkling wood), trace a history (the very gait of the proud, beautiful girl she once was, before the red wine got her, is suggested), and point a moral. The singer's line lurches on the word "trunken," staggers and recovers at "singt im Wald"; the intervals grow wider, until the words "überlistet der rote Wein" swoop through an octave. The song is hectic, but its performance must be controlled: this is not the collier woman herself singing; she is overheard, not impersonated.

Miss Schwarzkopf was in top form. Bold and free, the voice rang out in the second song, Mozart's high-spirited *Meine Wünsche*. Many of her, and her admirers', favorites were included: Schubert's *Gretchen am Spinnrad*'; Brahms's *Ständchen* and *Vergebliches Ständchen*; Mahler's merry settings from *Des Knaben Wunderhorn*; five gems from Wolf's *Italian Songbook*, that gallery of men and women in and out of love, whose fleeting emotions, whose very features are set down in sure, tiny strokes. There were also new pieces in her repertory: two fine Schuberts—the serene admonition of *Die Sterne* and the sunburnt mirth of *Erntelied*. Carnegie Hall is really too big for a song recital (Town Hall is the place), and once or twice Miss Schwarzkopf made an effect on slightly too large a scale. In the last phrase of Wolf's *Wer rief dich denn?* she is wont, with a sudden change of timbre, to reveal the heartbreak that lies beneath the girl's expostulations. This interpretative gloss proves most affecting when it is a delicate suggestion, nothing more; on this occasion it became a signal that must have reached the backmost rows of the top balcony. Miss Schwarzkopf is an audacious executant. Everything she does, however, is carefully and lovingly prepared. We can be sure that no nuance has been left unconsidered. Both words and music have been probed for meaning. Because of this, we may find one quality missing in her work: the direct, unaffected, spontaneous utterance of such a singer as Elisabeth Schumann. But, also because of this, Miss Schwarzkopf can reveal the details of a complicated song in a way that makes other performances of it seem lifeless, no more than half-realized. True, she can be artful. In a simple song she may show simplism. She can be naughty, and coo the *o* of "Castiglione" (the last word of Wolf's *Ich hab' in Penna*) too coyly altogether. But who can resist, say, the artful young miss she portrays in Strauss's *Hat gesagt*; who not share with a smile in that naughty triumph when she boasts of her ten lovers in Castiglione?

The care extends to all details of Miss Schwarzkopf's performances. They are joint interpretations with her pianist; she and Geoffrey Parsons make a finely tempered

duo. By her demeanor she can hold even a New York
audience silent through a piano postlude (though Mr
Parsons was so funny, and so wickedly precise, as he
fingered the fumblings of the hesitant violinist in Wolf's *Wie
lange schon* that a ripple of mirth passed through the hall).
By presence and posture she can set, and afterward sustain,
the mood for a particular song, then change it in preparation for the next one. The platform lighting is planned. The
piano will have been tried in various positions to secure the
best sound in the hall. These things matter. In only one
respect did this Carnegie Hall recital betray the high
Schwarzkopf standards: the program-book was a wretched
thing that did not contain the texts of the songs (there were
merely translations) or even identify the poets. Since
Schubert wrote four songs called *Die Sterne*, we should have
been told which one (it was the Schlegel setting, "Du
staunest, o Mensch," D. 684).

Poets' names, poems, and English translations were all
duly present in the program-book of Jess Thomas's first
New York lieder recital, in Alice Tully Hall. Unfortunately,
the good deed was nullified by darkness in the hall for the
first half, but in the second the lights were turned on and all
was well. Mr Thomas cares about words. He pronounced
them with feeling and sounded their sense. A memorable
moment in his recital was provided by the soft, clear peal of
his tone through the syllables of "Morgenglocken," in the
last line of Wolf's *In der Frühe*. But his line was not unflawed.
A voice muscled to tackle the heroic Wagnerian roles
opened up too forcefully in climaxes. In the phrase "Hat
mit tiefem Seufzen" (Wolf's *Wo find' ich Trost?*), the sigh
became a yell of anguish. If the young Siegfried had learned
Liszt's *In Liebeslust*, he might have cried it out to forest and
field in the exuberant tones Mr Thomas used; "Ich sing' es

laut durch Wald und Feld" indeed—but within the confines of Tully Hall it need not be sung so loudly. There was also much delicately scaled soft singing. Wagner's Wesendonk Songs were sensitively done: *Der Engel* was smooth and rapt, marred only by two hefty an emphasis on the word "Engel"; *Schmerzen* was long-phrased; the gentle, quiet, throbbing urgency of *Träume* was beautifully captured, as if by a Tristan both passionate and tender. Mr Thomas's dynamic registers need finer adjustment to the demands of lieder; his intentions and his intelligence are already admirable.

ℐust about all Berlioz' music was inspired by words. His *Damnation de Faust* suggests Goethe's *Faust* read by flashes of lightning; a page here, a paragraph there, each leaving an afterimage that then takes vivid musical shape. The work was composed in a series of inspirations—"in my carriage, on the railroad, on steamboats, and even in cities. . . . In Pesth, by the light of a gas-jet in a shop, I wrote the choral refrain of the peasants' dance, one night when I had lost my way; in Prague I got up in the middle of the night to set down a melody that I feared I might forget. . . . I did not look for my ideas; I let them come; and they presented themselves in the most unforeseen order." Eventually, in Paris, Berlioz fitted the various "fits" together to make his *légende dramatique*, and devised the link passages. Sir Georg Solti, with the Chicago Symphony Orchestra and Chorus, gave a wonderfully coherent account of this piece, which has often been deemed scrappy. His reading of it was urgent and energetic. It is not the only way to tackle Berlioz' big dramatic cantatas. Last month, in Toronto, I heard Seiji Ozawa, with the Toronto Symphony and Mendelssohn Choir, give a *Roméo et Juliette* that depended for its effect on intensity of colorful detail, not long musical line, and proved no less whelming than this *Damnation*. But Sir Georg's drive, coupled with the high polish of the Chicago playing, carried the day. Not everything was ideal. Orchestra and chorus were perhaps cramped on the Carnegie Hall platform, and the balance suffered. In the finale, the solo violins were far too loud; their accompaniment figure drowned the main tune. The sound of the flutes was sometimes lost. The choir, expert body though it is, should have been urged to a more sostenuto singing of the Easter Hymn; when Berlioz indicated an octave portamento he presumably wanted it to be sung with portamento. But these were small things, to be noted only lest the blanket approval now generally given to the Chicago Symphony and all its works blunt discernment of its particular virtues; the performance as a whole was magnificent. Josephine Veasey, Stuart Burrows, and Roger Soyer were an excellent Marguerite, Faust, and Mephisto, Miss Veasey's smoothness in "D'amour l'ardente flamme" and Mr Soyer's elegant handling of the Serenade being of special note. A libretto with original text and parallel English translation was provided gratis.

The words went for nothing in the consequently pointless performance of Bach's Cantata No. 48 that opened last week's Philharmonic concert, conducted by Pierre Boulez. They were not even printed in the program-book; there was only a loose English verse paraphrase, not easily legible in the depressant gloom favored by the Philharmonic. But to the music of a Bach cantata the words are crucial; even the instrumentalists should know exactly what is being said if they are to invest their melodies with the due expression. An English translation was provided for following the fifty minutes or so (the closing scenes of the first act) of Pfitzner's *Palestrina* presented (in German) by the New Jersey Symphony at its Carnegie Hall concert last week. The translation held a howler or two ("Weiden" can mean willows as well as meadows; Palestrina's harp was surely hung on the willows, not "thrown in the pasture") but was better than nothing. The lighting, once again, was a shade too low to make reading easy. Pfitzner's solemn, searching, beautiful music is always a joy to those who enjoy it (and I'm a *Palestrina* nut who has even stood through performances of that immensely long opera). Henry Lewis conducted with love. Nicolai Gedda sang the title role with tone and expression that could not be faulted. In the first half of the concert, Mr Lewis gave an ardent, glowing account of a suite drawn from Prokofiev's *Romeo and Juliet*. He has a graceful action. From the New Jersey orchestra he drew richly colored, zestful, and accomplished playing. An exhilarating concert.

December 23, 1972

Recent research has shown that Bist du bei mir, *traditionally ascribed to J. S. Bach, is a composition by G. H. Stölzel; see* Georg von Dadelsen's Editorial Report on Series V, Volume 4, of the Neue Bach Ausgabe.

Phoenix

Hans Werner Henze, born in 1926, has long seemed to me the most interesting and important composer of his (and my) generation. Following his progress, we find the swift-moving musical history of our day refracted in a brilliant, poetic creator's mind. He has been prolific. His career has taken some surprising turns. But through the long list of compositions, in every genre, there runs an unbroken thread of steady artistic development in which romantic and technical adventures are combined. In almost textbook fashion, Henze lived out for a while the life of a Great German Artist. He had that thorough, practical training which is regular in Germany and uncommon elsewhere—working in small opera houses as coach and *répétiteur*. With his first opera, *Boulevard Solitude*, a modern treatment of the Manon story, he burst on the public as a brilliant youth with all the latest techniques at his fingertips and something of his own to say—a composer who had absorbed from Stravinsky and Schoenberg whatever he needed to express his personal, romantic visions. He could have had the country at his feet. Instead, like Jean-

Christophe, the hero of Romain Rolland's novel, he sickened of and fled the musical "market place"—the world of publishers, press relations, buttering up the right conductors, and all that—and in traditional German fashion made his Italian Journey and experienced the Italian Idyll. In Ischia he settled, and for four long years to the immense score of the opera *König Hirsch* he confided, as if to a diary, his Mediterranean musings and excitements. *König Hirsch* was mocked by young progressives when Berlin staged it in 1956. Henze remained in Italy; in a cello concerto called *Ode to the West Wind* and in the ballet *Ondine* he continued to waken the blue Mediterranean from his summer dreams. The early 1960s brought a rapturous outpouring of love music—*Ariosi, Being Beauteous, Cantata della fiaba estrema*—charting his emotional adventures. In these compositions, an expressed desire for Latin clarity of rhythm and line is in fruitful conflict with his fondness for intricate, softly luminous, close-woven textures. The cast of *König Hirsch* had included a young dreamer who mused, spellbound, amid the enchanted wonders of the forest; in the opera *Der Prinz von Homburg*, Henze's "deGermanized" version of Heinrich von Kleist's play, Prince Friedrich escapes from the world of Prussian militarism into gentle, moonlit dreams. Henze's next opera, *Elegy for Young Lovers* (1961), deals with a Great Poet who ruthlessly sacrifices friends, admirers, and lovers in the cause of his compositions.

The opera *Der junge Lord*, first performed, in Berlin, in 1965 (and due at the New York State Theater in March), opened a new chapter, The Return to the Fatherland—not to live but to be accepted. Henze was back in the center of the market place—lionized, recorded, published, conducted by Karajan! The Collected Essays appeared. At the time of the première, Intendants, music publishers, reporters, and television cameras clustered thick about him. An even bigger opera, *The Bassarids*, had already been composed in preparation for Salzburg, the costliest and glossiest of Europe's festivals, and Henze announced that with *The Bassarids* he had "made his peace with Wagner." Peace before a storm. For a couple of years, Henze composed mainly concertos in which his musical sinews grew tougher. His Second Piano Concerto was commissioned, for fifty thousand marks, to celebrate the opening of a *Kunsthalle* in Bielefeld named after Richard Kaselowsky, an early member of the Nazi party. The storm broke on the eve of its first performance, in 1968, when Henze published in the Bielefeld *Presse* a declaration entitled "Mein Standpunkt." It ended, "Unnecessary are new museums, opera houses, and world premières. Necessary, to set about making dreams come true. Necessary, to abolish the dominion of men over men. Necessary, to change mankind, which is to say, Necessary, the creation of mankind's greatest work of art: the World Revolution."

Later that year, I went over to Hamburg to hear the first performance of his oratorio *Das Floss der Medusa*. It had been commissioned by the North German Radio, for eighty thousand marks. It was not performed. Students set up a red flag and a Che banner (the work is dedicated to Che Guevara). The RIAS Chamber Choir of West Berlin, with that admirably crisp diction and attack that mark all its performances, set up a refrain of "Under the Red Flag sing we *not!*" Some mild scuffles broke out—and then, as if on cue, in marched a gang of steel-helmeted police troopers, who roughly removed the student demonstrators, scooped up on the way the elderly, distinguished librettist of the piece, Ernst Schnabel, and then patrolled round the hall in a show of force. Henze announced that because of the police intervention he would not conduct the work, and instead he led a section of the audience in a chant of "Ho! Ho! Ho Chi Minh!"—a rallying cry, incidentally, whose rhythm provides the ostinato figure ending the oratorio. The event raised many questions, some of them crystallized in one of the SDS manifestos showered upon the Hamburg audience: "This concert should have taken place before an audience of workers, not the bourgeoisie. . . . But in the future Henze will write revolutionary music, and see to it that it is heard and understood by those for whom it is written."

What sort of music? What sort of audience? The official music of the socialist countries is seldom revolutionary but, rather, an orthodox, "bourgeois" musical treatment of socialist texts or programs. Meanwhile, in the capitalist West, small socialist performances play to small converted audiences, while large ones—such as the Kurt Weill *Mahagonny* at Washington's Kennedy Center last week—provide aesthetic pleasures, and perhaps a fleeting pang or two, for educated, elitist audiences that can afford the ticket price. Britten composes an anti-church *War Requiem*, opposing to "the old lie, *dulce et decorum est pro patria mori*," a declaration that to die while trying to kill people is degrading and vile; we perform it in cathedrals amid the proud banners of battle. The bourgeoisie is adept at drawing the teeth of socialist art. In East Berlin, the satire of Henze's *Junge Lord* satirizes something across the border; in West Berlin, the audiences watching it smile indulgently at seeing their follies portrayed. Given his whole musical personality, Henze could hardly, after *Das Floss der Medusa*, turn his hand to writing workers' songs. What would he do next?

What he did was to dramatize his own problems in works that might be called self-illustrating. In a conflict of styles they projected the conflicts within him. Two of his most recent compositions are *Der Langwierige Weg in die Wohnung der Natascha Ungeheuer*, called a "show for seventeen," presented as part of Lincoln Center's "New and Newer Music" series in Alice Tully Hall, and *Heliogabalus Imperator*, an "allegoria per musica," commissioned by the Chicago

Symphony Orchestra to commemorate its eightieth anniversary, played first in Chicago last month, and then in Washington. *Natascha* has the librettist of *Versuch über Schweine*, the first piece Henze wrote after *Das Floss*. He is Gastón Salvatore, a Chilean poet, who in *Versuch* urged his friend to stop arranging thoughts and dreams in beautiful patterns, to stop asking clever, sensitive questions and, instead, to pick up a gun, as it were, and act! Henze's action was to set the exhortation to music. Natascha, in the new work, is a siren who "promises the leftist bourgeois a new kind of security that permits him to preserve his revolutionary 'clear conscience' without taking an active part in class warfare."

The show, which was commissioned by the European Broadcasting Union, first performed in Rome last year, and broadcast Europe-wide, lasts nearly an hour. There are eleven numbers, with titles—"Planimetry," "Geodesy," "Metaphenthes"—that suggest they are addressed to an audience with a classical education. Casual allusions to the Kaiserin-Augusta-Strasse and Anhalter Bahnhof, to "the carefree beds of the Keith-Strasse," need footnotes outside Germany. But the general drift of the poem is clear. In musical form, *Natascha* is a development of Henze's *El Cimarrón*, a "recital for four players" with a text based on the memoirs of the former Cuban slave Esteban Montejo, taken down by Miguel Barnet (and published in English as *The Autobiography of a Runaway Slave*). One of the original four players was the baritone William Pearson, who also created the role of the leftist intellectual in *Natascha*; another was the percussionist Stomu Yamash'ta, a performer of rare virtuosity and electric presence, who prowled and danced amid his instruments, restless and beautiful, suggesting both the wonders of the Cuban forest and the ranging of Montejo's fierce imagination. *El Cimarrón* is music theater for the concert platform. So is *Natascha*. Singer and percussionist (in New York, Paul Sperry and Gordon Gottlieb) again have the main roles, but the musical forces (directed on this occasion by Dennis Russell Davies, who struck me as a brilliantly able young conductor) are larger. A quintet of the instruments used in Schoenberg's *Pierrot Lunaire* "is meant to symbolize the old, sick bourgeoisie." A jazz quintet conjures up one easy, carefree way of escape. A brass quintet, set high, sounds the warning, repressive voice of authority as if from a watchtower. Natascha's cajolements trickle honeysweet from a prerecorded tape. Through these opposing sounds, singer and percussionist are free to wander, the first on his inconclusive journey, the other as a kind of jester-commentator. "The leftist bourgeois, with whom this work deals, refuses to go the full way to the apartment of Natascha Ungeheuer" (in the program notes, Mr Salvatore is once more pointing out the path he wants Henze to follow), but "he has not yet discovered his way to the Revolution. He knows that he must turn back on the way he has gone so far, and begin again." But Henze is too honest, and too much a musician, to renounce readily all that he has achieved. How is the composer of so much elegant, elaborate music to make a new start? *Natascha* is a poignant as well as a vigorous and vivid composition. Not without a pang does its creator recall the past styles in which he was happy. Natascha is not easily resisted.

Heliogabalus, the Chicago piece, dedicated jointly to Mr Salvatore and his friend Nono, a protest-singer (now deceased), is composed in Henze's most brilliant, full-blooded, and exuberant manner. It is a tone poem dealing with the Emperor Antoninus, called Heliogabalus or Elagabalus (218–22), and some events of his dissolute reign. Henze agrees with Gibbon that "it may seem probable the vices and follies of Elagabalus have been adorned by fancy and blackened by prejudice"—or, as the composer puts it, "Today we can see that nothing took place except that

which was opposed to the traditional Roman concept of
virility and respectability: these things [the enthronement of
Baal, the banquets, the drag balls] were simply part of the
ecstatic cult, however provoking they may have been."
There is no censure in the music. The piece, which lasts half
an hour, opens with an evocation of the gay, glittering
Syrian court in which Antoninus grew up. A long section for
strings is meant as a physical description, feature by feature,
of the supremely handsome young man. To a coruscant
paragraph for five percussionists he appears before the
Senate. According to Gibbon, "the grave senators confessed
with a sigh that, after having long experienced the stern
tyranny of their own countrymen, Rome was at length
humbled beneath the effeminate luxury of Oriental despot-
ism"; Henze omits the sigh. A series of woodwind solos,
bizarre, diverting, and capricious (and based on the novel
techniques explored in the concertos), depicts the lovers to
whom Heliogabalus distributed the dignities of the empire.
But at length the Romans rebel. To the strains of a ferocious
jig the Emperor is hunted down and killed.

It was an odd experience to sit in the Presidential Box of
Kennedy Center's Concert Hall and hear this uninhibited
glorification of license. From the Chicago Symphony, under
Sir Georg Solti, the work had a dazzling performance.
Henze has reveled in the resources of a large virtuoso
orchestra undeterred by fiendish rhythmic demands. Player
after player emerged as a colorful, cogent soloist. The
musical idiom is largely that of Henze's Sixth Symphony,
composed for the Cuban National Orchestra—a fizzing,
energetic, and joyful piece. We can pick up echoes of other
earlier works: the similar "physical description" attempted
in *Being Beauteous*, the percussion rhapsodies of *Natascha*, the
wild hunt of *The Bassarids*. *Heliogabalus* sounds as if it were
composed in tearing high spirits. Invention flows, technique

is at its most masterly, and the clear-cut paragraphs of the program keep things from sprawling.

December 30, 1972

Henze's music is all published by Schott (represented in America by Belwyn Mills), and most of the compositions mentioned above are recorded by Deutsche Grammophon. In particular, Das Floss der Medusa *is on 2707041,* El Cimarrón *on 2707050, the Sixth Symphony on 2530261, and* Natascha Ungeheuer *on 2530212. Ernst Schnabel describes the non-performance of* Das Floss *in his essay "Zum Untergang einer Uraufführung" and his Postscriptum attached to the edition of his libretto published by Piper Verlag, Munich.*

Network Message

Not all operas are political, but some of the greatest operas contain a political element, and perhaps it is listeners with sharpened political sympathies who respond most keenly to, say, *The Marriage of Figaro, Fidelio, Don Carlos, The Ring, Wozzeck*—and Kurt Weill's *The Rise and Fall of the City of Mahagonny.* Mahagonny is, in the words of its founder, Widow Begbick, a "city of nets" spread to catch fowl worth the eating. Weill's opera—chosen by the Opera Society of Washington for its first production of the season, in Kennedy Center, and due again in April from the Opera Company of Boston—is itself a reticulate work that continues to trap many kinds of human and political experience. In this it is like *The Ring*, and unlike many operas written by men who may have their hearts in the right place but give to their work no more than local and topical, and hence fleeting, significance—or by men who, quite simply, do not compose very good music. The allegory of *Mahagonny* is no more cut-and-dried, straightforward, or pat than that of *The Ring.* "Do not forget," said Bernard Shaw (in *The*

Perfect Wagnerite, still the best introduction to Wagner's masterpiece), "that an allegory is never quite consistent except when it is written by someone without dramatic faculty." Neither Weill nor Bertolt Brecht, his librettist, lacked dramatic faculty. Shaw's four successive prefaces to *The Perfect Wagnerite*, dating from 1898 to 1922, reinforce his point. In the last of them, he writes of "Rhinemaidens walking out with British Tommies . . . Marx enthroned in Russia, pistolled Romanoffs, fugitive Hapsburgs. . . . All this has so changed the political atmosphere in which Wagner lived . . . that it says much for the comprehensiveness of his grasp of things that his allegory should still be valid and important." *Mahagonny* is not so comprehensive or so important a work as *The Ring* (though it is one of the most important operas of our century), but what it shows and sings of likewise remains "frightfully real, frightfully present, frightfully modern."

Social "relevance" is no new thing. Operas have long been composed with an express political purpose. Hundreds of eighteenth-century pieces extolled, in mythic or classical analogy, the virtues of the rulers at whose courts they were first performed. A few others were critical: Beaumarchais's *Le Mariage de Figaro* was still a banned play in Vienna when Mozart used it for music. When I cited *Figaro* in my first sentence, I did not, of course, mean to suggest anything so silly as that the piece is primarily a political opera. *Figaro* is above all a human comedy and a musical exploration of love in all its aspects: full-hearted, all-forgiving love, lust, flirtation, possessive jealousy, suspicion, the hurt of betrayal —a gamut that includes Marcellina's championing of women's rights and Don Basilio's bachelor cynicism. But a performance of *Figaro* must nevertheless be deemed incomplete that at no point reminds us, on a historical plane, that in 1786 the Revolution was but three years away, and, on a topical plane, that Almavivas—men who think that by rank or riches they are entitled to privileges unjustified by character or accomplishment—are with us still.

The part that nineteenth-century opera then played in formulating political sentiment is well known. The Brussels riots of 1830, which drove the Dutch from the country, broke out after a performance of Auber's *Muette de Portici*. Verdi's early biographer, Folchetto, noted that in *Nabucco* and *I Lombardi* the composer "began—at first, I would say almost instinctively—to serve political ends with his music. . . . Foreigners will never be able to understand the influence exerted, during a certain period, by the ardent, impassioned melodies to which Verdi set situations, or even single lines, that recalled the unhappy state of Italy, or her memories, or her hopes. The public found allusions everywhere." So the "abhorred embrace" of an elderly guardian from which Elvira, heroine of *Ernani*, calls upon her lover to rescue her was equated with Austrian rule. A stirring line in *Attila*—"You can have the universe, provided I keep Italy!"—roused inordinate enthusiasm, though in context it is cried by an Italian traitor proposing a deal with the Hun. Today, while these things slip through the net, other emotions may be caught. In Verdi's *Don Carlos*, Posa announces that he has come "from a country once so fair! It is now but a desert of ashes, a place of horror, a tomb! There, the orphan who goes begging and weeping through the streets stumbles, as he flees from the fires, over human bodies! Blood reddens the water of the rivers; they flow laden with corpses. The air is loud with the shrieks of widows mourning their slaughtered husbands!" The ruler who has ordered the destruction of a country and its people replies coolly that this is the price at which he intends to buy peace. Aghast, Posa exclaims, "The peace of a cemetery! O King! Let not future ages say, at the mention of your name: He was Nero!" "Il fut Néron!" To the mind of the baritone who sings these words, and to the minds of an audience from whom their directness has not been cloaked by our fondness for hearing our operas sung in foreign tongues, another name than Nero's must now occur.

"All a poet can do is to warn"; Britten set Wilfred Owen's words as epigraph to his *War Requiem.* "It is only the poet," said Shaw, "with his vision of what life might be, to whom these things ["our sordid capitalist systems, driven by invisible proprietorship, robbing the poor, defacing the earth"] are unendurable." J. M. R. Lenz's play of 1776, *Die Soldaten*, dealing with the moral degradation brought about by military life, and Bernd Zimmermann's opera drawn from it in 1959 both warned of things that have come to pass. The poets', the playwrights', and the opera composers' warnings have often been censored. In the Archives Nationales, in Paris, we can read the comments of Napoleon III's Imperial Ministry of Fine Arts on the speech of Posa cited above, and especially on Posa's cry of "Donnez à vos enfants, Sire, la liberté!" "This cry, which a great composer will surely not fail to invest with all the fire and all the intensity his art can muster—can it be uttered without danger in the present circumstances?" Not only Verdi but such apparently uncommitted spirits as Bellini and Donizetti felt the hand of the censor. Sometimes the objections were ecclesiastical (all those betrothals before notaries reflect a ban on the stage representation of sacraments), sometimes monarchical (Donizetti's *Maria Stuarda*, in which a queen confesses to murder, could not be played unaltered in Naples; at the dress rehearsal the Queen of Naples had fainted). In the Soviet Union, censorship still acknowledges the power of art to affect people's thoughts. But few composers have suffered so thorough a suppression of their work as Kurt Weill. The series of pieces begun in 1927 in collaboration with Brecht—notably, *The Threepenny Opera*, *Mahagonny*, and *The Seven Deadly Sins*—had established Weill as the most important theater composer of his country, after Strauss. Then, in 1933, the Nazis imposed a total ban on his music. From abroad, scores and orchestral materials were recalled by the publishers, and destroyed along with the material still in Germany. In this country, the exiled composer wrote musicals, but the Weill of the great years was effectively silenced. He died in 1950. It was not until the mid-1950s that the major works began to be heard again, and the process of rediscovery, and of actual physical reconstruction of his music from precious sources that survived the Nazi decree, still continues.

Several revivals, particularly of *Mahagonny*, have been bedeviled by two misconceptions. First, that this music is exclusively an emanation from the Berlin of the late 1920s: enjoyable enough but not to be taken very seriously—only with a grain of affectionate, slightly patronizing nostalgia (a corollary of this is that Jenny is a role for a night-club *diseuse* rather than the lyric soprano of Weill's intention). The perceptive critic T. W. Adorno, after a Berlin production in 1931, called this a "misconception of *élan,* jazz, and infernal entertainment." To hear no more than that in *Mahagonny* is like hearing no more in *Figaro* than the tunes the Prague citizens danced quadrilles to and whistled in the streets. The second misconception derives from Brecht's having appended his notorious essay on "culinary opera" to the published text of the libretto. *Mahagonny* is treated as if it were a Brecht play with incidental music, whereas it is an opera through and through, one that "works" in exactly the ways of traditional opera. Neither misconception marred the very intelligent, very impressive Washington performance, produced by Ian Strasfogel and conducted by Gunther Schuller. The musical values of a score with its roots in Bach, Mozart, and Mahler were fully realized by Mr. Schuller, his orchestra, and his cast of opera singers. Mr Strasfogel and his designers, Douglas W. Schmidt (scenery) and Jeanne Button (costumes), cunningly avoided the too specific location, either in Berlin or in the Wild West, that reduces the scope of the allegory.

It strikes me that the opening paragraphs of *The Perfect Wagnerite*, which provides so many texts apt to *Mahagonny*, may actually have suggested to Brecht and Weill the plot of their opera. Shaw's essay appeared in German in 1907. It begins, "Let us assume for a moment that you are a young and good-looking woman. Try to imagine yourself in that character at Klondyke five years ago [he was writing in 1898]. The place is teeming with gold. If you are content to leave the gold alone, as the wise leave flowers without plucking them, enjoying with perfect naïveté its color and glitter and preciousness, no human being will ever be the worse for your knowledge of it. . . . Now suppose a man comes along . . . a man with common desires, cupidities, ambitions, just like most of the men you know." In time, the gold finds its way to the great cities; there, as in Klondike, men turn their backs on love "and upon all the fruitful, creative, life-pursuing activities into which the loftiest human energy can develop it," and single-heartedly set about gathering gold "in an exultant dream of wielding its Plutonic powers." The inevitable course, says Shaw, "is plain enough to those who have the power of understanding what they see as they look at the plutocratic societies of our modern capitals." It is the course charted by *Mahagonny*. The drop curtain of the Washington production was a frieze of dollar bills in which the portrait of George Washington had been replaced by a golden calf. In the great finale, people bearing banners parade to the strains of a Mahlerian funeral march that gathers up into its tread all the main melodies of the opera. Brecht and Weill several times revised the slogans inscribed on these banners; Mr. Strasfogel boldly left them blank, and let a more terrible image on the back cloth, an inferno of devastation by roaring fire, remind us what love-denying, life-denying pursuit of the golden calf can lead to. Between these "statements" he avoided, as some other producers of *Mahagonny* have not, any obvious attempt to jolt a comfortable audience into realizing what the music is about.

Jolts are not needed. Weill's music is ever apt to get under people's skin and rouse violent emotions, prompt almost hysterical denunciation or enthusiasm. Adorno in that 1931 review spoke of "music with a circumspect sharpness which by means of its leaps and sidesteps *makes articulate* something which the song public would prefer not to know about." (Operas are written to make articulate something more than words alone can say.) A professor at London's Royal College of Music used to cite *Mahagonny* as an instance of positively *evil* music. The music of *Mahagonny* gets under my own skin to an extent that almost makes me distrust the passionate admiration I feel for it—the tingling of the scalp and coursing of the blood that are set off by a glance at almost any page of the vocal score. I can take refuge in cool analysis, demonstrate how a four-note musical "cell" (it could be represented as G-sharp, A, E, D), first heard in the phrases to which Begbick founds the city, generates all the main melodies; how it gathers power in the D-minor music of the hurricane, and then releases tension in the major of Jenny's "As you make your bed, you must lie there"; how its omnipresence provides a sound reason for the finale's being no mere potpourri reprise but a clinching and overwhelming musical statement. I can praise Weill's harmony, his textures (those neoclassical inventions sustained over firm basses), his orchestration, his judging of the instrumental comment on a vocal line, his precise control of form. But these things are not enough to explain the feeling of joy in men's and women's goodness that floods me as I hear the score, mingling with the horrified contemplation of our society's wickedness.

It is not a flawless work. Before *Mahagonny*, Weill and Brecht had written a *"Mahagonny* Songspiel" that had no consecutive plot; the "Songspiel" numbers were later incorporated into the new dramatic structure, but some of them fit awkwardly. The "God-game" episode seems to me musically on a lower level. The Crane Duet, though it is a beautiful piece of music, has no place in the scene of commercial love. Weill inserted this setting of one of Brecht's early love sonnets only when the original version of the scene proved unpalatable to managements, but he insisted that the original version should be used once theaters had the "courage" to do so. Washington left the duet in the love scene; it works only a little better when moved to Act III. A translation by Arnold Weinstein and Lys Symonette was used—less musically sensitive than the version of David Drew and Michael Geliot. "The dice rolls the way you have cast it; win or lose: it is all up to you" is at once less singable, less sensible, and further from the German than "As you make your bed, you must lie there, and no one will care what you do." (As a matter of fact, neither version correctly articulates the melody to which "Denn wie man sich bettet,/so liegt man" is set.) The Drew-Geliot "We *need* no roaring hurricane" puts a strong word on the strong beat of "Wir *brauch*en keinen Hurrikan," where Weinstein-Symonette have "We *do* not need a hurricane." And so on. Despite this, most of the words were surprisingly clear. William Neill made a first-rate Jimmy Mahoney, the free, frank, vigorous, life-asserting, romantic, unsentimental hero. Pamela Hebert perfectly caught the directness—innocence, even—of Jenny, an honest girl who must live in a dishonest world. *Mahagonny*, said its creators, is meant to be fun as well as "an experience." It was.

January 6, 1973

Bernard Shaw's The Perfect Wagnerite *has been reissued in paperback by Dover Publications.* Mahagonny, *with Lotte Lenya as its heroine, was recorded in 1956 (Columbia KL 243); Lenya's voice in the early 1930s—the clear, candid, light operetta soprano for which Weill composed much of his music—can be heard in the recording of excerpts from the opera reissued on Telefunken 23. David Drew's "The History of* Mahagonny," *in* The Musical Times, *January 1963 (Volume 104, No. 1439), describes the genesis and early history of the score. Brecht's essay "Anmerkungen zur Oper* Aufstieg und Fall der Stadt Mahagonny" *appears in Volume 17 of the* Gesammelte Werke, *in* Versuche 1-4, *and in the separate edition of the libretto (all Suhrkampf Verlag, Frankfurt).*

Spade Work

The Metropolitan Opera has revived Tchaikovsky's *Piko-vaya Dama*, or *Queen of Spades*, the only Russian piece in its repertory this season. This production was first given, in 1965, in an English translation by Boris Goldovsky; it has been brought back in Russian. On the whole, pleasure in hearing the sounds of the original seems to have outweighed the regret of people whose Russian was not fluent enough to enable them to follow the drama in detail and understand the sense of each line as it was sung. Several people have written to me expressing some surprise that I don't take it for granted that opera is always best sung in the original language. Of course I don't—any more than I take it for granted that opera is always best sung in the vernacular. There is no simple "best" about it. There is, however, an ideal that can be simply stated: Ideally, an opera is performed in the language in which it was composed, by a cast and to an audience that understand that language perfectly. The ideal can be achieved on occasion—when, say, Virgil Thomson's *Four Saints in Three Acts* is sung in New York (as it will be next month, in the Forum Theatre, when

the Piccolo Met gets going), when *Aida* is sung in Milan,
Don Carlos in Paris or Geneva, and *Prodaná Nevěsta* (*The
Bartered Bride*) in Prague. But once an opera crosses a
language border there must be compromise. Any decision
about what form that compromise takes should depend on
the particular work concerned, the cast available, local
circumstances (is there another production of the work in
the same city? what language was it done in last?), and, not
least, the quality of current translations. In other words, no
automatic answer, but for each opera, in each production, a
separate decision. Either way—in the original language or
in translation—something is lost. Is the work a comedy that
will fall flat if the jokes are not understood, or a broadly
lyrical drama in which detailed attention to the text hardly
matters? Will it be presented as "music drama" or "opera"?
(Stravinsky's distinction: "I believe 'music drama' and
'opera' to be two very, very different things," he wrote,
when introducing *The Rake's Progress* to the American
public.) Will the cast be national or international? How
familiar is the plot? How familiar have recordings made the
original libretto? How widely is the language of that libretto
understood? How well has it been, or could it be, translated? (*Pelléas* into English won't go.)

Happy the city with two companies that can offer both
kinds of experience and spread the losses between them (loss
of dramatic directness in one place, of original sound values
in the other). Even then, each work is a special case. All
things considered, I think, the New York City Opera is right
to introduce Henze's *Der junge Lord* in English, wrong to do
Der Rosenkavalier in German, right to do *Lucia di Lammermoor*
in Italian, wrong to do *Les Contes d'Hoffmann* in French. All
things considered, I think, the Metropolitan is right to do
most of its performances in the original language (all of
them, this season). *Der Rosenkavalier* at the State Theater
should be in English, because it is in German at the

adjacent house, and the two productions might as well be complementary instead of competing; also, because Hofmannsthal's libretto needs to be understood word by word, and a good singing translation does exist to open the work to people who don't speak German. But *Lucia* should be in Italian at the State Theater, though it is also in Italian at the Met, because in this case, I think, more is lost than gained by translation; also, because Beverly Sills is so good in Italian. Julius Rudel's flexible policy for the City Opera is right, even if some of the particular decisions may be questioned. What is wrong is dogmatic general assertion, one way or the other, made before all things have been considered.

Queen of Spades in Russian? Of that language, many people have perhaps a dozen or two words, just enough to realize when characters are talking, as in opera they often do, of things like "love," "death," "truth," and "God," and to know which of the *tri karty* in the Countess's winning formula—"troika, semyorka, tuz"—Herman stakes on. But anyone else who has heard *Queen of Spades* in English a few times, and listened to recordings while reading text and translation in parallel columns, can probably recall more or less what is being said at any point. Following an opera in this vague sort of way, without real attention to the words that are being uttered, listening only to the sounds, can be enjoyable—more so, indeed, than hearing all too clearly an English translation whose tone and diction are obtrusively wrong, or whose lengths, stresses, and inflections lie awkwardly on the music. But a performance without verbal communication from the singers makes special demands of them; they must be doubly eloquent in the sounds they produce, in their phrasing, in their acting. The leading role in *Queen of Spades*, Herman, was taken by Nicolai Gedda, whose theatrical personality is not especially vivid—even if more daemon than usual was revealed by his rolling eyes and jerky gestures. He sang impeccably, and it was not his fault that the orchestra at the close of Act I broke the dynamic bounds that Tchaikovsky set, and covered his defiant apostrophe to the tempest. The Lisa was Raina Kabaivanska, a decent, reliable soprano, clear and steady of voice, who became something more than that in the arioso of Act III, "It is nearly midnight," which she sang with much energy and passion, in long, well-knit phrases. (Her opening words were drowned by those wretched, unmusical scenery-applauders, who cannot see a fall of paper snow without shutting their ears and clapping their hands. Snow in late spring?—or are we supposed to assume that many months have passed since the first scene? And if it was snowy winter, why did Lisa wear no gloves?)

The first Herman and Lisa were Nicolai Figner and his wife, Medea Mei-Figner, he a Russian tenor and she an Italian soprano of exceptional smoothness—each note pressed close to the next—and intensity of utterance. (Both made records.) Something of their style survives even today in Russian performances of Tchaikovsky's opera, and it is a style that depends on a much freer approach to meter, a greater readiness to linger, than was shown by Miss Kabaivanska, Mr Gedda, and their conductor, Kazimierz Kord. Mr Kord, in his Metropolitan début, displayed energy and a nice care for pointing up the varied instrumental accompaniment to each verse of the strophic songs. The orchestra's playing was crisp and incisive. But too often the brass tended to overpower string melodies. The orchestra's last paragraph, an envoy that starts *ppp* and closes *pppp*, while the curtain slowly falls, was begun most beautifully. No one heard how it ended, for those beastly premature applauders got to work again well before the opera was over.

Henry Butler's staging was pretty dowdy. The St Petersburg backcloth of the first scene showed a crumpled sky.

The climax of the ball scene—a tease that builds up toward
the appearance of the Tsarina and is cut short by curtainfall
just as she is due to enter (since imperial personages could
not be represented on the Russian stage)—was muffed and
mistimed. In the last scene, the ghost of the Countess, which
is supposed to vanish after nine bars, stayed on to the end in
a spotlight—in a vulgar, obvious tableau that took our
attention away from the dying hero. Tchaikovsky planned
his opera on a grand scale. Though he was no great master
of form, *Queen of Spades* is carefully planned, and extensive
cutting throws it out of balance. At the Metropolitan the
principal omissions were of the children's chorus in the first
scene, the Russian song and *gouvernante*'s arioso in the
second, the trio of the pastoral divertissement, and Tomsky's
song in the final scene.

If Mr Kord in Tchaikovsky was a conductor reluctant to
linger, Erich Leinsdorf in the final *Walküre* of the season
showed positively indecent haste. He managed to clip a
further three minutes from the already too fast timing he set
at the opening performance, and raced through the wonders
of the work in a brisk, stingy, efficient fashion. This was a
pity, for there were two débuts, one scheduled and the other
not, worth hearing in happier circumstances. I have long
wanted the chance to praise Rita Hunter's singing of
Brünnhilde. In London I can't, since she sings the role there
in my translation. Her first Brünnhilde in German was
marked by warmth and directness of expression, naturalness, and long, easy phrasing. She used portamento more
amply, and more eloquently, than any of her colleagues.
She learned the role with Reginald Goodall, who is the last
of the big, broad Wagner conductors in the line of
Furtwängler and Knappertsbusch. If Mr Leinsdorf's *Walküre* is the fastest on published record, Mr Goodall's is the

slowest; Miss Hunter is even better, more moving, when she has time to be expansive. Hans Sotin's was the surprise début, as Wotan (taking over from an indisposed Thomas Stewart). His bass is an organ of rare beauty and firmness, and when he knows the role more fully, has studied it in detail with great conductors and great producers, he may well become what we have long needed: a Wotan with a real "Wotan voice," grand, powerful, and heroic.

After grumbles at excessive speed, a word of praise for Roberto Benzi's unhurried approach to the first act of *Faust*, also at the Metropolitan. In almost all modern performances, *Faust* becomes trivial when the hero, asked to name his heart's desire, rejects riches, glory, and power, and bursts into the tripping 6/8 strains of "À moi les plaisirs, les jeunes maîtresses!" But Mr Benzi, a romantic, lyrical conductor equally good at the sober and the lyrical episodes, paced things so well that any suggestion of triviality was removed. The cry burst poignantly from the old philosopher's heart.

January 13, 1973

Et, O ces voix d'enfants...

What's in a name? A good deal, I think, when it comes to the popular acceptance of a new piece of music. George Crumb is a good namer. *Vox Balaenae* is an uncharacteristically formal title for his enchanting piece of sea music based on the song of the humpback whale. *Echoes of Time and the River* and *Black Angels* (rather than, simply, String Quartet) are more typically attractive titles; *Ancient Voices of Children* is a winner. So is the piece. It was composed in the summer of 1970, and first performed in October that year, in the Library of Congress. Arthur Weisberg's Contemporary Chamber Ensemble brought it to New York. Boulez billed it in his first series of Prospective Encounters. In 1971 it won a UNESCO prize in Paris. A Nonesuch recording gave it wide currency, and at least three ballets, perhaps more, have been danced to it: Milko Sparemblek's, in Lisbon, soon to be taken up by the Dance Theatre of Harlem; Vassili Sulich's, in Las Vegas; and, most recently, John Butler's *According to Eve*, done by the Alvin Ailey company in New York last November. In London this season, the work figured in a Sinfonietta program, along with Weill's *Der Jasager* and Stefan Wolpe's Chamber Concerto. And last week it figured in a Philharmonic program, along with Telemann, Stravinsky, and Richard Strauss.

Ancient Voices of Children, in fact, seems to be the latest in the series of vanguard works that have caught the public's fancy. Others have been Schoenberg's *Pierrot Lunaire*, Boulez' *Le Marteau sans maître*, and Karlheinz Stockhausen's *Gesang der Jünglinge*. In common, they have had novelty of sound, audacity of technique, kaleidoscopic patterns of timbre, catchy titles, and sufficient extra-musical elements to stimulate a listener's imagination and assist his "hearing."

It might be suggested that, given his ingredients, Crumb simply couldn't go wrong. *Ancient Voices*, like several of his other works, is based on Lorca, and thus the music has a starting point in some of the most direct, prime imagery that any creator can call to his assistance. He sets five poems, or sections of poems, breaking the sequence with two brief dances. The work lasts about twenty-seven minutes. Onstage, there is a mezzo-soprano; offstage, a boy treble answers the woman in the clear, touching tones of innocence. An ensemble of seven players is involved: oboe, piano, mandolin, harp, and three percussionists. "¿De dónde vienes, amor, mi niño?" asks the woman. "De la cresta del duro frío" comes back a childish cry from the distance. "¿Qué necesitas, amor, mi niño?" "La tibia tela de tu vestido." How can it fail to be moving? Would it be possible to set the couplet "Todas las tardes en Granada,/ todas las tardes se muere un niño" in a way that was not affecting? And when it is noted that after that couplet (which is chanted to a soft, tender flamenco pattern, rising from a chord of C-sharp softly thrummed from marimbas, hummed by the percussionists, and gently blown, by one of the players, on a mouth organ) a toy piano steals in with *Bist du bei mir,* from the Anna Magdalena Bach Notebook, or that during the final song the oboist, moving farther and farther into the distance, gently muses on that plangent cry which punctuates the Abschied of Mahler's *Das Lied von der Erde,* while the boy walks onstage and joins his voice to the woman's—well, of course, any tough, suspicious old critic thinks that he is being got at, and worked over emotionally by a battery of tearjerking devices such as Puccini himself might envy.

But I've lived with the *Ancient Voices* for some time now. At first encounter, I was bowled over, like just about everyone else. Further encounters dispelled all incipient suspicion and steadily increased my admiration for what seems to me one of the most delicate, poetic, and beautiful compositions of our day. Crumb's use of the collage ingredients is scrupulous and principled. I'm not, I confess, a great score-reader beyond the line of duty; unlike Verdi, I don't keep a row of scores, along with the volumes of poetry, beside my bed. But the score of *Ancient Voices* (which is only seven and a half pages long—though they are large pages, sixteen by twenty inches) has become a favorite piece of reading. It is easily read, since there is never a great deal happening at any one time, and is a pleasure to the eye as well as a delight to the inner ear. But only a performance of the work can reveal the subtleties of its sound with precision, since Crumb has just about the most adventurous command of small, delicate shades of timbre of any composer around. I know of no other who has invented so many fascinating new things for singers and instrumentalists to do, or has used the older, familiar inventions (such as a voice singing into the undamped piano strings to provide an aeolian-harp halo of resonance) with such exquisite finesse.

At the Philharmonic concert, I sat, for the first time, in the topmost terrace of the hall (and there, for the first time, enjoyed decent acoustics). The work came over perfectly, memorably. Jan DeGaetani, the singer to whom it is dedicated, is a simply astounding performer. Basically, she has a beautifully clear, secure, even tone. She can be limpid and cool, or passionate and wild. She can project a pianissimo murmur that is perfectly audible, and cry a high C, *tutta forza*, without a trace of edge or impurity. In addition, she has a flexibility of tongue, lips, and mouth and a control of breath that enable her to achieve a virtuosity of vocal sounds unheard since the late Elsie Houston made those famous records of Brazilian folk songs. The treble was David Ulin, poised and true. The Philharmonic players, under Boulez, were sensitive. The program book ignored the composer's direction that both Spanish texts and English translations should be printed; a sheet with the latter only was provided.

The concert began with that oft played, oft recorded Telemann A-minor Suite for flute and strings, with Julius Baker as flutist. Boulez is an oddly dull conductor of eighteenth-century music. Can it have something to do with the fact that he never uses his hands to mold an expressive line? Instead, they only demarcate a rhythm or define a dynamic level. Then the Crumb, and after the interval Stravinsky's *Ragtime*, for eleven instrumentalists, and his *Reynard*, for nineteen and vocal quartet. Neither Stravinsky work made much effect in so large an auditorium. The Forum Theatre is probably the place for *Reynard*. Finally, the symphony orchestra appeared for Strauss's *Till Eulenspiegel*. The piece was given a hectic, highly colored, but humorless performance—hectic in point of instrumental balance (not of rhythm, which was carefully controlled), and too loud both at the start and in the epilogue. It was short on charm but had plenty of energy.

January 27, 1973

The score of Ancient Voices of Children *is published by C. F. Peters; the recording is Nonesuch H 71255.*

Bouleversement

There is plenty of new music to be heard in New York—less than in London, it is true, but enough to keep any interested listener very busy. There is no dearth of lively composers and no shortage of expert performers. Yet to a newcomer the "new-music scene" here presents some puzzling features. To embark on any large-scale criticism after but a few months' acquaintance would be both rash and impertinent; let me venture just a few midseason observations, based chiefly on the work of Pierre Boulez in his triple role of conductor, compère, and composer. Mr Boulez should be the center of new music in New York. In the summer of 1971, before embarking on his first season as music director of the Philharmonic, he stated his intention: "What I want to do is to create models of concert life in two cities—London and New York. After that, anyone can do it. But if I don't, I fear nobody will. . . . And that's why I've been invited by the New York Philharmonic and the BBC. It's not just because of my ability as a conductor. There are plenty of conductors as good as I and some who are much better in parts of the repertory. But it's the ideas I want to put into practice that count. I want to create conditions in which the music of our own time is once again an integral part of concert life. That's a creative task and that's why I accepted it."

It is possible for one man to change the concert life of a great city—provided that he controls the city's major concert-giving organization. I watched it happen in London. The man was William Glock, his organization the BBC, the largest patron of musicians—both performers and composers—in the world. Glock, appointed BBC Controller of Music in 1959, made the music of our own time central to the BBC Symphony's concert series, to the Proms (that enormous "festival" of orchestral music which for over eight weeks fills the Albert Hall, and over the air reaches a wider audience still), to the countless concerts and chamber and solo recitals promoted by the BBC both in public halls and in studios, to the broadcast relays of new works up and down the country, to recordings and relays from abroad, and to the broadcast talks about music and the printed commentary and discussion appearing in the BBC's publications. Within a few years, Stravinsky could call London "a great capital of contemporary music" (a footnote in his *Expositions and Developments*). He said this had been brought about "to a large extent by the accession of an intelligent younger generation in the musical press," and he was possibly too generous to the profession. It is true that Glock's arrival coincided with the appointment, to major critical posts, of several young writers sympathetic to his ideas; there was also a crop of exceptionally gifted young composers, and another of instrumentalists adept in the techniques of, and eager to perform, contemporary music. All things conspired; the conspiracy succeeded because Mr Glock, who is now Sir William, was there to lead it, and had the BBC's vast resources behind him. Moreover, for ten years before that, as director of the Bryanston and Dartington Summer Schools, where men like Stefan Wolpe, Elliott Carter, Luigi Nono, and Luciano Berio had taught and inspired a new generation of British musicians, Glock had been training his lieutenants. Boulez arrived as his most brilliant general.

In New York, Boulez has a harder task. There is nothing like the BBC to his hand. (The Philharmonic is important, but less dominant in the musical life of New York than the BBC is in London.) Nor is there anything quite comparable to the Arts Council of Great Britain to support him in his campaign. London has five major full-time symphony orchestras. The BBC Symphony is paid from television license fees; the four others are sustained by both the nation (through the Arts Council) and the city, and a proportion of their income is dependent on the programming of new native music. In addition, there are chamber orchestras and ensembles specializing in contemporary music which draw most of their income from the public purse. I mention these things not to suggest that they order this matter better over there (and by Continental standards British subsidies to music are still meager); the intricacies of American subsidy still escape me. (For example, though federal, state, and city grants to the Philharmonic amount to only $331,000 in a budget whose total expenses are $5,293,000, there must also be good deal of "concealed subsidy" in the form of the tax rebate on the gifts from corporations, foundations, friends, and patrons.) Nevertheless, when from the latest report of the Arts Council of Great Britain, covering the year March 1971–March 1972, I pull some figures, I wonder whether those of this country are comparable. During that period, the people of England, through their taxes, commissioned from their composers, and paid for the performance of, sixty-six new musical works: the Scots, five; the Welsh, thirty-eight—this in addition to the commissions from the BBC, other bodies, and individuals. Maybe the American record is more impressive. The very fact that I don't know indicates a failure of publicity. Such a failure, in this of all countries, is surprising.

In New York, I miss the musical press—equivalents to the British monthlies *The Musical Times* and *Music and Musicians,* and that quarterly review of modern music *Tempo,* which contain essays on and introductions to forthcoming works, and informed discussion on those that have been recently performed. America is not short of good writers on music, but there is nothing quite like those magazines, which circulate among the ordinary concertgoing public. They are on sale in London's concert halls. Since I have, after all, embarked on comparisons, let me add that in Lincoln Center I miss the bookshop that on the South Bank (London's complex of concert halls) sells not only all the musical magazines and a wide range of books on music, and pocket scores, but also the particular scores, so far as they are published, of all the works due for performance throughout the place. I miss the monthly brochure that should list, with detailed programs, all the events in the five theaters, the big Philharmonic Hall, the recital halls of the Juilliard School, and the auditorium of the Library of Performing Arts that make up the Center. I miss a detailed monthly calendar, such as *The Musical Times* publishes well in advance, of all the musical events scheduled for the city, and an equivalent of the *Music and Musicians* monthly calendar that announces all the major events of the country (impracticable in this huge land—but the interested New York musician should at least be able to know when something unusual and worthwhile is happening in Washington, Philadelphia, Buffalo, Boston, Hartford, and anywhere else within easy reach). There is a lack of information—information that could stimulate attention and insure that the numerous good things available are fully enjoyed. It is rather like—let me get all my limey grumbles off my chest!—the way the efficiency of New York's subway and bus systems is vitiated by the lack of clear, simple signposting, such as any logical person could devise in an hour or two. How early do the promoters get together to compare plans and programs, and avoid clashes that must divide a potential audience? The signposting toward new music is inadequate: often one comes across it too late, when already irreversibly headed for something else; at other times, on arrival, there is too little helpful related information.

One little example, of a small, simple piece of further guidance that could have been given but wasn't. Three of the four works billed at this season's Prospective Encounters concerts, conducted by Boulez, had already appeared on record: Jacob Druckman's *Incenters,* Peter Maxwell Davies' *Eight Songs for a Mad King,* and Mauricio Kagel's *Match.* It would have been easy to tell people this and print the record numbers on the program sheet; if Boulez thinks the pieces are worth doing, he must think there are people who may perhaps want to hear them again, after the concert is done, or even hear them in advance. Not everyone can make sense of, say, Davies on just one or two hearings. A line about whether a score is published, and by whom and at how much, would not be amiss. An indication of which scores and which records are available at the Lincoln Center library, for borrowing or for reference, might prompt continuing interest, a less brief encounter. It would no doubt be too expensive to produce a magazine specifically connected with the Encounters, such as the *Domaine Musical,* which Boulez edited when he was director of the Domaine Musical concerts in Paris in the 1950s. That magazine, with its fiery, stimulating manifestos, got into hands the local likes of which probably never open the covers of *Perspectives of New Music* (a magazine less readable than *Domaine Musical*—partly, I suspect, simply because by nonspecialists it is less read).

Boulez' Domaine concerts, charged with new works and explosive new ideas, left an enduring mark on Paris musical life. They became the talk of that talkative town. As the critic Antoine Goléa put it, they were "the crucible, the brain of avant-garde French music." Boulez' Prospective Encounters here have not been comparable—in part because they have been largely retrospective. Last week's began with William Bolcom's *Morning and Evening Poems*, for soprano and chamber ensemble, texts from Blake, composed in 1966. The composer wrote in the program, "This piece is in a style I don't compose in any more . . . but I think its lyricism might save the piece, along with the extraordinary text." It was saved for me by the beautiful singing of Phyllis Bryn-Julson, which gave distinction to a score otherwise modest, "healthy" (Boulez' word), and of no special musical interest or marked character. Kagel's *Match*, of 1964, was billed to follow, but that particular encounter remains prospective, since Boulez said the performance was not ready. Instead, Paul Jacobs played Stockhausen's Piano Piece XI and, joined by Robert Miller and Morris Lang, the same composer's *Refrain* (1959), for piano, celesta, and vibraphone. Mr Jacobs' spoken introduction to the works was fluent, laconic, and engaging. Of the piano piece he gave two very accomplished, gripping performances; the execution of the trio was confident, cogent, arresting, not quite precise. Afterward, Boulez suddenly became interesting, even eloquent, as he talked of his fellow-composer's early attempts in these pieces to marry fixed notation with some elements that shift in each performance—a problem that had also concerned him at the time. He described how in *Refrain* each new event began only when its predecessor had faded into silence, and asked the players to demonstrate with an example. Then, one had the impression of everyone in the hall listening, with hushed breath, for the moment when a musical sound died. It was the kind of intent, electric stillness that a great singer can sometimes induce when she has the house hanging spellbound on a single, soft-spun note. It should have been followed by a second performance, which might all have been listened to in that way. Boulez said there was no time for that, so we had no six-minute *bis*, only half an hour's more rather dull chat.

Stockhausen is the most important composer so far Encountered, and these unscheduled performances of his relatively early works provided much the most vivid musical experiences of the series. For the rest, I have found the concerts disappointing, with too much loose gab and too little music. The criticisms David Hamilton made of the first series still hold. (Mr Hamilton's thoughtful assessment appears in the current *Musical Newsletter*. Now there's a magazine that every intelligent concertgoer should read; it is not on sale at Lincoln Center—only by subscription.) The Loeb Student Center of New York University is not quite right for these events, either in feel or in space. Weak or middling pieces have been included in a repertory so small that only the strongest will do. Boulez is not a skillful compère. Like Mr Hamilton, I wish that he would tell the audiences he draws about the other, abundant new-music series that New York provides. (Amplified and annotated, the monthly broadsheet of announcements published by the Center for New Music—a good start, though far from complete—might well be included with the program.) Last week, he could have said that some of Mr Bolcom's later music was available on record; referred anyone interested in pursuing the remarks on randomness to his essay "Alea," in a 1964 *Perspectives*; announced that three days later, in the Juilliard Theatre, he would in a public master class be pulling to pieces some compositions by Juilliard students. These sporadic Encounters will serve small purpose if they don't send people questing after other new adventures.

The first of the Juilliard School's series of Boulez master classes in composition, last month, was most interesting for the light it shed on his own current ideas and practice. As instructor, he was, surely without realizing it, at his most odious and crushing. He all but sneered at the two student composers, Andrew Violette and William Komaiko, for writing for means so old-fashioned and conventional as, respectively, piano and string quartet, instead of a fashionable chamber combination. He told Mr Violette, whose *Dream Maze,* though nothing special, was a perfectly agreeable modern-romantic piece by a youth who knew his Berg Sonata and Berio *Sequenza IV,* that if he had written some sections all in the treble and some all in the bass, the work would have "acquired a profile." He chided him for not exploiting more extravagant and unusual ways of getting sound from the piano, such as he, Boulez, had pioneered. He mocked and parodied a rather striking effect of repeated chords. He subjected the opening bars to instant recomposition. From separate movements of Mr Komaiko's Second Quartet, a work whose basic idea is the presentation of each instrument as an individual, he pulled two passages that were rather similar in mood, in order to refute with a triumphant smile the composer's declaration that he thought each movement did have its own character. (As if moments of tender reminiscence were now taboo.) Oh, he was hateful! And no doubt for the best reasons: to spark spirited defense from the budding composers (but how do you defend yourself against a man who brooks no contradiction?) and to ram home his central thesis, the unremarkable one that every piece should show a clear "idea"—favorite Boulez word—clearly executed.

As a composer, Boulez has lost the verve that made his *Le Soleil des eaux* (1948), *Le Marteau sans maître* (1955), and

Pli selon pli (1960, but many years in the making) just about the most exciting, colorful, and powerful pieces of their day. In his latest work, . . . *explosante/fixe* . . . , as in its predecessor, *cummings ist der dichter*, he seems to be picking over a small, if striking, "idea" and executing it with a great deal of elaboration and technical resource. Both pieces are attractive to the ear; both have left me wondering whether the results were worth all the effort and expense involved in their performance. . . . *explosante/fixe* . . . went through various metamorphoses before it reached the version commissioned by the Chamber Music Society of Lincoln Center, and performed in Alice Tully Hall as a world première. As one of the eighteen *Canons and Epitaphs: In Memoriam Igor Stravinsky*, by various composers, published in the magazine *Tempo*, it was a page of music followed by six pages of performing instructions—in effect, a "composition kit" for a piece that could not be performed until considerable work had been done on it. Boulez suggested an instrumentation of two violins, two flutes, two clarinets, and a harp. Last year the composer "realized" a version, for flute, clarinet, and trumpet, that was performed in London, together with the other *Canons and Epitaphs*, to mark the anniversary of Stravinsky's death. It lasted about ten minutes. The version for the Chamber Music Society is longer (about half an hour), more elaborately scored, and equipped with electronic effects supplied by a device called the Halaphone. The flute opened proceedings, solo, with its "explosion"—a skittery, jittery, captivating pattern of sound, exquisitely played by Paula Robison. In turn, viola, cello, trumpet, harp, vibraphone, clarinet, and violin "exploded" (though the word is really much too violent to describe what seldom rises above a delicate patter) and then continued, each with "its set of variations on an individual level, *fixe*." The work has a "profile," since the notes are contained in a range of two octaves. It has a clear and easily grasped "idea"—but one that outstayed its welcome, I thought, even when the Halaphone came into action to provide variety and complexity of texture. This machine—nine hundred and forty-seven pounds of equipment brought over from the experimental studio of the Heinrich-Strobel Foundation, in Freiburg-Günterstal—was controlled by a crew of three, led by its inventor, Peter Haller. It picks up the sounds of the individual players, can mix and modify them as required, and project them, through a series of speakers around the hall, to produce effects of circling or stalking. Seated at one side of the hall, I missed these marvels, and heard merely rather curious and interesting combinations of live player on the stage and distorted descant in various places. At the second performance, the machine went wrong.

At the regular Philharmonic Hall concerts, there has been surprisingly little new music. Boulez' programs look particularly timid by comparison with those of the Chicago Symphony; Solti has certainly made the music of our own time an integral part of Chicago concert life, and has concentrated—wisely, it seems to me—on music composed for a large, virtuoso symphony orchestra. But to the Philharmonic programs—and program-books—I must return another time.

January 30, 1973

Perspectives of New Music, *a semi-annual, is published now from P. O. Box 271, Yardley, Pennsylvania 19067.* Musical Newsletter, *a quarterly, is published from Box 250, Lenox Hill Station, New York N.Y. 10021.*

The Canons and Epitaphs *appeared in two issues of* Tempo: *Set 1 (*Tempo *No. 97, 1971) by Edison Denisov, Boris Blacher,*

Peter Maxwell Davies, Hugh Wood, Lennox Berkeley, Nicholas Maw, Michael Tippett, Harrison Birtwistle, Luciano Berio, and Alfred Schnittke; Set 2 (Tempo No. 98, 1972) by Elisabeth Lutyens, Aaron Copland, Elliott Carter, Roger Sessions, Darius Milhaud, Alexander Goehr, and Pierre Boulez.

In May 1973, Boulez next brought out a revised version of . . . explosante/fixe . . . , slightly longer than that heard in New York (about thirty-five minutes) and with modified electronics (supplied by the South West German Radio). First performed by members of the BBC Symphony Orchestra in Rome, and broadcast Europe-wide, it was given its London première at a Promenade Concert in August. Other performing versions of the work have been made by Heinz Holliger (1972 Salzburg Festival, and broadcast throughout Europe) and by Karl and Margaret Kohn (for two pianos; Los Angeles, April 1973). See Susan Bradshaw's article on the piece in Tempo No. 106 (September 1973).

Mutual Ordering

Scorn not the string quartet: Boulez, you have frowned, and dubbed it an old-fashioned form—but there are at least three good, linked reasons that composers continue to write the things. One is that, ever since Beethoven showed the way, they have found that two violins, viola, and cello provide a medium in which their most secret, personal, and intimate thoughts can well be shaped. (Consider Smetana's *From My Life*, Janáček's *Private Letters*, or the long series of quartets in which Shostakovich traces his spiritual autobiography.) Another is that, ever since Haydn and Mozart showed the way, composers have used the string quartet to test novel procedures of rhythmic or textural interplay, to break untrodden harmonic ground, and to try bold new devices of form. As H. C. Colles put it in the essay on chamber music which has run through successive editions of Grove's Dictionary: "Chamber-music combinations, and particularly the string quartet, have been found to be a peculiarly convenient medium for all those experiments with atonality, polytonality, quarter-tones and other divisions of the scale which are characteristic of the restless technical enterprise of today"—and likewise, he might have added, for all those experiments with metrical and rhythmic resource, with polyrhythms, "measures" unmeasured, elaborate subdivisions of the beat, and ever-altering time signatures. The third reason grows from these. Since composers have already cast so much of their most serious and striking music in string-quartet mold, since the quartets of Haydn, Mozart, and Beethoven, of Brahms, of Bartók and Shostakovich are worth playing, they are played—and so there exist ensembles with minds, ears, and fingers finely tuned to subtleties, technically skillful, responsive to new ideas, and prepared to rehearse long hours together. The more adventurous of these ensembles like to undertake new music, and commission it. And so for the composer of a string quartet there is at once the challenge of the past, the chance of fresh exploration, and the assurance of finding worthy performers.

Internationally, Elliott Carter, born in 1908, is now America's most famous living composer. He unites two qualities that, particularly in their combination, strike a European as especially American: a breadth and range of cultural experience (not only musical), evinced in his education, his writings, and his compositions, that can make many otherwise comparable European creators seem nationalist, even local, and a "ruggedness" of artistic temperament, a heroism most conveniently termed Ivesian, which, when all the worlds of music lie known and open to him, leads him to choose and pursue his own unfaltering path—not blinkered but with a full, commanding view over the paths that others are taking. Only Roberto Gerhard, the Catalan exile who settled in Cambridge, England, comes to mind as a composer similarly farseeing and resolute, openminded and single-hearted. Carter's orchestral pieces are perhaps closer to being repertory works in London than in New York (there is no Carter composition billed in the Philharmonic programs this season), but scarcely a week seems to go by here without performances of his chamber music. This week's bills, for example, show the First String Quartet in Carnegie Recital Hall on Monday, the Sonata for flute, oboe, cello, and harpsichord at Hunter College the same night, and on Thursday the Woodwind Quintet in Carnegie Recital Hall. Last week, on Tuesday, his Third String Quartet was given its first performance, by the Juilliard Quartet, in Alice Tully Hall. The place was full, the atmosphere electric. All musical New York seemed to be there. It was "an event"—as the unveiling of a Third Quartet by the composer whose First and Second Quartets are landmarks in the course of contemporary music could hardly fail to be. After the performance, both Carter and his interpreters were cheered.

Carter has been drawn to the string quartet for all three reasons mentioned in my preamble. The First Quartet, dedicated to the Walden Quartet, of the University of Illinois, dates from 1951, and the Second, commissioned by the Stanley Quartet (but first played by the Juilliard Quartet), from 1959. The Third, commissioned by the Juilliard School for the Juilliard Quartet, was completed in 1971. When Carter embarked on his First Quartet, the second reason—the need to try new procedures—was uppermost; as the composer recalled later, "There were so many emotional and expressive experiences that I kept having, and so many notions of processes and continuities, especially musical ones—fragments I could find no ways to use in my compositions—that I decided to leave my usual New York activities to seek the undisturbed quiet to work these out. . . . As I wrote, an increasing number of musical difficulties arose for prospective performers and listeners. . . . I often wondered whether the quartet would ever have

any performers or listeners." It did have them. It became
Carter's most oft performed composition. "It even received
praise from admired colleagues." The work had gathered
up and deployed in masterly fashion ideas that had been
stirring in American music, while its liberating effect on
young composers is a matter of history; as Martin Boykan
wrote in the spring *Perspectives* of 1963, "It spoke, in fact, for
the America of the fifties, in the same way that the *Sacre*
spoke for the Europe of half a century ago." The Second
Quartet had a similar Janus quality. Its language, said
Carter, "emerged almost unconsciously through working
during the fifties with ideas the First gave rise to," while
from its elaborate notions of concurrent but unsynchronous
time scales, of character interplay between the four members of the quartet as individuals, and of scores as "auditory
scenarios for the performers to act out with their instruments" there arose the Double Concerto (1961), the Piano
Concerto (1965), and the Concerto for Orchestra (1969).
The first two string quartets are recorded (by the Composers
Quartet, on Nonesuch). Listening to them intently, again
and again, provides the best possible introduction to
Carter's later orchestral pieces—and to the new Third
Quartet. Already, in the First Quartet, we can hear his
fondness for passionate, rapturous melody measured against
the beat of regular time; for the sudden dissolution of a
long-breathed line into a rapid *scorrevole* scurry; for the
tender, almost Wagnerian romance of long-held thirds and
tenths, *tranquillo*, soft-shining high above the staff, which
provide fleeting, elusive points of tonal reference. In the
Second Quartet, we can learn that recurrence does not
mean literal repetition (a tone, a manner, the general shape
of a gesture recur); that the growth of a theme can be like
the growth of a plant (no two leaves quite the same but all
recognizable as belonging to one particular species); that
counterpoint may be like a sapling twined with ivy (the

slower, sturdier growth setting limits to and determining the general direction of the tendrils that scramble around it, the two related yet distinct); and that time can be measured by different clocks (the simplest example is the cello cadenza, freely declaimed while time ticks by at two different speeds). These are ideas that are developed in the Third Quartet. (Other things, such as the moments when the four voices draw together in a single statement, or when they suggest four-part harmony in the almost "classical" way inherent in a cello-based texture, do not recur.) When we have learned the ways that Carter's melodies move and grow, each in accord with its own time scale, we are ready to listen to the Third Quartet.

The new work, like the Second Quartet, lasts about twenty minutes, or about half the length of the First. The demands it makes of the four players are immense—and no praise can be too high for the Juilliard Quartet's achievement in having mastered so technically formidable a score and presented it so cogently. The players are divided into two duos—Duo I, of violin and cello, and Duo II, of violin and viola. Each duo pursues its independent dialogue, discourse, what you will. Duo I plays a kind of rondo made of the recurrence, in irregular order, of four episodes of contrasting character. They are marked *Furioso*, *Leggerissimo*, *Andante espressivo*, and *Pizzicato giocoso*, and each episode is heard three times. (The sequence could be represented schematically as FLAP, LFPA, LPFA.) Meanwhile, Duo II plays what can be most simply described as two movements. The first of them is an "arch form," in which episodes marked *Maestoso*, *Grazioso*, and *Pizzicato, giusto meccanico* are symmetrically grouped either side of a central *Scorrevole* (as it were, MGP-S-PGM). The second consists of two couplets, alternations of a *Largo tranquillo* and an *Appassionato*, interrupted by a return of the *Scorrevole* from the first movement (LAL-S-A). Thus, each episode of Duo II is heard twice.

Though independent, the discourses of the duos are simultaneous; though they progress at different speeds, their coexistence in time is precisely defined, for their measures, four hundred and eighty-one of them, are ruled by the same bar lines. (Very rarely, however, is the first beat of any measure clearly marked by a simultaneous note from both duos.) The sequence of recurrences is so organized and overlapped that each of one duo's episodes is at some point heard in conjunction with each of the other's. Moreover, there are moments when each duo falls silent for a few measures, as if to draw breath, and these moments are so distributed that each of the ten episodes involved can be heard for a while in isolation (except, for some reason, Duo II's *Appassionato*, which never achieves more than two consecutive measures "unaccompanied").

That is the "scenario," the "dramaturgy," of the piece. The effect might be likened to that of two intricate films projected simultaneously, each of which must be followed both in its own right and in relation to the other, since the coincidence of images is never the result of chance but is precisely calculated to provide what Carter calls "a sense of ever-varying perspectives of feeling, expression, rivalry, and cooperation." The film simile must not be pressed, since the Third Quartet is a "living" double dialogue; if Carter had wanted to achieve automatic precision he could have composed the work on tape, but the element of four distinct players, individuals in twin ensemble listening and reacting to one another, is inherent in his conception.

When the eye, as opposed to the ear, first meets the score, it boggles. The work is rhythmically complex to a degree which makes it appear impossible of comprehension, or, for that matter, of execution. Metrical elaboration is nothing new in Carter. Consider the *Presto scherzando* movement of his Second Quartet, marked to be played "with rhythmic precision in all parts." To achieve rhythmic precision in the first measure, that measure of five quarter-notes (which lasts only one and seven-tenths seconds) must be divided into sixty equal parts. The first violin must enter on the counts of twenty, twenty-five, and twenty-nine; the second violin on one, sixteen, thirty-one, and forty-six; the viola on forty-nine and fifty-eight; and the cello on one, thirteen, twenty-five, and thirty-seven. In the first measure of the new quartet, similar precision would require a count of one hundred and eighty (in a measure lasting three and four-tenths seconds), and in the final bar (where the scheme is twenty-one against fifteen against nine against six) a count of six hundred and thirty! But these things are a matter for the composer and his interpreters. They need not worry the listener. Let me venture a homely analogy. On the table where I write, there lie two natural objects that please me: a strip of bark from a silver birch, and a helix. The bark is patterned with small striations of differing lengths and intensities, and the dark-brown shell is spattered with white triangles, no two alike, in similarly irregular spacing. If I attempted to "notate" the rhythmic periodicity of these two pleasing natural patterns, I should arrive at something mathematically far more elaborate than anything in Carter's Third Quartet; yet I can contemplate them without boggling. Again, the analogy must not be pressed—Carter's quartet is not an *objet trouvé*, nor is it composed in simple emulation of nature's intricacy ("fashioned so purely, fragilely, surely")—but it may serve to suggest why the listener need not be daunted by the technical difficulties of the work and can "contemplate" them with an unworried ear. He will probably never know exactly how precise any particular performance is. But just as, without counting himself, he can, when listening to one of Messiaen's rhythmically tortuous compositions, quickly discern the difference in effect between a performance that has been scrupulously counted and one that is merely approximate, so in Carter's piece he will no doubt be more deeply moved by accurate than by loose executions. It should, however, be added that only Duo II is required to play "in quite strict rhythm throughout" (that "quite" is ambiguous, until a further *giusto sempre* defines it as "completely"); Duo I plays "quasi rubato throughout."

On the basis of two hearings (a rehearsal and the first public performance), some time spent with the score, and a trust in the composer inspired by the way some of his previous works that proved baffling at first encounter have become ever more dear and rewarding, I am prepared to affirm that Carter's Third Quartet is a major new composition, a piece that is passionate, lyrical, and profoundly exciting. It was not exactly baffling at first; response, though largely intuitive, was ready. But a myriad details passed by uncomprehended. May it soon be recorded. Once, string quartets were composed as much to be played as to be listened to. Now, the phonograph has brought chamber music back into the private chamber, and made possible an intimate acquaintance with works far too difficult for amateur fingers to compass.

February 3, 1973

The Nonesuch recording of Elliott Carter's First and Second String Quartets is on H 71249. Pocket scores are published by Associated Music Publishers.

Modern Pleasures

Ruth Crawford Seeger (1901–1953) was but a name to me—mainly for her work on American folk song—until, last Monday, in Carnegie Recital Hall, the Composers String Quartet played her String Quartet of 1931. The piece crops up in accounts of contemporary American music, where it is described as uncommonly advanced for its date. It certainly is. Study in Berlin and Paris had preceded the composition, but influences are harder to discern than pointers to the future. Some of Elliott Carter's rhythmic procedures are foreshadowed in the first movement, and while the softly shifting cluster-chords of the slow movement may owe something to Berg's Lyric Suite, closer parallels can be found in Ligeti and Lutosławski compositions of recent years. In the first movement, melodies that are subtly varied either by free repetition or by free inversion progress in different meters, often against fixed points of reference in the form of long-held notes. In the scherzo, the instruments seem to be nudging one another forward in merry, friendly play. The slow movement moves mysteriously to a fierce climax, then sinks to silence. In the finale, the first violin is a wild beast to whom the other instruments whisper rapidly in octaves; he becomes ever less violent, less abrupt, more lyrical in his utterances, while the others do exactly the opposite, until midpoint is reached. After a pause there, everything is spun out in reverse, a semitone higher. The first violin begins the movement with an exclamation of a single note, then one of two notes, one of three, and so on, while the others respond with a phrase of twenty notes, then one of nineteen, progressively reducing until their single note marks the turning point of the palindrome. It is highly schematic, but the effect is not one of mere contrivance. Before the eye has worked out the ground plan of the movement (a score is published by Merion Music), the ear has already welcomed a quirky, shapely, and fascinating stretch of music. Ruth Crawford Seeger's quartet is a good example of the string quartet's aptness as a medium for testing new procedures, which I wrote about last week. In 1931 it was an audacious piece, and completely assured in execution. All four movements have a strong, positive flavor that can still be enjoyed. (A recording by the Amati Quartet is available on special order from Columbia; a new recording, by the Composers Quartet, who played it very well, is due from Nonesuch.) The recital continued with David Del Tredici's *I Hear an Army*, for soprano and string quartet, a work of imaginative and picturesque incident (though Catherine Rowe, the singer, lacked beauty of tone), and ended with Carter's First Quartet; rightly, the evening took its part in a series titled "The Pleasures of Modern Music."

Handel's Italian operas are a musical treasure house too seldom entered. The listener needs a feeling for history, and some experience, to accept their conventions: the soprano or alto heroes; the action confined to recitative;

the long strings of arias, broken but rarely by ensembles, each aria ending with its singer's exit. But once these conventions are accepted, he can respond ardently to the marvels that Handel achieved within them. In the expression of emotions, Handel stands among the greatest. He is the most generous and copious of musical inventors. He writes superbly for the voice. His instrumental textures are always diversified, always just. He has immense variety, and the sequences of apparently isolated arias build into satisfying wholes. Plots that look tortuous in synopsis become clear in the theater when the works are performed in translation, or to an audience that has studied the libretto in advance. But little service, I fear, was done to the cause of Handel opera by the Handel Society of New York's concert performance in Carnegie Hall, on Tuesday, of his *Ezio*. Of the twenty-five arias in the work, all in *da capo* (A-B-A form), only nine were given complete. Two were omitted altogether; in two, the third section was reduced to a brief instrumental reprise; the others were shorn down to the first section only. The more nearly complete a Handel performance, the more evident is his control of form. The operas, however, are long, and so they are always cut. One way of cutting is to retain, as here, at least some of almost every number but few numbers complete; another way, which I think less unsatisfactory, is to remove the more dispensable arias altogether but leave whole what is left. Yet in this performance a fault more serious than the abridgment was the undramatic conducting of Stephen Simon. The music plodded along where it should have danced; the rhythms were lifeless; the slow tempi sagged. Seldom did he set a natural, inevitable-seeming pace for a number or sustain an easy flow. Everything came out at much the same dynamic level. The singers were not urged to give full expression to the emotions of the music.

Ezio, composed to a Metastasio libretto adapted for

Handel's use, was first performed early in 1732. The action
begins more or less where that of Verdi's *Attila* ends; the
Hun has been defeated, and General Aetius returns to
Rome in triumph to be greeted by the Emperor Valentinian
III. "Action" is perhaps too strong a word; the situation is
that Valentinian decides to reward Aetius with the hand of
his sister Onoria, though Aetius loves Fulvia, the daughter
of Maximus, a schemer who plots against both the Emperor
and his general. Valentinian also loves Fulvia, and Onoria
loves Aetius. This is tangle enough to provide the necessary
scenes of misunderstanding, constancy, despair, delight, and
rage before everything is tidied into a happy end. The most
interesting plight is Fulvia's; she despises her father's
duplicity yet is restrained by filial duty from denouncing
him in public. To save her beloved Aetius, she pretends to
have accepted the Emperor's hand, but then bursts out with
her true feelings when she sees Aetius's distress. Death,
rather than deception! This role, with its splendid array of
arias, was composed for Handel's faithful Anna Strada. She
must have had a more powerful, a more dramatic and
richly colored voice than Judith Blegen's, but after a
somewhat pallid start Miss Blegen (who had learned the
part at short notice to take over from an ill Evelyn Lear)
became better and better. She crowned her performance
with an affecting, exquisitely turned account of "Ah! non
son io che parlo," an aria that Burney rightly described as
"admirably composed in a grand style of theatrical pathetic." It includes octave leaps, from trill to trill, which
Miss Blegen took most featly. She was the only singer who
sounded really at home in the Handelian style.

Handel used only one castrato in *Ezio*, but he was the
great Senesino, in the title role. His voice centered on the F
above middle C, and Handel wrote for him to the fifth
above and the fifth below, with occasional excursions
beyond. This is an awkwardly low tessitura for women who

wish to sound brilliant and heroic. (Janet Baker often lifts the music a tone or two when she undertakes the Senesino roles.) They are better suited to the poignant moments, as Gwendolyn Killebrew was—but she was fuzzy of focus. Valentinian was composed for Anna Bagnolesi, a contralto; Corinne Curry, a mezzo, sometimes switched octaves in mid-phrase, with disconcerting effect, when the line ran low. Onoria's music was delivered in a regal manner by Betty Allen. Maximus, one of Handel's rare tenor principals, was taken by Raymond Gibbs; he made little of a characterization that should be fairly subtle. There is a sixth member of the cast, Varus, prefect of the Praetorian Guard, who plays a subaltern part in the action but is musically interesting, for this was the first role Handel composed to display the range, power, and accuracy over wide intervals of the bass Antonio Montagnana. In "Nasce al bosco," Varus leaps an eleventh, from C to high F, and in the next measure he plunges a twelfth, from middle C to the F below the staff. He is awarded the final aria, in competition with a trumpet, "in Handel's fullest and best style of martial Music" (Burney again). Morley Meredith only just coped.

An English translation of the text was provided free of charge. A libretto with parallel columns of Italian and English, such as was published in 1732, would have been more helpful, and worth a dollar or so of any Handelian's money. The cast sat "offstage," to one side, when not actually singing; the theatrical shape of the opera would have been better defined by the provision of some "onstage" chairs as well, to make it plain exactly who was concerned in any particular scene.

The Metropolitan Opera's current production of Verdi's *Macbeth* is a limp, bloated relic of the famous presentation of the piece that Carl Ebert directed and Caspar Neher

designed for Berlin in 1931; they brought it to Glyndebourne in 1938, revived it there after the war, and
expanded it for the Metropolitan in 1959. The opera is a
thing of contrasts—musical, scenic, and dramatic. As Boris
Goldovsky demonstrated in his interval talk last Saturday,
during the Texaco broadcast, Verdi pits the F minor of
guilty remorse against the bright E major of bloody
resolution. After the black scene of Banquo's murder, the
curtain lifts on the hectic brilliance of the Macbeths'
banquet; this was a great moment, literally dazzling, in the
Glyndebourne edition of the Ebert-Neher presentation, and
at the old Metropolitan it also came in for praise. But in the
revival the banquet was a drab, glum affair (there wasn't
even anything to eat). All the scenic contrasts were flattened
by a lighting plot tenebrous from beginning to end, except
where the follow-spots cast their crude circles of radiance
around the principals. No sudden blaze to match the shouts
of victory. The appearances of Banquo's ghost were feebly
managed. (How chilling when it is suddenly there, calmly
seated at the table, among the guests; in this version the
specter stalked on amid a flashing of lights.) In the sleep-
walking scene, huge gouts of blood splashed all the scenery.
The shadow play that opened the battle was rather
effective.

The show could have been saved by stronger, subtler
interpreters of Macbeth and his Lady, though what it
needed above all was more vigorous musical direction than
that provided by Francesco Molinari-Pradelli. America
must surely be filled with young conductors who would not
refuse a chance of attacking this score, of inspiring singers to
the soft, intense, energetic declamation that it so often
requires, of coaxing from orchestra and chorus both the
fiery and the dark, sinister sounds that are called for. Mr
Molinari-Pradelli rolled out the music like a routineer; the
marvelous score made little impact. Martina Arroyo's

warm, soft-grained voice was ill-suited to her part; a Lady Macbeth needs metal in the timbre, and a more combative personality. In the title role, Sherrill Milnes was dull. He acted as if he knew the story in advance. He did nothing to make us hang upon each word as it was uttered. In general, the handling of the text was not nearly vivid enough. (Verdi told his first cast to concentrate on serving the poet before the composer.) For some years now, Mr Milnes has shown the promise of becoming a very fine Verdi baritone, but he lacks *school*. He is uneven. A noble phrase will be followed by a raw one. We can still call him promising, since the splendid vocal material seems unharmed by the heavy use he has made of it; I wish we could call him exciting. Ruggero Raimondi gave a straightforward, imposingly sonorous account of Banquo's part, and Franco Tagliavini was a decent Macduff. It was interesting (for once) to hear the 1847 close, rather than the long victory chorus of the 1865 revision or the composite version (Macbeth's 1847 soliloquy plus the new chorus) favored by Ebert. One day I should like to hear the aria for Macbeth that originally ended the apparitions scene; the duet that took its place, "Ora di morte," is not especially distinguished.

Apart from dropping in for an occasional breakfast in Alaska, I first set foot on American soil in Washington, D.C., one night, and was taken by my hosts straight to the Lincoln Memorial, where are inscribed the Gettysburg and Second Inaugural Addresses. It made an impressive and powerful introduction to a new nation conceived in liberty and dedicated to the proposition that all men are created equal. On dark days, I have clung to that first, lofty vision of American nobility and goodness. It is not surprising that the Presidential Inaugural Committee should have decided against a recital of Lincoln's Second Inaugural Address at the concert celebrating the start of Mr Nixon's second term—and surprising only that the committee should have suggested that text in the first place to Vincent Persichetti when inviting him to compose a work for the concert. In the event, Persichetti's *A Lincoln Address,* deleted from the Washington program, was performed first in St Louis last month, by the St Louis Symphony, and then in New York last Thursday, when the orchestra visited Carnegie Hall. The address was declaimed by William Warfield. The music that accompanied it, drawn from Persichetti's *Hymns and Responses* and *Liturgical Symphony,* did no more, alas, than deck its simple grandeur with "movie-music" gestures. Portentous strains began it. A big crescendo for "And the war came." After "Neither party expected for the war the magnitude or the duration which it has already attained," a roll on the side drum and another crescendo. A solo flute for "Both read the same Bible," strings in pious pastoral for "The Almighty has His own purposes," and a suggestion of an underlying Shaker tune. And so on, to a quiet, Vaughan Williamsy close. Worthy, well-intentioned music, but conventional in its responses and uninspired.

The concert, which was conducted by Walter Susskind, began with a clean, nicely poised account of Mozart's "Prague" Symphony, notable for shapely string articulation (the violas especially firm and strong) and a delightfully woody bassoon tone. The flute did not come through strongly enough; when Mozart (or Haydn) is played the rampart of strings across the front of the platform should be breached to let the woodwinds sit well forward. Janet Baker sang Mahler's *Kindertotenlieder* in grave, beautiful tones, but Mr Susskind's contribution was jerky. (No text in the program-book—merely inadequate epitomes.) Dvořák's Slavonic Dances, the first set, were done with a lilt, with verve. Silly prudes hushed the applause that broke out naturally after the jolliest numbers—as if these dances were a great symphony that should be heard out in solemn silence. St Louis has a sound, spirited orchestra.

February 10, 1973

The Nonesuch recording of Ruth Crawford Seeger's String Quartet is H 71280. David Del Tredici's I Hear an Army *is recorded on CRI SD 294, by Phyllis Bryn-Julson and the Composers Quartet.*

Errant Knight

Balanchine's *Don Quixote* may not be a straightforward, easily acclaimed success, but it is a ballet more interesting, more rewarding to contemplate, more subtle, and more disturbing in the afterimages it leaves than most other full-length dance narratives. I felt that I "knew" the piece long before I had actually seen it, because Edwin Denby's essay "About *Don Quixote*" (reprinted in his collection *Dancers, Buildings and People in the Streets*) had so vividly, and so lovingly, described and evoked its episodes, its dance manners, and its atmosphere. But the first live encounter, during the New York City Ballet's current season at the New York State Theater, proved disconcerting. Some of the action was different; I was prepared for that, because *Don Quixote* has been through many editions since it was first performed, in 1965, but unprepared for quite so drastic a shift of emphasis from the drama of Don Quixote to the dance divertissements. For *Don Quixote*, I had thought, must be the exceptional work in a canon otherwise true to Balanchine's Petersburg-based, pre-Fokin credo. The second of Fokin's Five Principles, formulated in 1914, stated that "dancing and mimetic gesture have no meaning in ballet unless they serve as an expression of dramatic action." In 1962, when Balanchine was in Moscow, he declared, contrariwise, "The ballet is such a rich art form that it should not be an illustrator of even the most interesting, even the most meaningful literary primary source. The ballet will speak for itself and about itself. . . . I am always sorry when an excellent ballerina depicts with her movements only some literary theme." Three years later, he composed *Don Quixote.*

In the first act of the ballet, where once there were some village dances, there is now a long, irrelevant pas classique espagnol, led by Karin von Aroldingen and Peter Martins. She is hard, brilliant, and commanding; he is allotted choreography that seems to imply a quicker, more compact sort of dancer, and he does not really get his long limbs round the movements quite crisply enough. The costumes are strident and unbecoming. But it is a wonderful set of dances, superbly fashioned—a suite in which the soloists and a *concertante* group of twelve girls are deployed in ever varied textures. One is dazzled, as always, by the prodigality of Balanchine's invention, and shares the evident delight with which he created new, surprising sequences and patterns while limiting himself to the formal language of "classical-ballet Spanish" as established by Petipa. I long to see this episode again. It "speaks for itself"—though it does not really speak about *Don Quixote.*

The witty, quirky divertissements of the second act—entertainment at the ducal party—fall more naturally into the dramatic structure of the piece, and are framed by court dances in which elegance and cruelty are combined. Esteban Francés's black-and-gold scene, his black-and-gold costumes, and these cold, precise dances in which aristocratic formality suddenly takes on the accents of menace conspire to suggest the Spain of Philip II. The dances are

not irrelevant, for Don Quixote is present, and finally
shamed, during them; through the chilly glitter of a
chivalry that has become a mere code of manners his true,
warmhearted chivalry moves like a steady flame amid
flickering agate. The courtiers mock his childlike simplicity
with spiteful, childish tricks.

Most of Act III is another suite of dances—a vision scene,
a dream that turns to nightmare, a whirl of knightly
exploits, romance, and sorcery, in which reminiscences of
the adventures we have seen mingle with those we know
that the knight has read about. It is Don Quixote's dream;
the poetic sequence of enchanted dance images portrays his
reeling fancies. But surely he should be on the stage,
sleeping uneasily beneath a tree (as in the last act of
Massenet's *Don Quichotte*). The Lady Dulcinea's appeal
when she is threatened seems to be addressed to him—but
he is not there. He has gone off into the wings, as Albrecht
goes off in the second act of *Giselle,* though the plot demands
his presence; as Aurora and the Prince, in the last act of *The
Sleeping Beauty,* often fail to show up at their own wedding
celebration until the moment for their pas de deux has
come; as Odile, in the second act of *Swan Lake,* no sooner
arrives than she is whisked offstage by her Prince until they
are due back for the pas de deux. In all these cases, the
narrative is sacrificed to "pure dance," and there are people
who argue that it should be so. I prefer productions that
make sense of the story as well. Whatever Balanchine may
have said about literary themes, in *Don Quixote* he essayed
one. Though Petipa's ballet of the same title has very little
to do with Cervantes, and a great deal to do with a display
of brilliant, diversified dancing, Balanchine knew and loved
the melancholy knight: the prologue, the harsh, horrifying
scene in which he is caged, the beautifully simple, profoundly affecting death scene all show it. When Balanchine
next revises *Don Quixote,* I hope he will think himself back

into the title role he first portrayed, and insure that it is once again central. For that is the way to make the piece more theatrical, more readily "effective"—not by adding divertissements, however stunning they may be. Though he may be happier devising new, joyful classical pas, from the time of *The Prodigal Son,* in 1929, Balanchine has also been a master of expressive, dramatic ballet. So little of it remains in the repertory—his *Fairy's Kiss* has been reduced to *Divertimento,* his *Firebird* has all but lost its plot, his *Swan Lake* has become a suite—that his admirers cannot, without protest, allow him to think of his *Don Quixote* as no more than a framework for glorious dancing. There is nothing, alas, that can be done about Nicolas Nabokov's wretched score, which lays a deadening hand on the evening. It is short-breathed, repetitive, feeble in its little attempts to achieve vivacity by recourse to a trumpet solo or a gong stroke. The marvel is that it did not inhibit Balanchine's invention; it merely dulls our response to it unless we are able, so to speak, to "see through it" to the wonders of the choreography. The vulgar *Don Quixote* music that Minkus wrote for Petipa had more life in it, and Roberto Gerhard's score for Ninette de Valois more character and subtle emotion.

Not without a pang does one see for the first time a role—in *Don Quixote,* in *Jewels*—shaped for the style and movement of Suzanne Farrell and realize that one will probably never watch Miss Farrell dance it. Dulcinea remains a beautiful portrait of the dancer who for a while was Balanchine's Muse (and is now wasting herself in Maurice Béjart's troupe). Seeing that this was so did not lessen appreciation of Sara Leland's light, lucid, tender, and delicately inflected account of the role in all its aspects, from serving maid to radiant vision. I went to *Don Quixote* with a Covent Garden ballerina. She, too, was seeing it for the first time. Like me, but with a technical appreciation that makes her opinion more valuable, she was raptured by the steps that Balanchine has created; enthusiastic about the dancers of his company; distressed by the music; and puzzled that he should permit the total effect of so many rare and precious things to be untheatrical.

A few months before *Don Quixote* was first done, Balanchine wrote *Harlequinade*—a new version of the Petipa *Harlequin's Millions*, to music by Drigo, in which he had danced as a boy. In its latest edition, *Harlequinade* has also acquired a new divertissement—a *ballabile des enfants*, based on the choreographer's childhood memories. The children of the School of American Ballet, here as in *Nutcracker*, are never cute, coy, winsome, or sentimental but poised, intent little classical dancers, perfectly disciplined—and perfectly delightful. Act I has a plot of sorts, though it is dissolved into dances. The action of Act II occupies about twenty seconds, while the Good Fairy showers on Harlequin his millions, and all the rest is happy dancing. Patricia McBride (Colombine), Edward Villella (Harlequin), Gloria Govrin (the Good Fairy), and Deni Lamont (Pierrot) still dance in their original roles. Miss McBride was captivating. Mr Villella had all his wonted courtesy and romance but less than his old brilliance; his dancing was dapper, not breath-taking. The lighting was crude. Rouben Ter-Arutunian, to whom it is credited, may have meant to suggest a rude commedia-dell'arte theater but can hardly have wanted his follow-spots to stop short of the dancers' feet.

A word for Gelsey Kirkland and John Clifford, who together (in the central Rubies panel of *Jewels*, the third movement of *Symphony in C*, the Andante of *Brahms-Schoenberg Quartet*, a pas de deux of *Don Quixote*) and separately (notably, she in *Nutcracker*, he in the Sarabande of *Agon* and the first variation of *Four Temperaments*) have been dancing so vividly and well this season. The two extended pas de deux in *Jewels*—that of Rubies in Balanchine's liveliest Stravinskian vein, and that of Diamonds (now movingly danced by Kay Mazzo and Peter Martins) in his grandest Maryinsky manner—seem to span a century of classical ballet, though both are so evidently by the same creator.

After *Jewels,* it was hard to look kindly on the classical confections of the American Ballet Theatre during its City Center season. This is a company of able dancers without an individual style and without a choreographer or group of choreographers (such as once it had) to provide its staple repertory, care for its revivals, and compose for its artists the new roles they need if they are to develop as artists. In this it resembles such troupes as London's Festival Ballet and the Dutch National Ballet—though there are stars of greater luster on the Ballet Theatre bills. Both the repertory and the manner of execution are what is often termed "commercial." It is what many people want. Where the City Ballet dancers invite us to share, if we will, in their dedicated rites (which can be bubbly and buoyant as well as calmly beautiful), the Ballet Theatre dancers seem to fling their offerings over the footlights and defy us not to break into applause. The first two programs I attended contained four ballets each; on each occasion three of the four (*Les Patineurs,* the Gsovsky *Grand Pas classique,* and *Graduation Ball*; the *Paquita* divertissement, the *Flames of Paris* pas de deux, and *Graduation Ball* again) contained fouetté sequences. I'm partial enough to a nice bout of thirty-two, twenty-four, or even just sixteen fouettés, especially when they are neatly paragraphed by doubles in the right place. Cynthia Gregory's were just about impeccable, and Eleanor D'Antuono's were pretty exciting. But at best they are applause-catching things; such programs make altogether too open a bid for applause.

Within a company, roles in the company ballets can
generally be handed down from generation to generation of
dancers and still fit—or be made to fit if the original tailor
or his deft successor is at hand. But the Ballet Theatre
dancers borrow a lot of their finery from all over the place,
and some of it does not suit them. Their version of Ashton's
Patineurs is tattered and pulled out of shape. Their account
of Lichine's *Graduation Ball* is too broad and brassy. They do
better by Rudi van Dantzig's dance-drama *Monument for a
Dead Boy,* which was composed in the first place for a
similarly eclectic company. (Whether it is worth doing all
over again is another matter.) Alvin Ailey's new *Sea-Change,*
to the music of the Sea Interludes from Britten's *Peter Grimes,*
is, like much of his recent work, fluent and agreeable but
lacking in what Boulez calls "profile." My grumpy comments raise the question of whether a company and its
dancers can ever thrive without a resident choreographer to
direct their progress. I can't think, offhand, of any company
that has. And what a pity that no one should be using, say,
Miss Gregory, who has such rare equilibrium, speed, and
precision, and a charming, distinctive personality as well—
or, for that matter, a dozen other remarkable artists in this
talented troupe. Dancing is not enough. They need something of their own to dance.

February 10, 1973

Edwin Denby's Dancers, Buildings and People in the Streets
and his earlier Looking at the Dance *are reissued in paperback by
Curtis Books; no one has written better about dance than Mr Denby.*

An Encyclopedic Heroine

Bellini's *Norma* was composed for a special occasion—the début at La Scala, in December 1831, of Giuditta Pasta. She was already celebrated, and at a smaller Milanese theater had recently won a triumph in Bellini's previous opera, *La sonnambula,* but for some reason she had not yet sung at La Scala. Felice Romani, Bellini's regular collaborator, chose as the basis of his libretto a play by Alexandre Soumet which had just been given with success in Paris. It provided a tremendous role for the heroine. Soumet related with pride how his leading lady, Mlle George, had "run the whole gamut of passions that can be contained in the female heart," and had been, in turn, Niobe, Lady Macbeth, and Velléda (the heroine of Chateaubriand's *Les Martyrs*) before rising, in the final act, to "heights of inspiration that can perhaps never be reproduced." With justice, Bellini told his leading lady that she would find she had a role suited to her "encyclopedic character." Bellini's and Romani's Norma remains one of the most demanding parts in opera, both vocally and dramatically. It calls for power; grace in slow cantilena; pure, fluent coloratura; stamina; tones both tender and violent; force and intensity of verbal declamation; and a commanding stage presence. Only a soprano who has all these things can sustain the role. There have not been many such sopranos. The critics of the nineteenth century delighted to describe and compare the fine points of the performances by Pasta, Giulia Grisi, Malibran, Adelaide Kemble, and, later, Lilli Lehmann. The Germans even acclaimed Jenny Lind's Norma as "maidenly"—which, as the English critic Henry Chorley remarked, was "praise original, to say the least of it, when the well-known story is remembered." Chorley liked Grisi, who had originally played Adalgisa to Pasta's Norma. Grisi's performance of the title role was modeled on Pasta's but was "perhaps, in some points, an improvement on the model, because there was more of animal passion in it," wrote Chorley. "There was in it the wild ferocity of the tigress, but a certain frantic charm therewith which carried away the listener." Lilli Lehmann, whose Norma won a eulogy from Hanslick, introduced the opera to the Metropolitan, in 1890. Rosa Ponselle sang it there from 1927 to 1931, Zinka Milanov between 1943 and 1945, and again in 1954. Maria Callas made her Metropolitan début as Norma, in 1956. The current Metropolitan production dates from 1970, when Joan Sutherland (who in London twenty years ago played Clotilde, the handmaiden, to Callas's Norma) was its heroine. Now the part is being taken by Montserrat Caballé.

Mme Caballé first sang Norma in Barcelona three years ago. On the opening night, according to reports of the event, she charged her tones with dark, dramatic colors, as if in emulation of Callas's famous interpretation, but then on the second night essayed quite another rendering, in clear, limpid timbres. I can believe it, now that I have heard in quick succession two such different vocalizations of the role as Mme Caballé's on the RCA recording of the opera and Mme Caballé's at the Metropolitan last week. The recording, just published, was made in London last summer. The soprano put in a busy studio stint that also included Liù in Puccini's *Turandot*, Mathilde in Rossini's *William Tell*, and the title role of Verdi's *Giovanna d'Arco*, so it is perhaps not surprising that her recorded Norma lacks dramatic intensity and vividness of detail. Of Pasta it was said that with three notes she could stir an audience to the depths of its being. Callas could do the same when she uttered the three notes of "Sì, Norma," upon confronting her betrayer in the final scene, or of "Io stessa," while confessing her guilt and gently drawing the priestess's garland from her brow. At these points in the recorded performance, Mme Caballé disappoints us, but she sings the role with a full, clear voice, generous, flexible, powerful in climaxes, and affecting when it is fined down to a gentle thread of exquisite sound. At the Metropolitan, on the other hand, she used, too consistently, her darkest, most resinous and bitter tones. She gave a more emotional performance, but one that fell less gratefully on the ear. It sounded as if she had been studying the Callas recordings. Moreover, it looked as if she might have been influenced by those photographs of Callas as Norma, with arms extended and hands held high. Last December, Mme Caballé was doing the part at La Scala, in a new production by Mauro Bolognini, and she comes to New York with an assured theatrical command of its phrases, and complete stage aplomb. She made a superb entrance. Throughout the evening, she looked magnificent and moved with unaffected dignity. Her flashing eyes and aquiline profile created a noble portrait of the high-mettled priestess.

There was nothing tentative about either the singing (despite some moments of pitch trouble in the first act) or the acting. But much of the time it was a generalized grandeur of manner that she offered. She maintained scarce-varied tones of grief, or anger. The utterance of individual phrases still lacked that specificness which Callas has taught us to expect. The most moving passages were the solo verse of the duet "Mira, o Norma" and the long recitative that introduces the final scene. There the darkness cleared from the timbre; the phrases were limpid, delicately shaped, and sounded with the utmost beauty of tone. Several fast episodes she took too fast for the music to have much meaning. Vocally, she has just about everything a Norma needs. When she combines her "clear" and her darkly dramatic approaches into one properly "encyclopedic" portrayal, she should be tremendous.

Adalgisa, a soprano role, has long been appropriated by heavy mezzos. It was taken here—as on the RCA records and in the new Scala production—by Fiorenza Cossotto. The two ladies played together in masterly fashion. They sang together rather less well, since Miss Cossotto's tone spreads under pressure and the run of thirds could not be precisely tuned. For the first time in my experience, Adalgisa looked younger and prettier than Norma, as the story requires; her kittenish charm contrasted well with the chief priestess's severe, grief-clouded beauty. Miss Cossotto was less monotonously loud than in the recording, and more various in her phrasing, but one vulgar trick she retained. The first note of the phrase "Io l'obbliai" (when Adalgisa tells Pollione, before their duet, that she has forgotten their love), a high A, was marked by the composer to be sung "con messa di voce assai lunga"; Miss Cossotto delivered it without *messa di voce* (a swelling and then diminishing of the tone) and as a tuned scream, *tutta forza*. John Alexander (stepping in for an ill Carlo Cossutta) made a dull, reliable Pollione; Oroveso needs a grander bass than Giorgio Tozzi's.

Norma, a late and admirable example of *opera seria*, is worth treating as more than an exercise in vocal connoisseurship. The Metropolitan version is handsomely staged by Paul-Emile Deiber, with impressive choral assemblies. Norma's children need quieting down; playing hide-and-seek and pat-a-cake, they steal attention during some of their mother's most poignant phrases. Desmond Heeley's rocks and menhirs build into imposing scenes—though his failure to provide any *querce antiche* forces Norma to scoop the air with her sickle and produce mistletoe as if by a conjuring trick. Rudolph Kuntner's lighting is picturesque and carefully executed, if too constantly nocturnal. Visually, the opera was treated with due seriousness. But Carlo Felice Cillario was an unworthy conductor, who handled the score in a superficial fashion. The first finale was heavily cut. The "Guerra!" chorus retained its beautiful *maggiore* close—reminiscent of the Pastoral Symphony—which is often omitted, but Mme Caballé sang neither the fierce cries that should propel it nor the swelling arpeggio that should rise (like Leonora's at the close of "La Vergine degli angeli," in *La forza del destino*) through the closing bars. An intrusive interval interrupted the progress of Act II.

Mahler's Sixth Symphony, a work once rarely encountered (in my young days I crossed the North Sea to catch it), has been played six times in New York this season: four times by the Philharmonic, under Boulez, and since then by the Cleveland Orchestra, under Claudio Abbado, in Carnegie Hall, and by the Boston Symphony, under

James Levine, in the Brooklyn Academy of Music. Abbado had already shown his considerable merits as a Mahlerian, conducting the Second Symphony with the Philadelphia Orchestra in Philharmonic Hall earlier this year. Of the Sixth he gave a warmer, more picturesque and emotional account than Boulez' yet one that was equally well controlled in point of form. The Cleveland Orchestra is as excellent as ever—sterling tone in every department, uncommonly true tuning, no striving for glamour, no screaminess or stridency in climaxes, and plenty of disciplined energy. The Boston players, under Mr Levine, proved less distinguished, less poised, and less accurate. The brasses tended to glare; the solo flute at the close of the Andante wobbled too generously. Mr Levine cut the repeat of the first movement, which spoiled its shape, and in general he missed that inevitable-seeming relationship of one tempo to the next within movements which made both Mr Boulez' and Mr Abbado's readings flow so coherently.

The Dance Theatre of Harlem, a black classical company, made a fine impression when it appeared earlier this month at the Klitgord Center, in Brooklyn, as a part of the New York City Community College's Festival of the Arts. Within a few years, Arthur Mitchell and Karel Shook have produced a troupe worth watching—a troupe with a style and character of its own—and in Lydia Abarca it has a long-limbed, fluent ballerina whose carriage, placing, and precision of musical accent suggest that she was born to dance Balanchine. The Dance Theatre's account of Balanchine's *Agon* is bouncier than the City Ballet's; the dancers convey a sense of conscious delight in having conquered such difficulties, which is captivating in its way. In his *Holberg Suite*, a classical divertissement, and *Rhythmetron*, a classical *Sacre* with ethnic accents, Mr Mitchell shows himself a skillful and resourceful choreographer; his inventions stretch the dancers, but not beyond the limits of their technique.

February 24, 1973

The RCA recording of Norma, *with Caballé and Cossotto, conducted by Cillario, is on LSC 6202.*

So Much Virtue

An auditiorium holding about fifteen hundred people probably provides the best general home for opera. Such a house, well designed, can be large enough for Wagner (the Festspielhaus in Bayreuth is only a little bigger, seating eighteen hundred) and not too large for Mozart. Everybody can see and hear well. Strong, seasoned voices are not constricted, and young voices are not strained. Massive effects can be achieved without mammoth forces, while small details can strike home. Words can be heard. Moreover, financing should be easier, since Menotti's Law—the larger the house the larger the subsidy that must be poured into it—has yet to be disproved. But even companies that play in theaters of this moderate size generally feel the need for a studio-type auditorium as well, where the products of modern music theater and also small-scale treasures of the past can be staged at slight cost and in greater intimacy. (Most of the German opera houses built since the war include a "workshop," or studio.) Big companies with any sense of artistic adventure need such an outlet even more. So La Scala built its Piccola Scala. The

State Opera in Munich reconstructed the little Cuvilliés-Theater. Covent Garden has plans for a small modern theater beside the nineteenth-century house, and meanwhile supports the itinerant English Opera Group to perform works by Purcell, Britten, and young men like Harrison Birtwistle. Now the Metropolitan Opera has taken a step in this direction by presenting three weeks of chamber opera in the Forum, that tiny theater (fewer than three hundred seats) beneath the Vivian Beaumont, and close to the parent house. Richard Dufallo is principal conductor and artistic adviser. Marit Gentele is program adviser. The repertory, drawn from the seventeenth and twentieth centuries, is choice: Maurice Ohana's *Syllabaire pour Phèdre* and Purcell's *Dido and Aeneas* on a double bill, and Virgil Thomson's *Four Saints in Three Acts*. The program-book vouchsafes no information about the troupe, but it apparently consists chiefly of young professionals (several of them members of the Metropolitan Opera Studio), together with some Juilliard students and a few seasoned hands such as Evelyn Lear and Thomas Stewart, in the title roles of the Purcell, and Betty Allen, as Commère of the Thomson. A small band of deft instrumentalists has been brought together for the occasion.

Dido and Aeneas is not just the best school opera ever written (it was composed, probably in 1689, for performance by the young gentlewomen of Josias Priest's boarding school, in Chelsea) but one of those works that can be mentioned in a breath with Monteverdi's *Ulisse* and *Poppea* and Gluck's *Orfeo* as holding in a new, marvelous balance those tensions—between words and music, declamatory recitative and lyric aria, straight dramatic progress and subtle, dexterous musical forms—that have ever given to opera its special affecting power. The work is utterly direct in its communication—a listener needs no historical training to appreciate its dramatic force—and utterly natural-

seeming in its advance from amorous passion to noble
tragedy, yet examination of the score shows it to be filled
with carefully wrought technical devices. The plainest
instance is the way Dido's first air and her final lament are
freely declaimed in phrases of three, four, five, six, or seven
measures, in each case over a regular and recurrent bass
figure—four and five measures long, respectively. The
melody flows and surges with the heroine's thoughts, breaks
off, rings out again, repeats words with a new, fierce
intensity; meanwhile, the ground bass moves forward
inexorably. The outer acts belong to Dido. In the central
act, she has but one phrase to sing, and by its isolation it is
thrown into prominence and becomes important: her words,
"The skies are clouded," are ominous; the harmony (a
decorated fanfare in D major) points to the G minor of her
final entrance and her lament; the figuration adumbrates
the phrases in which she finally dismisses Aeneas. Modern
editors do wrong, I think, to supply extra music to close the
act with witchy song and dance in D, even though (like
some other episodes for which there is no music in the
surviving scores) they are mentioned in the libretto. The
act, and its action, come to a climax in the great closing
soliloquy for Aeneas, where the harmonies are wrested as
violently as his heart, and his E-major cry of "Yours be the
blame, ye gods!" provides an ironic echo to the passage in
Act I in which he has boasted of defying the feeble stroke of
destiny. Aeneas, in Acts I and III a suppliant, a foil to
Dido's more active passion, here becomes a heroic character
in his own right. Witches at this point are an anticlimax; we
should move directly to the quayside of Act III, where the
sailors' carefree farewell to their Carthaginian nymphs
prepares for the tragic parting of the principals. Purcell's
control of dramatic movement—his sense of when to bate
and when to press on—is as notable in the long span as in a
single phrase. The development of the courtiers from a

light-spirited crew to a compassionate chorus whose final elegy flows gently from the last chord of the lament is masterly. "Whence could so much virtue spring?" Dido, like Sophie von Faninal, is good on pedigrees; she knows her classical mythology, and answers this question about Aeneas with "Anchises' valour mixt with Venus' charms," doing so in strains that recall now Lully's grace, now Carissimi's vividness of word painting. Purcell's virtue springs from his command of both the French and the Italian approaches to text setting. By tempering formality with freedom, he rediscovers the methods of Monteverdi, and then transforms them by his perfect ear for the stresses, lengths, and inflections of the English tongue. Unerringly, he places each phrase in a vocal register where it simply cannot take the wrong expression. One tiny point more. (I could go on for pages about the big points.) What a pretty, piquant device it is that the spirit world should throw back its echoes of the witches' dance with slight, subtle distortions of the harmony.

Dido came into town—from the Thames-side village of Chelsea—early in the eighteenth century, and then disappeared from the boards again until it was revived by London's Royal College of Music in 1895. (The Juilliard School gave the first staged performance outside Britain, in 1932.) Purcell's autograph is lost; his music survives in two eighteenth-century manuscript copies, in which a mixed choir is employed (though the choruses can easily be reconstructed for girls' voices). Aeneas is the only solo role for male voice; at the Forum the roles of both Sailor and Spirit were usurped, not unsuccessfully, by tenors. The edition used was that "realized" by Benjamin Britten and Imogen Holst. Under Britten's own direction, it comes off superbly, but I do not think it a completely safe edition for performers who may not have Purcell's music in their blood. It is liberally—perhaps too liberally—larded with expression marks, with changes of tempo and dynamics, and with instructions like "forceful," "more intense," "animated." These are indications provided by two master Purcellians toward an eloquent performance, but they seem to have led Miss Lear and Mr Stewart (as, in a French production, I once heard them lead Teresa Berganza and Gérard Souzay) to adopt an overromantic, overrhetorical manner. There were affecting moments, but dialogues that should have flowed swiftly became sticky. Moreover, choruses and dances, under Mr Dufallo, sometimes chugged when they should have skipped. (The very look of the notes on the pages of the edition by Thurston Dart and Margaret Laurie is crisper; is it fanciful to suggest that their score prompts a livelier performance?) That producer who lurks in every critical breast wanted to call a rehearsal in which the text was spoken, not sung, so that the natural tempi might be established. The Belinda—Susan Belling, whose tones were clear and sweet—might also have thus been encouraged to make more of her words.

Rhythmic lethargy was one thing wrong. Another, and no fault of the performers, was that the Forum, attractive little place though it is, is inimical to opera. Acoustically dead, it mercilessly exposes any impurity of tone, and abets such impurity by tempting the singers to try to force a response from their echoless surroundings. The band has been placed in a narrow gallery; there is nowhere else for it to go. This arrangement can work in even smaller theaters (such as the little Mermaid in the bottom of a St John's Wood garden, where Kirsten Flagstad once sang Dido), where the singers and the players remain close together, but when, on the bare thrust stage of the Forum, Dido is singing a Purcell melody under one's nose, while at the other end of the theater the harpsichordist picks his way through a countermelody by Britten, extraneous spatial effects are introduced that mar the music.

hana's *Syllabaire pour Phèdre,* composed six years ago, is, in effect, a brief cantata for a virtuoso ensemble of singers, piano, harp, harpsichord, two citharas (one of them tuned in third-tones), a fashionable array of percussion (four players), and some passages on tape. Performed on a record by the virtuosos of the French Radio, under Marius Constant, to whom it is dedicated, it makes delicate and beautiful sounds. The chorus patters the syllables "Hip-po-lyte" like drumbeats. A coloratura soprano, invited to soar higher than the Queen of Night, sings sweet vocalises. Third-tone melodies from cithara and voices add exotic touches. The percussions serve Bouleztin sauce. Phaedra both speaks and sings; Hippolytus and Theseus speak. Most of the language is broken into the sounds of vowel and consonant, but intelligible whole phrases do emerge which narrate in elliptical fashion the progress of the tragedy. It is a skillfully made and attractive piece. According to a note in the libretto, "the inner structure of the work . . . provides an open field for a visual imagination to fill with a ritual of gestures, lighting, colors, profiles, and volumes, all of which may vary with each performance according to the state of the trance attained by the participants." The Forum staging, directed by Paul-Émile Deiber around a truncated spiral staircase by Ming Cho Lee, and lit by Shirley Prendergast, added nothing to the score except a certain embarrassment while the principals walked round and round in front of us, or reeled, writhed, and fainted in coils on the steps. No more than *Dido* is *Syllabaire* a piece that takes easily to a thrust stage. The musical realization had evidently been rehearsed with care, but the hall dried the enchantment out of the sounds. Cynthia Barnett has the right sort of sweet, high, true soprano for the coloratura role.

In common with Purcell, Virgil Thomson sets the English language to melodies whose speeds, stresses, note values, and rise and fall are so sensitively precise that, once heard, they sing again in the mind at a mere reading of the text. It is not just a question of "fit." Thomson found an implicit music *in* the lines of Gertrude Stein's libretto *Four Saints in Three Acts,* but that was just a starting point; next, he had to create from it a music *for* those lines that would propel them, set them winging into the theater. The theme of *Four Saints* is, in the composer's words, "the religious life—peace between the sexes, community of faith, the production of miracles—its locale being the Spain Gertrude remembered from having traveled there." Perhaps—Thomson suggests as much in his autobiography—there is also a hint of the artistic community in the Paris of the late 1920s where *Four Saints* was conceived and composed, where Stein and Joyce, like Saints Teresa and Ignatius of the opera, had their bands of disciples and produced their miracles. Thomson put the text on the music rack of his piano and improvised music for it. "When the first act would improvise itself every day in the same way, I knew it was set. . . . Then I wrote it out." The melodies and harmonies that occurred to him recall hymn tunes and childhood ditties ("running from Gilbert and Sullivan to Morning Prayer and back") filtered through a fine and discerning ear. Memories of Ávila met memories of Kansas City, Missouri, the Harvard Glee Club, the organ loft of King's Chapel, Boston—and, in a Paris where Erik Satie's influence still played, *Four Saints* was created: a work that is tender, ecstatic, at once uninhibited and exquisitely controlled. As Miss Stein remarked in *The Autobiography of Alice B. Toklas,* "And it is a completely interesting opera both as to words and music."

It is tempting to speculate on what might have happened if the Darmstadt Opera had taken up the piece, as at one time seemed possible. (Apparently, Karl Böhm quashed the project.) The opera would doubtless have been scored more amply. It might have made the rounds of Germany, and prompted more successors from Thomson than *The Mother of Us All* and *Lord Byron* (works in which the fruitful crossplay of verbal and melodic rhythms, and of textual and musical forms, is further developed). In the event, *Four Saints* was first staged, in 1934, to inaugurate the Avery Memorial gallery of the Wadsworth Atheneum, in Hartford. That première—produced by John Houseman, staged and choreographed by Frederick Ashton, designed by Florine Stettheimer (some of whose designs for it are currently on view in the Low Library of Columbia University), and conducted by Alexander Smallens—is part of history. The 1952 revival of the opera was based upon it. It is understandable that the directors of the new production should have wanted to essay something different. Maurice Grosser, who first fashioned a working scenario (it is printed as a preface to the vocal score) from Stein's distinctly "open" text, counsels freedom for later stage directors and choreographers, and suggests that the decorator should use any device, style, or invention that produces an effect of brilliance. There is plenty of evidence to show that the original presentation was brilliant, light, bright, and shapely. Those epithets do not apply to the current Forum production, staged and choreographed by Alvin Ailey and dressed by Jane Greenwood. As a spectacle, it lacked any marked character; the elegant punctuation of both the text and the score was not reflected in the action. It looked as if Mr Ailey had not made up his mind just what the opera is, or might be, about. Roland Gagnon's musical direction, however, was expert and to the point: the tempi were well set, the rhythms were nicely maintained, and, insofar as the Forum acoustics allowed, the balances were just. No complaints on that head. A few about the singers. Originally, Thomson used a black cast, because he found that blacks pronounced words clearly and acted and sang unself-consciously. The present cast is part black, part white. The new St Teresa I (Clamma Dale) and St Ignatius (Arthur Thompson) sang the music in a self-conscious way, as if their main thoughts were on voice production. David Britton, who took the role of St Stephen, had the easiest command of the style. There were other promising voices to be heard; Barbara Hendricks (St Settlement) deserves mention. In the chorus of the 1952 revival were Leontyne Price and Gloria Davey, and in the ballet was Arthur Mitchell; perhaps some of the singers in the current show will be famous one day.

A verdict on Opera at the Forum must begin by regretting that the Forum is no place for opera but must add that the idea of such a troupe is a good one and deserves support. No doubt the Metropolitan is already laying its plans for Opera at—well, where? If it decides to keep its child in the Lincoln Center area, the Juilliard Theatre, the Vivian Beaumont, and Alice Tully Hall—thousand-seaters each, roughly—would be possible places (though they might not be available). If, like the Philharmonic, it decides to move south for its more experimental presentations, perhaps the Mercer O'Casey, where Stanley Silverman's opera *Doctor Selavy's Magic Theatre* goes so well, might be considered; it seats only three hundred but has better sound than the Forum. In any event, good luck to the venture. The repertory waiting to be done is large. The performers are gifted, and they could have disarmed any disappointment at their present achievement by reciting Tom Durfey's Epilogue to *Dido and Aeneas,* which on the first night was spoken by Lady Dorothy Burk:

> . . . if some Critick here
> Fond of his Wit, designs to be severe,

Let not his Patience be worn out too soon,
And in a few Years we shall be all in Tune!

March 3, 1973

The Britten-Holst edition of Dido and Aeneas *is published by Boosey & Hawkes, the Dart-Laurie edition by Novello. The recording of Ohana's* Syllabaire pour Phèdre *mentioned above is Musical Heritage Society, MHS 1087. In 1947 an abridged recording of* Four Saints in Three Acts *was made with, substantially, the original cast; this is still available on RCA LM 2756.*

Frederick Takes Trouble

Eighteenth-century serious operas to texts by court poets
generally supported the existing order, and, in mythic
or historical parallel, hymned the clemency and benevo-
lence of a just ruler. *Montezuma*, devised by a ruler himself,
was an opera that urged reform. Frederick the Great, its
author, announced his intentions in a letter to his friend and
artistic crony Count Algarotti: Cortes would be the tyrant
of his piece, music would launch a sally at the barbarism of
the Christian faith, and opera itself would serve "à réformer
les mœurs et à détruire les superstitions." Reform was not to
be confined to the subject matter; the "abuse" of constant
da-capo airs would also be abolished. Frederick took pains
with his piece; Bayreuth, the scene of a later, greater
operatic reform, played a part in the story. The King,
having written *Montezuma* in French prose, sent the libretto
to his sister Wilhelmine, the Margravine of Bayreuth, and
asked her to have it enacted by her excellent French troupe
and then let him know what she thought of the dialogue,
the dramatic motion, and the effect of the whole: "I take
the liberty of laying at your feet a Mexican who is not yet

quite polished; I have taught him to speak French; now he must learn Italian. But before putting him to this trouble, I beg you to tell me frankly what you feel, and whether he warrants the effort." Wilhelmine presumably thought he did, for Montezuma was taught Italian by Frederick's court poet, Tagliazucchi; was set to sing by Carl Heinrich Graun; and reached the boards of the Berlin Opera in 1755—twelve years before Gluck, in the preface to *Alceste*, drew up his famous principles of operatic reform. Frederick had supervised rehearsals to insure that his cast acted in the spirit of the piece. The décor was by Giuseppe Galli Bibiena.

This most interesting score has been in print (as Volume 15 of the *Denkmäler Deutscher Tonkunst*) since 1904 but has seldom been performed. The American première was given by the Associate Artists Opera Company of New England last month, in the Boston Center for the Arts. The performance was not admirable—its best point was the lively orchestral playing, under John Miner, a conductor with a good feeling for tempo and accent—but the work proved enthralling. The royal reforms did not extend to enjoining upon Graun the "beautiful simplicity" that Gluck proclaimed as his first care, but they included more than just the virtual abandonment of *da-capo* airs. (The score includes only four numbers with a first-section repeat, and they are *dal segno* rather than *da capo*; that is, the orchestral introduction is not repeated.) Characters are allowed to remain on stage after singing their airs—which makes for a less artificial drama than one punctuated by exits after all major utterances. The length of the dialogues in *secco* recitative is interestingly varied, and reduced on occasion to a mere two phrases between numbers. Singers often strike into airs without orchestral preliminary. Similar things are found in operas by Handel and by Hasse, but less abundantly.

Students who use Oliver Strunk's *Source Readings in Music History* will recall J. F. Reichardt's comparison between the styles of Hasse and Graun, and his description of Graun's special virtue in limning tender complaint or cruel affliction. *Montezuma* contains a hit number that illustrates to perfection Graun's excellence in "the gentle and affecting": a lament by Pilpatoe, Montezuma's general, that his overconfident emperor should trust the foreign invaders. It is centrally placed, just before the "battle symphony," in which the Spaniards fire on their hosts. The last of the lament's three sections resumes the tempo and tonality but not the melody of the first. In Boston, this air, "Erra quel nobil core," was touchingly sung, with long breath and in sensitively molded phrases, by Wayne Rivera. Act III opens in similar vein: no prelude, but a long, impassioned, and many-hued *recitativo con stromenti*—a monologue for the imprisoned emperor—leading to a beautiful air, *largo e pizzicato*, which, in turn, reaches no cadence but breaks into *secco* recitative as the prison doors are opened. Reichardt noted that the cosmopolitan and immensely prolific Hasse had the bolder sense of immediate theatrical effect. His tunes are catchier and more simply accompanied. Graun, stuck in Berlin, perfected his own special style, and he did so with a grace, a skill, and a thoroughness of resource and invention that make his music interesting to modern ears.

Frederick's libretto does not mince words in denouncing the barbarism of the invaders; his Cortes has no redeeming virtues, such as Voltaire allowed to the conquistadores in *Alzire*. But the King's anti-imperialist, anti-Catholic sentiments went for nothing in Boston, since the opera was sung partly in Italian and partly in gibberish. The program-book contained no synopsis of the action. A bilingual libretto was on sale in the theater but was useful only to those who had studied it in advance. Graun wrote his piece for six sopranos or altos (female or neutered) and a single tenor; it was sung

in Boston by two sopranos and five tenors or baritones, and
the resultant octave transpositions spoiled the carefully
planned textures of voices and instruments and dulled the
bright ring of the heroic numbers. Charles Kondek's
direction hardly went beyond assigning moves; he had
certainly not taught his cast how to bear themselves. The
pistol shots, decisive in routing the Aztecs, who knew not
gunpowder, were omitted; at the Berlin première, Frederick
says, they were much applauded—and in the city where
Prescott, Montezuma's great chronicler, lived they should
not have been forgotten. Richard Conrad, as Tezeuco, the
only genuine tenor role, showed an uncommon command of
trill and roulade and, alone in the cast, a full understanding
of the style and the language. But his tone was not pleasing.
Mary Strebing, a clear, bright soprano, shone as the second
woman. The edition was admirably full; some recitatives
were shortened, but only one air was left out.

There was more opera in Boston last month: in the
Aquarius Theatre, an exuberant, exhilarating, and
altogether irresistible account of Donizetti's *The Daughter of
the Regiment*, directed and conducted by Sarah Caldwell for
the Opera Company of Boston. Miss Caldwell is surely the
single Best Thing in American opera: a marvel, with the
energy and gusto of the indomitable Dame Ethel Smyth,
Felsenstein's flair for theater, and Beecham's baton in her
hand (the little minuet was paced and phrased with a
charm and delicacy such as have not delighted me since
Beecham did the *air de ballet* from Grétry's *Zémire et Azor*); a
person whose passion for living opera is based on sound
scholarship and research into original sources; mistress of
the newest discoveries of stagecraft, the latest lighting
devices and scenic materials; a director who couples a clear
conception of what a work in performance should ideally be

with a genius for practical improvisation which makes the most of the available theater (on occasion, non-theater, since Boston has no real opera house) and draws the best from the available cast. Donizetti's opera, so popular in Victorian days, can seem thin, and it can be played for galumphing great laughs, but here it had grace, lightness, and a merriment all the more captivating because it sprang naturally from the characters and the music. The action spilled out into the house, launched from a background of pretty scenery, by Beni Montresor, which was borrowed from Houston—for this *Daughter* was a last-minute production, adopted in place of Rossini's *Barber* when Beverly Sills begged for an extra year in which to relearn Rosina in the amplified edition that had resulted from Miss Caldwell's researches. This Marie was the finest thing I have ever heard or seen Miss Sills do. Her Tonio, Enrico Di Giuseppe, overshot his high C's but was winning enough. Spiro Malas, as Sulpice, and Muriel Greenspon, as the Marquise, were both good. Only Kitty Carlisle struck a false note, by electing to play the Duchess of Crackentorp in a brassy, plebeian way. The opera has a weak dénouement; Miss Caldwell—changing only the spoken dialogue, not the music—gave it a strong one, so neat in its Gilbertian resolution that it seems mere inadvertence on the part of Donizetti's librettists to have omitted it.

Only one of Haydn's five puppet operas survives, words and music; the music turned up not long ago, in a copy in the Bibliothèque Nationale, Paris, which is at once incomplete, since the (detachable) prologue is missing, and, so to speak, more than complete, in that extra numbers by Gluck, Ordoñez, and Haydn himself have been inserted. This work, *Philemon und Baucis*, with its prologue *Der Götterrat*, was first performed in 1773, to entertain the

Empress Maria Theresa during her visit to Esterház; and in English, as *Philemon and Baucis*, with Alessandro Scarlatti's deft, dainty cantata *Endymion and Cynthia* as a pretty curtain-raiser, it was performed last week in the music room of the Otto Kahn house—now a girls' school, the Convent of the Sacred Heart—on East Ninety-first Street. The presence of two Esterházy countesses and of Mr Kahn's daughter added a pleasant touch of continuity; the palace (it is more than a house), bustling with attractive young life, made a perfect setting. *Philemon* is an endearing little opera, with an overture, opening and closing choruses, four airs, and a duet. Jupiter and Mercury (speaking roles) visit the earth in the guise of pilgrims, and walk through wicked Phrygia, where only the aged, pious couple Philemon and Baucis welcome them with warm hospitality. In reward, Jupiter brings back to life their son, Aret, and his betrothed, Narcissa, victims of a Jovian thunderbolt, and grants Philemon's request that his cottage should become a temple wherein he and Baucis can worship the god. A storm, the resurrection, the transformation of the cottage, and the final appearance of Jove in majesty give scenic opportunity to the puppeteer. Haydn's music is apt, graceful, and a little more cunning than a first encounter with it might suggest. The old people sing in simple songlike strains, but the cadences of Philemon's second air touchingly mirror the varied epithets that close the four strophes—"O glückliche/fröhliche/schreckliche/traurige Zeit!" Aret greets the world again in a more elaborate number, chastely sweet in a way that recalls Gluck. His voice duets with the oboe; first violins and the lower strings pluck soft chords while through them the second violins, muted, thread a smooth murmur of triplets. It is movements like this (there are others in the comedy *L'incontro improviso*, which Boulez is conducting at the Philharmonic this month) that make one love Haydn's operas despite their faulty theatrical timing. A gentle air for

Narcissa, borrowed from his *Il mondo della luna* and placed
next by whoever compiled the Paris score, provided an apt
companion piece; it has a tender bassoon obbligato.

The Nicolo Marionettes strode the little stage with
confidence. The music was very well played by l'Ensemble
du Sacre Cœur, under Michael Feldman; from a small
ensemble in a small hall every ravishing detail of a Haydn
score can be heard. There was an able quartet of singers:
Ida Faiella, Linda Mahoney, Thomas Bogdan, and—best of
all, for his tenor had a firm, forward sweetness that recalled
the young McCormack—John Aler, in the role of Aret. In a
place of learning, it was sad to hear sentences in the English
translation like "Let Baucis and I serve you," and the
names Philemon and Baucis both mispronounced. (A
glance at Webster could have put the performers right.)

At the Metropolitan, *Peter Grimes* has been revived with a
new conductor, Sixten Ehrling, in his début there. Mr
Ehrling did not bring to Britten's score that passion with
which Colin Davis almost wrenched it apart; his reading
was measured, carefully paced, highly accomplished. In the
title role, Jon Vickers has subdued his former unremitting
wildness but lost none of the intensity and power that make
his interpretation so cogent. The suddenness of his violent
outbursts is now even more alarming. Ellen Orford's music
consists largely of phrases in notes of equal length; Lucine
Amara sang them too equally, without the slight adjustment
to verbal values which warms them into expressive life. The
role calls for a rather fuller voice than hers, but in the
"Embroidery" aria she was exquisite. Donald Gramm's
Balstrode was first-rate. Tyrone Guthrie's production, cared
for now by Bodo Igesz, is careful, and was carefully
executed by the large cast. Just two stagy and inappropriate
"effects" marred it: the unrealistic lighting of the quartet,

and the billowing fog carpet—not naturalistic but, it seemed, an attempt to suggest a brain landscape—which Peter paddled through during the mad scene. Tanya Moiseiwitsch's scenery is the Covent Garden décor slightly reworked; Aldeburgh is in the Constable country—the Metropolitan's skies are all wrong. The chorus alternated unpredictably between feebleness and splendor. Some curious textual variants have crept in. Balstrode sang "death" instead of "dissolution"—better sense, though it breaks a rhyme. Peter, asked where his apprentice got bruised, shouted, "How should I know?"—which is less striking than the libretto's "Out of the hurly-burly."

This *Grimes* had a good deal more life in it than the Metropolitan's revival of *Il trovatore*. Attilio Colonnello's designs for the opera are picturesque and imposing but, literally, repetitive. Nathaniel Merrill's production is large and handsome but, at present, quite undramatic. Carlo Felice Cillario, conducting, seemed to grope his way toward tempi set by the singers, while their rhythms tended to flounder for want of a firm accompaniment. All in all, it was the sort of evening that brings grand opera into disrepute and keeps musical people away from the Met. Though Placido Domingo, having cracked at the close of "Di quella pira," sent word to say he was indisposed and needed our indulgence, he alone both sang and acted with consistent spirit and imagination. Montserrat Caballé was in uneven voice and was lazy about articulating small notes. Fiorenza Cossotto bawled much of her role. Robert Merrill stood and delivered, flinging out his right hand on the dominant, closing it to his breast on the tonic. All of them had good—even magnificent—moments; their efforts did not amount to a satisfactory account of the work. While composing *Il trovatore*, Verdi dreamed of creating an opera

whose acts would be single movements, proceeding unbroken, instead of a series of separate numbers. To his
librettist, Salvatore Cammarano, he wrote, "If the opera
could be, so to speak, all one number, I should find that
sensible and right." *Il trovatore* is hardly "all one number,"
but in the most gripping account of it I have ever heard (led
by Martina Arroyo and Shirley Verrett) there was no
mid-scene applause—not because the artists sang badly but
precisely because they sang so well, with such dramatic
intensity, that no one wanted to shatter the drama with
noises of his own. So, for example, the last note of Azucena's
"Stride la vampa" rang out fiercely, and then into a tense,
electric silence there stole the voices of the gypsies in
comment. Similarly, the knell announcing the Miserere
tolled softly into an attentive hush that followed Leonora's
"D'amor sull'ali rosee" (closed, as such an air should be, on
the middle, not an unwritten high, A-flat), and at the end of
the Miserere Leonora could pick up the words that lead
into her subsequent aria—"Di te! scordarmi di te!"—without having an audience racket break either the verbal
thread or the harmonic progression. But at the Metropolitan last week the singers after each number struck attitudes
that positively invited applause. History is on their side: in
the 1850s, at a first performance, the composer himself
would appear onstage in mid-scene, along with the singers,
to acknowledge the audience's appreciation of any number
that had especially pleased it. But the evidence of the score
is against them; for example, the Tower Scene—aria,
Miserere, aria, two-section duet—is one long sequence in F
and A-flat, one of the most extended scenas for a soprano
ever composed, and, like the closing scene of *Götterdämmerung*, it should be heard as such, without interruption after
each paragraph. With that Wagnerian simile, I exaggerate.
The conductor Gianandrea Gavazzeni exaggerated when
he called *Il trovatore* "the Italian St Matthew Passion." But

the time has come to treat Verdi's music as seriously in opera houses as it is treated by serious musicians. Much of the best work on Verdi is now being done in America. It may be unrealistic to expect the Metropolitan's general manager to set papers like Martin Chusid's on tonal structure in *Rigoletto* and *La traviata* as required reading for his prima donnas as soon as they are published (those two were read to learned congresses last year), but at least their contents should be mastered by the men responsible for directing his performers. *Pace* Caruso, *Il trovatore* calls for more than just the engagement of the best singers in the world.

March 10, 1973

Martin Chusid's "Drama and the Key of F major in La traviata*" will be published in* Atti del III° Congresso internazionale di studi verdiani, *his "Rigoletto and Monterone: A Study in Musical Dramaturgy" in the* Proceedings of the Eleventh Congress of the International Musicological Society. *Excerpts from Graun's* Montezuma *have been recorded, with Joan Sutherland as the heroine, on London 1270. Beverly Sills's Marie in* La Fille du régiment *may be enjoyed in the Rataplan ("pirate") recording, RA 200, made from a Carnegie Hall performance of the opera in 1970. A Vox recording of Haydn's* Philemon und Baucis *is no longer in print; the score has been published in the Joseph Haydn Werke (G. Henle Verlag, Munich-Duisburg) as Series XXIV, Volume 1.*

Crown Imperial

The City Opera has just staged Monteverdi's *L'incoronazione di Poppea*. It has not done well by the piece. I delight in the choice but deplore the execution; urge people to attend the show but warn them that *Poppea* is a more admirable work than what they will see and hear in this account of it.

In an age when contemporary opera has won little broad public support, the repertory has been enriched by revival and rediscovery. Early Verdi has come back. So has Donizetti. Meyerbeer is seen and heard when companies want to make a splash and can afford to. And, best of all, the works of Monteverdi, closely followed by those of his pupil and colleague Francesco Cavalli, have during the last decade been taken up by one opera house after another. Opera has never been more direct than in these Venetian compositions of the seventeenth century. To perform them is to restate the first principles of music drama. Moreover, they can be put on by small companies in small houses.

The first great opera is Monteverdi's *Orfeo* (1607). At the start of it, the allegorical figure of La Musica steps forward to tell us what opera is all about. "I am Music," she sings, "who in sweet accents know how to calm every troubled heart, and can inflame the coldest minds now with noble anger, now with love." Opera, the new art form, was barely ten years old at the time. It had been born in simplicity, as a kind of verse drama the expressive power of whose lines was heightened by recitative declamation modestly accompanied. Monteverdi lavished on the swift-growing child the other riches that the art of music could provide: madrigals, songs, and dances; formal structures of strophe, variation, rondo, and refrain to throw into relief the free declamation (or vice versa), contrasts of texture between solo voices and ensemble; and the varied colors of a large orchestra. The Orpheus myth is itself an allegory of music's power; within the opera we can discern other, small allegories of ways in which that power can be employed. For example, when Orpheus entreats Charon to grant him passage to Hades he does so in several stanzas of increasing brilliance and vocal virtuosity, punctuated by elaborate instrumental displays, but the stern boatman remains unmoved until the singer abandons coloratura and makes a direct, unaffected appeal in melody unadorned, patterned on the natural rise and fall of the words as a suppliant might speak them. There is a moral in that. There is no moral relating to operatic practice which cannot be illustrated from Monteverdi, no device which cannot be deemed a development of something he discovered, no "abuse" which cannot be viewed as a disturbance of the tensions he held in equilibrium, no "reform" which does not point a return to the principles of his work.

Orfeo was written for the Gonzaga court. *Il ritorno d'Ulisse* and *L'incoronazione di Poppea*, composed some thirty-five years later for the public theaters of Venice, are less complicated in facture, more modest in instrumental resource, but even subtler in construction, bolder in their progress, and keener and more masterly in their communication of human passions. *Poppea*, like *Figaro*, is about the varied aspects of love. The prologue announces a demonstration of the thesis that sexual passion exerts a greater influence than either chance or virtue on the conduct of human affairs. We move to first-century Rome, where the Emperor Nero is infatuated with the courtesan Poppaea and determined to make her his Empress. In Poppaea, love is at once happy sensuality and the instrument of ambition. In the proud Empress Octavia, it has turned to jealousy and vindictiveness. On both Octavia and Nero, the philosopher Seneca enjoins self-control; his admonitions are not heeded. A fifth character, Otho, dominates the first act. Still desperately in love with Poppaea, his former mistress, he comes in at the start to find Nero's troops on guard outside her door. The act mounts to a climax in a great confrontation between Poppaea and Otho (reduced to a fragment in the City Opera text); Otho attempts to find consolation by turning to another woman, Drusilla (to whom love means joyful self-sacrifice, and hang the consequences), but the curtain falls on his powerful line "Drusilla is on my lips, but in my heart—Poppaea!"

Act II depicts the destructive forces unleashed by selfish love, in two long sequences. Seneca, ordered by Nero to die, goes nobly to his final bath, amid the mourning of three disciples. Otho and Octavia conspire, with Drusilla's assistance, to murder Poppaea. Like Othello, Otho muses over the sleeping, still cherished woman he is about to kill. Love, embodied in the allegorical figure of Amor, makes him linger; Poppaea wakes and is saved. At the curtain, Amor cries of his victory. Between the killing and the attempted killing there is a playful little scene in which a boy, Octavia's page, and a girl experience the first quaint prickings of love; then, in an exuberant *madrigale a due voci*, Nero and the poet Lucan celebrate Seneca's death, the ending of restraint, and Poppaea's beauty. (It is not a lurching drunk scene, though it is often played as such.) In Act III, the conspirators are banished, Octavia sings an impassioned farewell to the city, Poppaea is crowned, and, finally, the voices of Poppaea and Nero—two equal sopranos, echoing, twining, and closing on a unison—ring out to hymn love's triumph.

The libretto, by Francesco Busenello, is a supreme piece of dramatic construction, subtle and searching in its characterization, beautifully controlled, varied but never diffuse. The smaller roles—the grumbling guardsmen who must keep watch while the Emperor makes love ("Damn love, Poppaea, Nero, and Rome, and the Army," in a rising sequence of exasperation); Poppaea's bustling, garrulous old nurse, Arnalta, so tender while watching over her charge; Octavia's nurse, who seeks to cheer the Empress with Despina-like advice; even the freedman who so reluctantly tells Seneca of Nero's decree—are also vividly drawn, in small, telling strokes. (Arnalta, who has three airs, should really be counted among the principals.) By comparing the text printed in Busenello's collected works (1656) with that set in the Venice manuscript score which is the main source for the music (both are available in the New York Public Library, the latter in facsimile), we discover that the composer, by small adjustments and omissions, made the drama more effective still.

I have described the original structure of *Poppea* at some length because it is obscured in the City Opera presentation, which is based on the uncritical acceptance of an edition of the piece made by Raymond Leppard. This matter of edition cannot simply be swept aside, since it affects every aspect of the performance. Mr Leppard's work is apt to inspire mixed feelings. On the one hand, his "realizations" of *Poppea*, *Ulisse*, and Cavalli's *Ormindo* and *Calisto*, for Glyndebourne, and of *Orfeo*, for Sadler's Wells, have been responsible, more than anything else, for the revival of Venetian seventeenth-century opera all over the world, and for this he earns respect and unstinted gratitude. He may well have left a permanent mark on operatic history. For conductors unwilling or unable to tackle for themselves the problems of modern performance, Mr Leppard has provided ready-made answers of proved effectiveness. Effective they are. Only a curmudgeon could resist the delights they have offered, or fail to acknowledge that the editor-arranger was moved by a passionate appreciation of these operas and a concern to share his joy in them with the widest possible audience. On the other hand, anyone who studies the material that Mr Leppard has elaborated—or, for that matter, anyone who encounters the works in other, chaster realizations, such as Alan Curtis's of *Poppea*—may well feel that Mr Leppard has gone too far and done too much. The main points at issue are not musicological mysteries; they can be most conveniently discussed under separate heads:

SCORING: In the Venice manuscript, the vocal lines of *Poppea* are supported only by a bass line with no indication of scoring, though there are occasional changes of clef that suggest a change of the accompanying (continuo) instrument that sounds the implicit harmonies. Leppard rings the changes, aptly, on continuo harpsichords, harp, lute, archlute, guitar, and flue and reed organs, plus cellos and basses. But sometimes he shifts instruments in a fidgety way (let the phrase "to my way of thinking and hearing" be understood in all these demurs), and often he writes out elaborate continuo parts that draw attention from the sung line. The bosomy harp swirls associated with Octavia are particularly distracting. When the music moves from recitative into arioso or aria, he composes full and generally elaborate string accompaniments; I itch to strike out page after page of them and let the melodies sing forth over simple continuo. The ritornellos, or instrumental interludes, of *Poppea* are composed in three parts; Leppard enriches them to five, believing that five-part ritornellos—found in *Orfeo* and *Ulisse*—were the norm.

STRUCTURE: At Glyndebourne, with its long dinner interval, operas fall most conveniently into two acts; the German houses also like a two-act scheme. Leppard breaks the three-act *Poppea* into two acts, the break coming after Seneca's death, and, having shifted the boy-girl flirtation to an earlier point, resumes with the Nero-Lucan madrigal. This destroys the careful dramatic structure described earlier. At Glyndebourne, the arrangement had its advantages; there is no need for other houses to follow suit. Sadler's Wells, though it performs *Poppea* from Leppard material, has restored the original act breaks; the City Opera should do the same. An hour and thirty-five minutes makes an uncomfortably long first act.

CUTS: Until audiences are ready to grant Monteverdi the time they willingly give to Berlioz or Wagner, his operas must be cut. Leppard's cuts are built into his edition; the conductor who may have a few minutes in hand has no chance of restoring, say, the great Poppaea-Otho duet in full, or an important monologue for Otho in Act II, or the brief duet for Nero and Poppaea that should open the final scene and balance "Pur ti miro" at its close. He may even think these things more important to include than the prologue. The small mid-scene snicks tend to pass unnoticed unless one is following in an uncut score; cumulatively, they alter the carefully controlled dramatic pace. Curtis's edition contains more of the music, and can be cut (or left whole) to suit individual circumstances.

TRANSPOSITIONS: Nero and the young page are sopranos; Otho is an alto. There is a case for reassigning the first and last roles to natural male voices, as Leppard has done (though to turn Cherubino's precursor into a tenor is absurd). To my mind, however, the "veristic" gain is outweighed by musical losses. Producers who think an audience could not accept a trim, bright-voiced woman playing Nero—or Handel's Caesar, or Mozart's Idamantes —and therefore spoil the music to save the sex underrate their listeners' power of dramatic imagination. Leppard's Nero is a tenor, and not a high one. By casting a baritone in the part, City Opera has now dulled the role still further. Though Leppard's first Poppaea was a soprano, Magda Laszlo, she, like every other singer of the part in my experience, was taxed by the high tessitura to which he transposes the final duet. When challenged, Leppard points to numerous indications for transposition in the Venice score (added, presumably, to suit the cast of a later revival), but the big shifts there affect only the subaltern roles; the main vocal characterization is little altered. Moreover, it is one thing to tailor an opera so as to make the most of an exceptional interpreter—as Leppard arranged *Ulisse* for the marvelous Penelope of Janet Baker—and another to give that special edition general currency.

TEMPI, DYNAMICS: Leppard himself is a Monteverdi conductor of uncommon sensitivity and eloquence. If he has a fault, it is a tendency to sentimentalize the tender passages —he especially favors "melting" closes—and this gets reflected in the expression marks of his editions. Conductors and singers with less than his feel for Monteverdi style can be misled by them, and by the succulent string writing, to adopt at times too sickly-sweet a manner. Most of his indications, however, are pointers to a lively, theatrically gripping performance.

This edition of *Poppea* was first performed, at Glyndebourne, in 1962. I was bowled over by the work and by the zest with which it had been brought to life. So was everybody who saw it. But the Leppard score has not stood up well to ten years of hard use—years, too, of increasing public familiarity with Monteverdi's music. It was generally pasted by the press when it entered the Sadler's Wells repertory, in 1971—after due respects had been paid to its pioneering importance and to its grace, richness, and skill. Perhaps, like Gluck-Mottl, Handel-Harty, and Bach-Stokowski, this particular example of Monteverdi-Leppard has now served its turn. (It must be remembered, however, that in Monteverdi's case there is no "original" that can be put on the players' stands; *Poppea* in performance must always be Monteverdi-another.) Leppard has owned that today he might approach the task of realization differently.

And so to the performance. In 1616, when Monteverdi received a libretto that did not please him, he wrote:

> I have observed that the personages of this drama are winds, and moreover that the winds have to sing. And how, my dear Sir, shall I be able to imitate the speech of winds? How shall I be able to move the passions by such means? Ariadne [the heroine of his opera *Arianna*, from which only a great lament and a few scraps preserved in a treatise on scenic music survive] moved the audience because she was a woman, not a wind, and likewise Orpheus moved the audience because he was man, not a wind. . . . This tale does not excite my feelings in the least. Ariadne inspired a true lament in me, and Orpheus a true entreaty; heaven knows what this tale will inspire in me!

The personages of *Poppea* are real—"living" men and women. (But, you ask, what about those few gods who appear from time to time? Well, it is a convention easily accepted that inner promptings or premonitions may find audible utterance in the form of supernatural voices.) Gerald Freedman, the producer of the City Opera show, did ill to prescribe so many fancy, artificial poses and to cluster round the actors a small corps of graceful ballet girls and ballet boys. A colleague wrote, approvingly, that "a quality of highly stylized dance permeated the entire production." To my mind, that summarizes what was wrong. Lloyd Evans' set is two lateral classical façades, awkwardly kinked as they approach the footlights; a raised platform at the back; a backcloth on which Bibiena scenes are projected. Beds pop on in a way to recall the Slumber Department sequences of the Marx Brothers' *The Big Store*. Poppaea's is red, Octavia's royal blue; Nero and Lucan tumble together on a daybed; a gleaming king-sized affair is borne on for the final duet. José Varona's costumes are handsomely designed, and most of the cast, whether dressed or near naked, look good.

That phrase "imitate the speech" in the Monteverdi letter quoted is important. Monteverdi, like Mussorgsky and Janáček, had theories about music as a universal language, springing from the imitation of speech inflections. He planned a treatise on the subject. It remained unwritten, but the madrigals and operas show his ideas clearly. It is not enough for the singers to sound the notes and pronounce the words more or less correctly. The roles require the declamation of great actors. The lines must be uttered with force, fire, and tenderness. Feeling for the words must dictate the phrasing. The life and lilt of the music depend on the text. The instruments are there only to accompany and support, with their quick, sensitive reactions, a dramatic declamation and to punctuate the dramatic progress with their ritornellos. The City Opera *Poppea* is sung in Italian. This seems to me a pity, since Busenello's play is far too good not to be followed in detail, line by line. (Mr Freedman essayed some quaint visual glossing. At the word "bocca," Nero advanced his mouth to Lucan's; an Oriental and a Negro super were brought on at the end to kneel at the line "A te l'Asia, a te l'Africa s'atterra.") The bilingual libretto on sale at the theater is a feeble, abbreviated affair that does not correspond to the performance. A new translator—he is needed, for the English text in the Leppard edition is poor—might find a starting point in the sensitive English version begun in Charles Ives's copy of *Poppea*, now in the New York Public Library.

Whenever *Poppea*, in whatever language, has been added to the repertory of an all-purpose company, it has taken the singers a while to learn the vivid declamation, free yet not unrhythmical, that is needed, and taken the continuo players a while to learn how to support them as an accompanist supports a lieder singer, so that one is not conscious of a conductor. At the City Opera, these things will probably come. Meanwhile, John Nelson, conducting, holds things together pretty ably. For the record, the main parts on the first night were taken by Carol Neblett (Poppaea); Frances Bible (Octavia); Muriel Greenspon (Arnalta); Faye Robinson, deputizing for Norma French (Drusilla); Alan Titus (Nero); Dominic Cossa (Otho); and Richard T. Gill (Seneca).

March 17, 1973

Alan Curtis's edition of L'incoronazione di Poppea, *which is to be published by Novello, is recorded on Cambridge 1901; Raymond Leppard's, published by Faber Music, on Seraphim S 6073—a somewhat abridged performance, given by the original Glyndebourne cast.*

The score of L'incoronazione *that formerly belonged to Charles Ives is on the reference shelves of the circulating library (in the Library and Museum of the Performing Arts at Lincoln Center), not upstairs in the Music Research division.*

Branching Out

hilharmonic Hall and the Metropolitan Opera stand as ancient monuments, new-built, to some fifty cherished and important years of musical history, but they are not the right places for hearing most of the music written during the seven centuries that today's music lover takes as his province. So in a week filled with interesting events none was more interesting and none, perhaps, of more moment than the concert of baroque music given by the Juilliard School in Alice Tully Hall last Friday. In innocence, I went along to it expecting to hear the music—by Bach, Rameau, Telemann, and Domenico Scarlatti—played on baroque instruments, at eighteenth-century pitch. America, after all, was the country where once I had stumbled into a gamelan class where not just a theoretical account of the thing, and not just a demonstration on a specimen instrument, but thoroughgoing practical instruction on a whole battery of instruments was in progress. America is the rich country where one expects technical teaching equipment to be superb whatever the field. And the famous Juilliard School would surely not be laggard in that field of baroque revival which during the last decade or two has transformed both the content and the perspectives of our musical life. The instruments, however, were modern. This was the Juilliard's first venture of the kind. It was a good one. Albert Fuller (artistic director, incidentally, of the newly established Aston Magna Foundation, in Great Barrington, Massachusetts, dedicated to the study and performance of baroque music) has fired his small band of instrumentalists with his enthusiasm for the period, and guided them toward the kinds of attack, phrasing, dynamic levels, rhythms, and ornaments that are required. They played with spirit and devotion; their zest and conviction were communicated to a packed and enthusiastic house. And when the Juilliard is equipped with baroque instruments the results will be even better. Let me chant once more that credo-refrain: the music of any age speaks most directly and eloquently to modern ears in the tones and with the accents of its own time.

The Overture to Rameau's *Zaïs*, which opened the concert, is an arresting composition, bold and wonderful. Rameau is the most neglected of great composers. Telemann's D-minor Quartet for flute, oboe, bassoon, and continuo (with a heavenly slow episode set into the finale) and Bach's Two-Violin Sonata were pleasing; Scarlatti's late, gravely tender *Salve regina* is very beautiful (the soloist, Lorna Myers, has a rich, soft-grained mezzo, though the music calls for a voice quicker to speak, more forward, and able to trill); but the revelation of the evening was the Prologue to Rameau's *Les Indes galantes*. The difficulty of staging Rameau's theater pieces lies largely in the dances, which are integral to the score, not detachable divertissements; one happy solution—as I noted when reviewing his *La Naissance d'Osiris* from Washington—is to re-create the dance style of Rameau's day. For this Juilliard performance, Wendy Hilton had set four of the Prologue dances—

the entrée, a musette, a polonaise, and a menuet—to eighteenth-century sequences. Student dancers and student players had worked together on their execution, and Rameau's dance music made a new sense as we discovered how musical and choreographic images fit so fascinatingly together. There was nothing merely quaint or self-consciously archaic in the enterprise; the dancers' Ailey-inspired grace flowed through the heavier, formal movements notated by Feuillet in the early eighteenth century. Mr Fuller's tempo for the *air gracieux* of cupids was, I felt sure, too brisk; if this number, too, had been danced, the proper tempo would have become apparent. Badiene Magaziner sang Hebe, the principal role, with the right quick, clear, forward tone and in good French; she was bright, fearless, and commanding in music that ranges boldly through the registers. Ahmed Tahir skipped Bellona's deep notes. (The goddess of war is here a bass.) Barbara Hendricks was a fleet, sweet Amor, though her French was unskillful. The choruses were omitted—but surely the Juilliard could have mustered a tenor to complete the harmonies of the finale. The next step is plain. With Mr Fuller and Miss Hilton as guides, the Juilliard's music, dance, and drama departments must combine to stage in their theater a complete Rameau opera. And after that they may as well show the City Opera how Monteverdi, and the Metropolitan Opera how Gluck, and the Piccolo Met how Purcell should be performed.

Since large orchestras still exist, composers still compose for them. Luciano Berio (born in 1925) is an inventive, colorful, and very canny composer, who draws inspiration from the remarkable interpreters for whom he writes (Cathy Berberian; the various soloists of his *Sequenze*) and in return provides them with virtuoso vehicles in which both their art and his are advanced. For the Philharmonic and the

Swingle Singers, in 1968 he composed his successful Sinfonia (expanded in 1970). His new Two-Piano Concerto, commissioned by the Philharmonic and first played at last Thursday's Philharmonic concert, is a distinguished and attractive composition, easily enjoyed. While not written "down" to its first audience, any more than were Bartók's American pieces (the Concerto for Orchestra and the Piano Concerto No. 3), it is, like those pieces—and like the Sinfonia—unformidable. The Concerto opens with a pantonal murmur from the two soloists, who are separated by the width of the platform. (Berio's only miscalculation is to start at a dynamic level lower than that provided by a coughing, chattering, and creaking audience.) Exclamatory incidents break through the gentle dialogue with increasing frequency until, after about five minutes, the orchestra enters. Berio uses a large orchestra (with triple or quadruple woodwinds, plus two saxophones) but does not use it very much. Knowing that the Philharmonic boasts a resident pianist of uncommon ability, Paul Jacobs, he assigns most of the virtuoso "accompaniment" to a third piano and otherwise writes fairly easy orchestral parts. Tuttis alternate with episodes where a single player—flute, violin, clarinet—engages with one or both of the soloists. Then the first piano has a rhapsodic cadenza of arabesque and filigree shot through with fleeting solos from various parts of the orchestra, and the second piano another, over long-held string tremolos. The soloists retire at last, before an orchestral *marche infernale* of miniature fanfares and repeated chords volleyed like grapeshot, and then they cut in again to launch a long, dazzling paragraph for the three pianos, an iridescent testudo of glittering tremolando chords that Gottschalk might have envied. After a final brief tutti, the music drifts gently, unexpectedly, toward silence while the first piano insists on G major and the second refuses to be bound.

The Concerto displays all Berio's virtues. His command of graphic musical gesture and his control of musical time conspire to make the score unfold before us like so many "scenes" of a drama. (Enter Clarinet; Enter Second Piano, with Followers . . . Exeunt; Scene change.) His ear, which has spent so much time analyzing the elements of musical sound, and his instrumental expertness insure a use of the instruments which is adventurous and unfailingly effective. The general form is clear. The details are finely worked and invite sustained attention. After a first, a second, even a third hearing, one only begins to grasp the subtle ways in which, it seems, the same "lines," repeated in a new set of circumstances, can lead to very different conclusions. The lines themselves are good; what Berio says is worth listening to, quite apart from the dexterous and elegant manners in which he says it. Currently the Concerto lasts twenty minutes, but the composer plans to enlarge it with some further dialogues between individual members of the orchestra and the soloists. I hope he does not alter the poetic dying fall of its sudden close.

It is surprising, and deplorable, that the Philharmonic concerts—New York's major orchestral series—are not broadcast as a matter of course. A work like this new concerto should have reached a larger audience than two hallfuls. No doubt it soon will: two-piano teams are prominent on the contemporary scene—what with Boulez' *Structures*; Stockhausen's *Mantra*, for the Kontarsky brothers; Henze's *Muses of Sicily*, for Rollino and Sheftel—and will want to tackle the Berio. The soloists of the first performance were Bruno Canino and Antonio Ballista, the most engaging team of all; their combination of lyricism and brio proved ideal. Pierre Boulez, associated with Berio since the early days of *Incontri musicali*, Berio's Milanese review, was a lucid, masterly, and totally convincing conductor. I wish he could be persuaded to do more contemporary music.

$\mathbf{S}$helley hoped that his play *The Cenci* would be performed at Covent Garden. Alberto Ginastera hoped the same for his opera *Beatrix Cenci*. In the event, Ginastera's piece was first given during the opening days of the Kennedy Center's Opera House, in Washington, in 1971, and last week it came to the New York State Theater. Shelley's play, for which he thought Edmund Kean and Eliza O'Neill would be the ideal interpreters, is a highly "operatic" piece—and was flamboyantly produced as such by the Old Vic in 1959. But in any consideration of the modern theater it also plays an important role, linked with the names of Seneca, Calderón, Artaud (whose famous version bombed so spectacularly in Paris in 1935), Barrault, and Peter Brook. Robert Edmond Jones left some stunning designs for it. Two operas by minor British composers, Roger Sacheverall Coke and Berthold Goldschmidt, have been based on the play, and Penderecki was at one time reported to be working on a version. *"The Cenci"*—as Stuart Curran remarks in his elegant, admirable study *Shelley's "Cenci": Scorpions Ringed with Fire*—"in somewhat altered form has the potential for a superb operatic libretto." Ginastera's librettists, William Shand and Alberto Girri, have altered it a good deal. Their two acts are cast as a series of short, largely sensational scenes, with narrative reduced to a minimum. Beatrice's trial is omitted; her rape, the murder of Cenci, and her torture are shown on stage. While not perhaps a "superb" libretto, it is a strong one, devised to need music for its fulfillment. Ginastera's music, alas, is not very interesting. There are some ingenious sound effects (notably an instrumental mimicry of Cenci's baying dogs). There are crashes, ominous "tension" passages, outbursts at the appropriate moments. Most of the time, the vocal line is a rather featureless declamation, without much character or dramatic life in it. The little State Theater program-book gave, as usual, almost no useful information about the piece, but since the conductor (Julius Rudel), the producer (Gerald Freedman), the designers (John Conklin of the sets, Theoni V. Aldredge of the costumes), the choreographer (Joyce Trisler), the two principals (Arlene Saunders as Beatrice, Justino Díaz as the Count), and the two assassins were those of the première, this was presumably a re-creation of the Washington performance. Miss Saunders was capable but not very moving as a heroine whom Duse longed to play. Mr Díaz, in, so to speak, a Chaliapin role, was vocally unimpressive, though his acting, in its hammy way, was quite powerful. (The State Theater is no friend to voices; elsewhere the singers might have sounded better.) Gwendolyn Killebrew, as Lucretia, was fuzzy-focused of tone. Vocally, the clear tenor of Gary Glaze, in the small part of Orsino, left the strongest impression. The piece was sung in Spanish. A bilingual libretto is published, and was on sale when one arrived in the theater, but that was late in the day; neither of New York's major music stores could provide it on the morning of the performance. All in all, the presentation was thoroughly efficient. It moved swiftly. The stage pictures were striking. But one cannot really recommend the opera to Covent Garden.

O ther things in brief. The twelve Solistes des Chœurs de l'ORTF, trained and directed by Marcel Couraud, form a vocal group of matchless virtuosity. Their Alice Tully Hall recital last week opened with their superb account of Messiaen's *Cinq Rechants*. Ivo Malec's *Dodécaméron* exploits in a fascinating, brilliant, and shapely fashion their ability to simulate anything from electronic "white sound," wails, and whistles to the patter of exotic percussion. *Nuits*, Xenakis's celebrated quarter-tone motet of cries, groans, and angry protests, strikes me as a contrived piece that palls quickly after a few hearings. A new work, Branimir Sakac's *Umbrana*, gave the choir difficult but uninteresting things to do. The group is less impressive when it has to sing music of a more traditional kind; in excerpts from Poulenc's motet cycle *Figure humaine*, which in any case calls for a larger chorus, the phrasing was not shaped to the words.

The Minnesota Orchestra, which is celebrating its seventieth-anniversary season, brought Szymanowski's Third Symphony, "Song of the Night," to Carnegie Hall. It is a glamorous, rapturous outpouring, heady, sensuous, and intoxicatingly beautiful, with a text by Rūmi, the Persian mystic. But it was done, disappointingly, without chorus. This involves a cut of some eighteen soft-shimmering bars in the first section; the conductor, Stanislaw Skrowaczewski, made another, needless cut in the central section. (In full, the symphony lasts only twenty minutes.) The orchestra played rather drably—hessian, where one wanted rich velvets touched by starshine.

Karl Weigl, who was born in Vienna in 1881 and died in New York in 1949, has been called "a figure of major importance." After hearing three string quartets and several smaller pieces, I think him hardly that but, rather, a minor composer whose works bear occasional revival, and fill in some of the background to that Vienna where Mahler and then Schoenberg, Schreker, Berg, and Webern were the giants. As Schoenberg once wrote, Weigl was "one of those who continued the dignified Viennese tradition." His Eighth String Quartet, given its first performance, by the Concord Quartet, in the auditorium of the Lincoln Center Library of the Performing Arts, on March 3, is a soundly made, unarresting composition with no harm in it and a good deal of careful craft. The recital ended with the second public performance—the first had been given a fortnight earlier—of Mahler's piano-quartet movement in A minor, a student piece from 1876, tuneful, richly wrought, and

sounding as if it might have been composed by Humperdinck.

A John Cage sixtieth-birthday "retrospective" in the
McMillin Theatre of Columbia University brought up some
attractive early works: a brief, chipper Clarinet Sonata of
1933; five E. E. Cummings settings of 1938 that sounded as
if Britten might have composed them thirty years later; and
a poised account of the *First Construction (in Metal)* of 1939.
Imaginary Landscape No. 4, though put on in style, with
twenty-four distinguished musicians at the controls of the
twelve little radio sets involved, had one of its less remarkable realizations, since nothing very interesting was picked
out of the ether.

March 24, 1973

Wagnerismo

Opera lovers feel at home in the Second Circle of Dante's *Inferno*, where the company includes Semiramide, Dido, lascivious Cleopatra, Helen, great Achilles, Tristan— and Francesca da Rimini, speaking words that later drift across the lagoon to the ear of Rossini's Desdemona: "Nessun maggior dolore/Che ricordarsi del tempo felice/ Nella miseria" ("No greater grief than to recall, in wretch- edness, the time of happiness"). Italian truck drivers, we are told, can recite Dante by the canto; cismontane and cisatlantic readers probably retain at least some of those lines so charged with emotion that whole tragedies seem to be compassed in their syllables: from the Francesca episode, perhaps "Noi, che tignemmo 'l mondo di sanguigno" and (as Francesca recalls how she and her brother-in-law Paolo read together the Lay of Lancelot) "Galeotto fu il libro, e chi lo scrisse;/Quel giorno più non vi leggemmo avante." In plain English: "We who tinted the world with scarlet blood" and "A Galahad [pander between Lancelot and Guinevere] was the book, and a Galahad he who wrote it; that day we read no further." But no simple translation of

the lines can render all they say. D'Annunzio's play
Francesca da Rimini, written for the Duse in 1901, amplifies
their sense with, on the one hand, a Pre-Raphaelite
profusion of medieval details lovingly observed and, on the
other, a Wagnerian richness of supercharged, voluble
passion. The publisher Tito Ricordi chose the play as a
libretto for his new young composer Riccardo Zandonai,
whom he was grooming as Puccini's successor, and made
the abridgment himself. D'Annunzio provided some new
verses to replace Paolo's account of his trip to Florence
(where he met a young poet named Dante Alighieri) with
the Tristanesque utterance "Nemica ebbi la luce,/amica
ebbi la notte" ("Light was my foe, night my friend").
Zandonai's *Francesca da Rimini* was first performed, with
acclaim, in Turin in 1914 and again at Covent Garden a
few months later. It reached the Metropolitan in 1916, with
Frances Alda and Giovanni Martinelli as the lovers. On
Thursday of last week, Eve Queler and the Opera Orchestra of New York revived the piece, in a concert performance, in Carnegie Hall. The evening was a great success,
satisfying to opera freaks of every complexion. There was
some lusty, full-throated singing to be heard and also—not
always incompatibly—some distinguished, intelligent interpretation, and in general the event offered a clear, sharp
view down a neglected byway of musical history.

The interest of *Francesca* lies in more than just the sound
of its music. It proves to be one of that crop of D'Annunzio-
based operas—from Pizzetti's *Fedra* of 1905 to Montemezzi's
La nave of 1918—that represents an ambitious movement
away from *verismo* toward a high-minded, heroic new
romanticism with its roots partly in classical tragedy and
partly in *Tristan*. Puccini's *Turandot* (1924) was an aftermath.
Since Puccini was a better composer than those mentioned,
or than Franchetti (*La figlia di Jorio*, 1906) and Mascagni
(*Parisina*, 1913), *Turandot* still holds the stage, while the other

works bear no more than an occasional revival. But such a revival can remind us, most fascinatingly, of those days when "serious" Italian composers were slightly ashamed of the popular Verdi and aspired to produce grand operas of a more intellectual cast.

At Carnegie Hall, a libretto with the Italian text and Arthur Symons' translation was on sale, and this was good, since *Francesca* while heard needs also to be seen by at least the mind's eye, and D'Annunzio's elaborate, explicit stage directions make this possible. The settings suggest Cardiff Castle, William Burges's High Victorian re-creation of medieval splendor. (For example, Act III plays in a "room painted in fresco, elegantly divided into panels, portraying stories out of the romance of Tristan . . . a beautiful alcove hidden by rich curtains . . . a sort of long chair without back or arms, with many cushions of samite"; round the octagonal hall of Act IV runs "a frieze of unicorns on a gold background.") For that matter, D'Annunzio's whole play suggests a heady, rich mixture concocted with ingredients from *Tristan*, Tennyson's *Idylls*, and Maeterlinck's *Pelléas*. Visconti might be the man to produce it. As Symons remarks in the preface to his translation, "D'Annunzio has learnt something from Wagner, not perhaps the best that Wagner has to teach, in his over-amplification of detail, his insistence on so many things beside the essential things, his recapitulations, into which he has brought almost the actual Wagnerian 'motives.'" Much the same could be said of Visconti's recent works—and also of Zandonai's score. The composer has learned things from Wagner, both directly and by way of Puccini and Debussy, but not the true principles of music drama.

The play has five acts, the opera four, the last of them comprising two scenes corresponding to Acts IV and V of the play. Both play and opera suffer from a structural weakness, in that four of the five scenes are built in a similar fashion: a long, leisurely preamble replete with picturesque local color and historical detail that are heavily—too heavily—charged with symbolism and dramatic irony, an action-filled close accelerating to a strong curtain. The first, third, and fifth scenes all begin with Francesca's women onstage (six small solo roles in the play, five in the opera). Zandonai writes pretty music for them, evoking timbres of the past with the strains of lute and viola pomposa. Act II is set in a bastion, where Francesca learns about Greek fire, an early Malatesta version of napalm, ignites some, and apostrophizes the fierce destructive flame. (Her monologue seems to have been cut from the opera at an early date, though it remains in the score.) Zandonai underpins the poet's symbolism by a conscientious use of leitmotivs. As the climaxes approach, his style tends to become cruder both in sound and in harmony. He veers between tasteful, well-made music, in the manner of early Pizzetti, and uninhib-ited Mascagnesque outburst. But the tunes don't stick—not even that of the big love duet after Francesca and Paolo "read no further." *Francesca* fails, in the end, because its melodies are unmemorable.

Raina Kabaivanska played the heroine. She is, in the old phrase, a gentlewoman in all she does, untouched by coarseness, and dignified even in her most passionate outbursts, and so she was a fine Francesca. Her powerful soprano lacks the warmth generally termed Italianate; equally, it is free from any squalliness and spread, being clear, forward, and impeccably focused. She is more Eames than Caniglia. One mannerism she indulged: a sudden *piano spianato* fined down to a level below the requirements of either word or musical phrase. Being a delicate kind of fault, it was easily forgiven. Her phrasing was smooth and sensitive. Her use of portamento was eloquent and well judged. Her words were tellingly uttered. Moreover, her demeanor on the platform was just right; there is an art of facial expression and pose—rather than overtly theatrical gesture—which helps to bring dramatic presence to concert opera, and Miss Kabaivanska understands it. Placido Domingo, as the fair Paolo, was in full, free voice. He made fine big sounds but brought no trace of intimacy to the gentle exchanges with Francesca. In a manner usually (but not rightly) associated with *Cavalleria rusticana*, he roared and sobbed and flung his arms about as if he were out to wow an Italian provincial audience. Matteo Manuguerra was an impressive Gianciotto—Francesca's husband, the King Mark or Golaud figure of the tale. His baritone is strong, vivid, and commanding, and his characterization was keen. The plot includes a third brother, Malatestino, a tenor, who plays Melot to Gianciotto's Mark; he, too, desires Francesca. Nuccio Saetta's singing of the part was as violent as his name but not inappropriately so in the role of a vicious young firebrand. The numerous small parts were capably done. As Ostasio, Francesca's brother, Harlan Foss produced a fresh, ringing baritone of such quality that one was sorry he had so little to do. Miss Queler has the measure of the score. She conducted it with a sure command of color and pacing. Though her baton technique may appear diffident, she proved—as in that vigorous *Lombardi* earlier this season—that she certainly knows how to bring an opera to life.

The night before, there had also been concert opera in Carnegie Hall: Act II of Borodin's *Prince Igor*, given by the New Jersey Symphony Orchestra, under Henry Lewis. The work is a patchwork of beautiful things, loosely stitched. There is almost no dramatic action. Onstage it can be a spectacular pageant based on the contrasts of Russian and Tatar. The music is bold, distinguished, and marvelously individual. In this performance, Marilyn Horne sang

Konchakovna in smooth, opulent tones. As Vladimir, David
Kuebler revealed a promising but still unfinished tenor. In
the title role, Tom Krause forced his voice until it lost pitch
and focus. Jerome Hines was a slightly worn but still
vigorous Konchak. I like the New Jersey Symphony.
Though the ensemble and the intonation may sometimes
stray, the sound is always warm, picturesque, and enthusiastic. The members play as if they loved the music, and such
zest is infectious. The act of *Igor* was preceded by a
full-hearted account of the Dvořák Cello Concerto, with
Lynn Harrell as a strong, glowing soloist.

March 31, 1973

More Than Monkeyshines

Under Julius Rudel, the New York City Opera has built up a repertory, wise, wide, and adventurous, that can bear comparison with any other in the world. All centuries and almost all schools of opera are represented in a nourishing mixture of the "classics" with less familiar fare. Of the six new productions this season, one has been from the seventeenth century, one from the eighteenth, two from the nineteenth, and two from the twentieth; the latest is Hans Werner Henze's *Der junge Lord*, presented last week. The level of execution, however, has been uneven and sometimes low. Any company adopting a repertory rather than a *stagione* system deliberately sacrifices, to some extent, excellence of performance to variety of offerings (*stagione* implies that fewer operas are done; each has a choice, stable cast, carefully rehearsed; and in any one week there may be no more than two or three pieces on the bill), and at the City Opera the disadvantages of the system have on occasion been compounded by eccentric and tasteless direction. But the production of *Der junge Lord*—or *The Young Lord*, since the piece is played in an English translation—

shows the work of the City Opera at its best. Although only
one of the principals—Kenneth Riegel, in the title role—
was first rate, the ensemble was admirable, and *The Young
Lord*, which contains some thirty solo roles and a great deal
of elaborate chorus work, is largely an ensemble opera.
Some things were wrong on the first night, but they were
details of execution, not flaws of conception. Sarah Caldwell
and Mr Rudel, the stage and musical directors, have
inspired their singers and players to a clear, true, and
entertaining representation of a work that looms large in
the modern repertory. This is the twenty-fourth production
—the second in America—of an opera that had its première, in Berlin, only eight years ago.

Why has *The Young Lord* been so successful? In part,
because it was skillfully planned to provide companies with
something that they had lacked since Richard Strauss's
Arabella (1933)—a large-scale new comedy that troupes
equipped for *Die Meistersinger*, *Falstaff*, and *Der Rosenkavalier*
could get their teeth into. The plot, drawn from an anecdote
in Wilhelm Hauff's *The Sheik of Alexandria and his Slaves*,
written in the early nineteenth century, is slight, and can
quickly be told: To the inhabitants of Hülsdorf-Gotha, a
small German town, an Englishman, Sir Edgar, presents his
lubberly nephew, Lord Barrat; the youth becomes the idol
of local society; his uncouth manners, ascribed to British
eccentricity, are enthusiastically aped by the townsfolk
until, at a ball, the young lord's fine, fashionable clothes fall
from him and he is revealed in his hairiness as—a trained
ape! Matter, one might think, for no more than a satirical
one-acter on the scale of *Gianni Schicchi*. Henze and his
librettist, Ingeborg Bachmann, have amplified it with
episodes of small-town life—five of the six scenes involve a
social gathering of some kind—and a romance that goes
wrong when Luise, ward of the local baroness, becomes
infatuated with Lord Barrat and abandons her poor-student

lover, Wilhelm. The worthies are wittily and precisely characterized in their utterances (though some of Miss Bachmann's specifically German sallies do not travel). Still, a disagreeable practical joke at the expense of *Kleinstadt* mentality, mockery of the bustling, snobbish burghers and of the *précieuses ridicules* at their literary tea, and some lyrical love music are hardly enough to fill an evening. *The Young Lord* is about something more, something dangerous as well as absurd: the bourgeoisie's readiness to embrace bestial ideas when they are presented, from above, behind a glamorous mask. This theme gives substance to the comedy, and, while obviously it is of especial concern to thinking Germans (and *The Young Lord* appeared at a time when liberals detected a resurgence of Nazi ideology in the new West Germany), it has wider applications that can be internationally understood. Many of the operas of the past now considered most stirring were in their day specifically political pieces at least in part—dramas whose text and music were fired by a revolutionary anger and pity so keen that today they move audiences who are not themselves suffering social, civil, or religious persecution, or a tyrannous foreign rule. The passions of a great musician remain potent. Moreover, a fable may fit more than the particular circumstances that gave it birth. Analogues to Berg's *Wozzeck* can easily be found in nonmilitaristic societies. The old situations gain contemporary force when, say, *Nabucco* is played in a subject country, *Fidelio* in a state that holds political prisoners, *Don Carlos* in a mighty nation that, by broadcasting fire and death, seeks to impose its will on a smaller one, and even *Figaro* in a land where aristocratic privilege is still honored. The world of Kurt Weill's *Mahagonny*—of justice perverted by cash, conspicuous waste encouraged for personal profit, and public good sacrificed to private gain, decency to dollars—is all around us, reported daily in the papers. Music can be a very political art.

Boulez' cantata *Le Soleil des eaux* deals ostensibly with river
pollution by industry—but only as a symbol of a wider
pollution of human life. And *The Young Lord* tells of more
than some fond, silly folk who mimicked a monkey. In his
next opera, *The Bassarids*, Henze treated the same theme—
Dionysus is its Young Lord—but this time in tragic, not
comic, terms.

At first, the political aspects of *The Young Lord* were
overlooked. The piece was commissioned by the German
Opera in West Berlin. It was the heyday of Visconti and his
luxuriously elaborate stagings. The work was played in a
loving, expensive re-creation of the little German town,
designed by the Visconti disciple Filippo Sanjust, and hazed
over with romantic nostalgia. Everything was realistic—except the ape, played by Loren Driscoll as an elegant
lordling in no way simian. The audiences enjoyed the
spirited comedy, and smiled indulgently to see their little
national weaknesses so prettily portrayed. Henze, who had
more or less shaken the dust of Germany from his feet
twelve years before, was welcomed back to the Fatherland
as a renegade reclaimed. It was some time before it became
clear that *The Young Lord* carried the seeds of the composer's
new and more radical revolt against his countrymen's way
of life. I next encountered the piece in Dresden. Here all
was fierce caricature except the two tenors, the ape and
Wilhelm, realistically portrayed as poles of unreason and
reason. A program-note likened the town's reception of Sir
Edgar to the *trunkene Landesorgie*, the besotted national orgy
with which the West Germans had just greeted Queen
Elizabeth. What Driscoll had uttered as graceful vocalise
the Dresden ape screamed in agony while Sir Edgar
tortured the beast into a semblance of human behavior. In
subsequent productions, the emphasis has constantly shifted
according to local circumstance. Wisely, Miss Caldwell has
in her version concentrated on what is generally true of

human nature, not specifically German, although with cunning touches she has made clear the social structure of the little town. Farce, fancy, and romance she has held in deft balance. Her handling is vigorous, inventive, and boldly individual. Twice only it failed us: at the start of Act II, when the children were not nearly cruel enough in their taunting of Sir Edgar's little black serving boy, and, surprisingly, in the crucial scene when the young lord's identity is revealed. This should come as a shock, but on the first night the lighting, grouping, and timing of the climax were so inept as to suggest that they had hardly been rehearsed.

With each hearing, Henze's score seems to grow in stature. It illumines—one might say that it embodies—the theme. During those moments when nothing of much consequence is happening on the stage, when people just appear to be waiting about, one should listen intently to the orchestra; plenty of dramatic action is going on there. The townsfolk are characterized by neoclassical music, often in C major, scored for a classical orchestra. A good deal of it is lifted bodily from Stravinsky, and the critic who found the derivations (which become especially noticeable in the setting of the State Theater, where Stravinsky's scores are played more often than anywhere else) "uncomfortably close" got the point without realizing it. The discomfort is intended, deliberately induced by the composer's equation of Apollonian neoclassicism with the bourgeoisie; Henze is questioning *idées reçues*. The closed world of Hülsdorf-Gotha is then invaded, first by the new sounds associated with the arrival of Sir Edgar (although the Englishman never speaks himself, his secretary speaks for him in courtly Straussian arioso, while his exuberant Jamaican—in this production, creole—cook, Begonia, introduces a more exotic element), and then by the wilder, more extravagant timbres, rhythms, and "irrational" melodies brought by a traveling circus.

The star of the circus is Adam, the all but human ape whom Sir Edgar later grooms as his jungle Dionysus. The different sound worlds interact. The secretary announces Lord Barrat's arrival in a civilized transformation of a circus tune, while Adam's cries are tamed into the two party sentences that his admirers find so exquisitely witty. Infection spreads—in the music, as in the fable. Stravinsky is swamped. The finale, which moves from monologue through duet, trio, and quintet to a Gadarene rout, is one of the most striking things Henze has written—a scene at once funny, tragic, and monitory. Mr Rudel's direction of this score had all the necessary punch and vigor, and he kept the textures clear, avoiding the danger, noted at the Berlin première, that the flavors of the intricate ensembles "run together like those of a dissolving Neapolitan ice."

The work was not really well enough sung. (Listen to the Deutsche Grammophon recording, with the original Berlin cast, to hear what it should sound like.) Luise, Wilhelm, and the Secretary need the full, smooth, easily romantic voices of a Mimì, Rodolfo, and Marcello; Patricia Wise, Gary Glaze, and Richard Fredricks were vocally small-scale, rather mousy, but on the right lines. Betty Allen as Begonia and Muriel Greenspon as the Baroness Grünwiesel projected strongly but not stylishly. As already noted, Kenneth Riegel made a first-rate Young Lord, and by some clever device the subhuman quality of his "speech" was strikingly suggested. Sir Edgar was played, a little too nervously, by Sir Rudolf Bing. Most of the small parts were sharply and amusingly etched—by, among others, Ruth Welting (Luise's friend Ida), Barbara Hocher (Frau Oberjustizrat Hasentreffer), John Lankston (Professor von Mucker), and David Ronson (Ökonomierat Scharf). The words were made uncommonly clear. The published English translation had been thoroughly and effectively revised by Mr Rudel. (One important line was lost, Wilhelm's declaration that the young lord behaves like a *beast*, whereupon all the ladies gracefully swoon; and "a mo . . . nkey" does not fit the notes Henze wrote for "Ein Aff' ist's!") Herbert Senn's scenery and Eleonore Kleiber's costumes are not smart, but dowdy in an apt and attractive way, and subtly colored. Economy may have dictated a return to the town square, instead of a ballroom, in the final scene.

April 7, 1973

The Deutsche Grammophon recording of Der junge Lord *is on 2709027.*

Cornerstone

Pierre Boulez has announced the Philharmonic programs for the 1973–1974 season. Native contemporary music is represented by the première of Peter Mennin's Eighth Symphony, Jacob Druckman's *Windows* (first heard, in Chicago, last year), and revivals of Aaron Copland's *Connotations* (composed for the opening of Philharmonic Hall) and of the Concertos for Orchestra by Elliott Carter (a Philharmonic piece of 1970) and by Gunther Schuller (1966). Contemporary Europe is represented by Alexander Goehr's *Pastorals* (1965), Bernd Alois Zimmermann's *Photoptosis* (1968), and Aribert Reimann's *Zyklus* (1971)—which, incidentally, must please the house of Schott, publishers of all three. So far as it goes, the choice is admirable: these are works which show that composers are still prepared to write for symphony orchestra (whereas during the current Philharmonic season several of the newer pieces—such as Stockhausen's *Kontra-Punkte* for ten players and George Crumb's *Ancient Voices of Children* for seven—may have suggested that the full orchestra had become a thing of the past). Boulez evidently intends to keep the whole Philharmonic, not just sections of it, alive. I regret, however, that he cannot be persuaded to bill his own compositions; his *Pli selon pli* is something that New York should hear. If the programs are further scanned for works written during, say, the last thirty-one years, then the following "modern" composers can also be added: Richard Strauss (Second Horn Concerto), Schoenberg (Piano Concerto, *Ode to Napoleon*), Prokofiev (Fifth and Sixth Symphonies, Sinfonia Concertante), and Martinů (Cello Concerto). There are also early works by Roger Sessions (the Suite from *The Black Maskers*, of 1923) and Michael Tippett (the Concerto for Double String Orchestra, of 1939—why not his stirring new Third Symphony?).

The Romantic theme for the season is Goethe's *Faust*, as reflected in Wagner's *Faust* Overture, Berlioz' *La Damnation de Faust*, Schumann's Scenes from *Faust*, and Mahler's Eighth Symphony. The Classical theme is Mozart and his concertos. About the latter I feel slightly unhappy. Boulez has declared that the Philharmonic "stage and hall were not made for contemporary music," but, as he has demonstrated, there is in fact a good deal of contemporary music to which they are well suited. What does not come over effectively in that large place is eighteenth-century stuff played with the reduced orchestral forces that Boulez, quite rightly, employs. (Handel's massive *Fireworks Music*, billed for the forthcoming season, is another matter.) This season, the Classical theme has been Haydn. Work after work of his has failed to make its due effect simply because the details do not register in the large spaces of Philharmonic Hall; even though they may be perfectly audible, they do not tell. The acoustic point was forcefully made when, at a master class in the Juilliard Theatre, Boulez and his student conductor let us hear a good deal of Haydn's Symphony No. 99. Whether by chance or design, it happened that the Juilliard Orchestra was deployed at exactly the strength (except for having one cello more) that Haydn's biographer C. F. Pohl lists for Haydn's own orchestra in the Hanover Square Rooms. There were eight first violins, eight seconds, and four each of violas, cellos, and basses. As a result the balance was not, as it so often is, top-heavy, and each marvelous detail, each shift of texture, every fine, subtle piece of woodwind writing could be appreciated in a hall whose acoustics are intimate, but not at all constricting. (At a later master class, the hall contained Stravinsky's *Rite of Spring* without strain.) I felt that I was hearing Haydn's music properly and keenly for the first time in months.

What should be is more easily stated than what could be, but moves can be made toward the former. Goeran Gentele felt that the Metropolitan Opera should come in two sizes, both of company and of theater, and Opera at the Forum was a first step toward achieving this. The Philharmonic should also come in two sizes, both of forces and of hall; the Prospective Encounters have been a first step toward achieving this, so far as the modern repertory is concerned, and the summer Rug Concerts—a new Philharmonic venture, a week during which the orchestra will be divided into alternate bands of thirty-five and seventy players—will be another. In addition, the Philharmonic programs should, of course, be planned in careful collaboration with those of the Clarion Concerts, the Little Orchestra Society, Musica Aeterna, the Juilliard School concerts, and the other groups whose work could help to fill some gaps in, for example, next season's Mozart-concerto theme. On the *Faust* front, I hope that one of the visiting virtuoso orchestras has been urged to bring into town Liszt's *Faust* Symphony, and that some choir has been encouraged to tackle Henze's *Chor gefangener Trojer*. Perhaps Henry Lewis, with the New Jersey Symphony, or Lukas Foss, with the Brooklyn Philharmonia, will be exploring Anton Rubinstein's "musical portrait" of Goethe's hero.

Still· on what should be—but what seems to me very easily could be: the Philharmonic should amplify its two themes by publishing two booklets, one on Mozart's concertos, the other on Goethe's *Faust* and why it has inspired so much music. They could be quite simple—just enough to enable the subscribers to see the season's "thematic" works in perspective, and perceive a little more fully why Boulez has chosen to gather them into one prospectus. Edward Downes's notes in the regular Philharmonic program-books are admirable and thorough, but they are directed solely to the individual works of the evening. And so this season, though Boulez has put on coherent and carefully planned "retrospectives" of Haydn and also of Stravinsky, they have been shows without a catalogue. There has been nothing to help the concertgoer see at a glance how the work he is hearing on one night relates to those he has heard on others, although the idea of appreciating and enjoying such relations is implicit in the very nature of the planning. There have been no suggestions for further reading or further listening. Rosemary Hughes's Master Musician on Haydn, and H. C. Robbins Landon's little introduction to the symphonies—to name only two simple, nonspecialist works intended for the average concertgoer—have not been on sale at Philharmonic Hall's "gift shop." (Next season, I trust that at least Stanley Sadie's *Mozart* and a paperback *Faust* will be there, duly announced in the program-book.) There has been no advice that across the plaza, at the State Theater, an even fuller "Stravinsky retrospective" has been on show, that in Grace Church a complete cycle of Haydn's masses is in progress, that an aspect of Haydn unrepresented in the Philharmonic programs—as a composer of puppet operas—could be discovered at the Convent of the Sacred Heart (or listened to on the air). (Next season, I trust, any New York performances of Gounod's *Faust* and Boito's *Mefistofele* will be brought to the Philharmonic audiences' attention.) There have been no recommendations of phonograph records that might increase listeners' delight and understanding. Do I sound too sternly didactic? I write only in the belief that the Philharmonic is not helping people to get the most from its offerings and that, more generally, music lovers' enjoyment could be increased by some connected guidance through the chaos of good things to be heard in New York.

Can the Philharmonic's concert performance of Haydn's *L'incontro improviso* be counted among those good things though it was inadequately cast and, by Boulez, rather dully conducted? On the whole, probably, yes, for *L'incontro* is a rich and beautiful work, and in the concert hall one can delight in its musical inventions, even in a poor execution, without being dismayed by the composer's lack of dramatic sense. Haydn's operas have been a discovery of our day, made possible by publication of the scores and increasingly frequent performances. (The fascinating checklist of operatic repertory in the United States from 1966 to 1972 just issued by the Central Opera Service at the Metropolitan reveals that eighty-four performances of Haydn operas were given during that period; he has a far higher score than more famous operatic figures such as Gluck and Weber.) Before they were known, these operas were generally deemed to be homemade little pieces, planned solely for a private princely audience, but probably containing some splendid music. In 1781, after completing *La fedeltà premiata*, the composer wished that the French could see it, and boasted that "no such work has been heard in Paris up to now, nor perhaps in Vienna, either; my misfortune is that I live in the country." But six years later, when Prague asked him for an *opera buffa*, he refused, "because all my operas are far too closely connected with our personal circle . . .

calculated in accordance with the locality." The reasons for this change of heart can, I believe, be summed up in a single word—*Figaro*. Once Haydn got to know Mozart well, he composed no more operas himself (except a late piece for London that remained unproduced until, in 1951, it became Maria Callas's only "creation"), even though for six years more he continued to direct a very busy opera company. Indeed, the sheer amount of operatic activity at Esterház—scores pouring in from all over Europe to be adapted to the talents of the troupe; over a thousand performances in the decade 1780–1790—is enough to show that Haydn was no rustic amateur but was in touch with all the latest developments. In *Die Entführung* and *Figaro* he must have found almost all that he had striven for in his own series of twelve well-varied works—and much more besides. His operas, like Mozart's, are rich in all forms of musical invention. The popular operatic composers of the day—Paisiello, Cimarosa, Anfossi, and the rest—wrote thinner stuff, and a great deal more of it. Paisiello composed about a hundred operas, and Anfossi over seventy; Haydn thirteen, and Mozart (from *Idomeneo*) seven. We can see what Haydn was up to when we compare *L'incontro improviso* with Gluck's *La Rencontre imprévue*, which provided its plot (and also a musical idea or two). Gluck's *opéra bouffon* moves swiftly in a series of short, simple, taking airs. Haydn, for the most part, writes long arias embodying his marvelous discoveries in the fields of thematic development, harmonic adventure, and instrumental texture. They are far too long to be effective on the stage. Haydn knew it; in his autograph several passages are struck through, and wonderful ideas are sacrificed. In most modern productions, still further cuts are made. We can see where Haydn failed when we compare *L'incontro* with *Die Entführung aus dem Serail*, which has the same basic plot, almost the same vocal disposition (two sopranos and two tenors—the noble pair and their respec-

tive attendants—and a buffo bass; Haydn has an additional
soprano attendant), and a musical likeness or two to suggest
that Mozart may have known Haydn's piece. In *Die
Entführung* the drinking scene is a vital part of the plot; in
L'incontro it is an unmotivated merry episode. When Mozart's lovers meet at last, their hearts overflow in music;
when Haydn's meet, the soprano launches into a comic
canzonetta in which she impersonates a rude corsair who
puffed smoke in her face. In Mozart, the captured lovers'
constancy in the face of death inspires a noble duet;
Haydn's response is two rather perfunctory phrases of
recitative. These things can be explained in part by
considering Haydn's troupe, that "personal circle" mentioned in his letter. The principal roles, Rezia and Ali, were
devised for Magdalena and Karl Friberth. From Haydn's
previous opera, *L'infedeltà delusa*, it is clear that Magdalena
had a great gift for spirited impersonation and that Karl
(who also wrote the libretto for *L'incontro*) enjoyed "character" roles. So each was given a chance to indulge a
specialty—at the expense of the drama. Haydn cheerfully
set a text that the mature Mozart would have scorned. But
any fool can perceive that Haydn was no Mozart. He was
not really a musical dramatist—but he was a great composer. Individual arias, whether passionate, poignant, or
bubbling with wit, are superbly made. Especially notable in
L'incontro are—but, no, any list would grow too long, for
nothing in it is negligible. It happens to be an opera I have
heard often, and each time with increasing love. To
mention just one aspect: the string textures—muted against
unmuted, pizzicato against legato murmur, in astounding
figurations that make picturesque points or sly, swift
jests—are miraculous.

Precisely because the piece was so "closely connected"
with the Esterházy company, to catch its spirit modern

performers need to have soaked themselves in Haydn's operas. Ideally, for example, the Rezia should know what kind of singer Magdalena Friberth was, in all her aspects, if she is to make the most of all the varied role. In the Philharmonic performance, only one singer, Sheila Armstrong, was wholly delightful. She was Balkis, counterpart to Mozart's Blonde. Her tone was sweet and true through all its range; her phrasing was lissome, her coloratura limpid. No one else produced consistently "real" notes or remained undefeated by vocal writing as taxing as that in *Die Entführung*—and at a concert performance, where all attention is on the music, the singing needs to be even more accomplished than in the theater. Ali's most difficult aria was omitted, and George Shirley barely got through the others. Maralin Niska's account of Rezia's music struck strident passages. Andrea Velis's Osmin (the Pedrillo part) was nimble and entertaining only until the music passed out of his effective range. Barbara Shuttleworth, the third soprano, and Spiro Malas, the buffo, were smudgy. The whole thing sounded somewhat underprepared; at times the Philharmonic's ensemble was so ragged and ill-balanced as to suggest sight reading. Boulez was more responsive to the romance than to the fun. Slow numbers were expressively molded, but some faster ones were handled in leaden fashion: Osmin's saucy opening *canzonetta* was treated as if it were a love song; two arias in 2/4 were plodded through at four beats to a measure. Six of the eighteen vocal numbers were omitted (among them, the dapper little drinking song, the pastoral-comical duet in which Ali reflects on the Peaceable Kingdom while Osmin remarks that lamb is still better for eating than lying down with, and Rezia's main romantic aria), but the others were done without cuts—without even Haydn's own cuts—and it was good to hear them in all their formal beauty. The recitatives were replaced by a jocular spoken narration. Stylish and pretty gracing of the vocal lines had been prepared by Christoph Wolff. No libretto was provided.

B oulez the conductor of *L'incontro* could, one felt, have profited by the advice of Boulez the Haydn instructor at the Juilliard master classes, who declared that "pulse is not cutting slices of time" and that shaping the phrase is often more important than indicating the beats, who pounced so quickly on flaws of rhythm and balance. The three classes—the first devoted to the First Brandenburg and Haydn's Symphony No. 99, the second to Berlioz' *Benvenuto Cellini* Overture and the *Parsifal* Prelude, the last to Webern's Six Pieces, in their original large-orchestra version, and *The Rite of Spring*—showed the *chef d'orchestre* at his most impressive. In closeup, we could examine what he himself aims to do when conducting. For the six students— two at each class—on the rostrum it cannot have been an easy experience; for the onlookers it was enthralling. There were so many things to be explained and put right, all in a hundred minutes or so: gestures, tempos, rhythms, rubato. So many techniques to learn: how to spot, and how most quickly to correct, errors of intonation or of balance; how to start a piece precisely; how to end it. So many points to consider in the whole complicated business of deciding first what sounds are wanted and then what gestures and glances can best elicit them. Boulez was not kindly, and he shared in the audience's mindless laughter provoked by a remark like "You think you are clever with that—and you are not." (But when the laugh was on him—as when he said he would demonstrate how to secure a unanimous attack and then drew a spatter chord from the orchestra—he merely spoke a mirthless "Ha-ha-ha.") Charm plays no part in his pedagogic method. In private life the man is easy, friendly, dazzling, and utterly delightful (years ago he bewitched me, and made me feel that all my ideas about music had been changed by two conversations); professionally he appears to be cold, immodest, funless, marvelously competent, and so self-sure in utterance that one almost begins to suspect a suppressed inner insecurity. (He could have won the audience's heart by a disarming reminder that his own performance of *The Rite* had been held in low opinion by Stravinsky.) His contempt for simple, winning graces and for ideas that do not accord with his are tempered by his evidently wholehearted, even passionate care for what he admires, and by his rare ability. The master classes reflected the qualities of his conducting. The last of them was particularly rewarding, for in the student conductor David Ramadanoff he found a musician of whom he plainly approved, one who deserved encouragement as well as correction. Between them, master and pupil and the patient Juilliard Orchestra regenerated that primal excitement in Stravinsky's score which is not always felt. Three sections were worked on—the Spring Auguries, the Ritual Action of the Ancestors, and the final Sacrificial Dance. One heard the performances take shape, gain power and precision, and then explode with resistless energy.

The last of the season's Prospective Encounters—those informal Philharmonic concerts given in the Loeb Student Center, on Washington Square, so titled that they are awkward to refer to in the past tense—was also the jolliest. Milton Babbitt was there to present his *Occasional Variations* for synthesized tape and *Correspondences* for string orchestra and synthesized tape, and though Mr Babbitt's written words can be chewy, his impromptu discourse is limpid, merry, and sage. He told us, frankly, that *Correspondences* had been but approximately performed—too little rehearsal, and bad balance between loud-speakers and live players. Less could go wrong with *Occasional Variations*, though it was played on only a two-track reduction of the four-track original. (Why, for heaven's sake? Inadequate equipment? Surely any manufacturer would be proud to lend the Philharmonic his finest wares for such an occasion.) It is an elegantly constructed and most attractive piece, scored in simulated instrumental timbres as if for an ideally proficient orchestra. One hearing was not enough. After the interval came György Ligeti's *Aventures* and *Nouvelles Aventures*—brief "imaginary operas" sung to nonsense syllables filled with intense expression. I called Boulez funless, and so he generally is, but with the Ligeti he had lots of fun, and drew aptly extravagant yet perfectly controlled executions from three superb soloists: Phyllis Bryn-Julson, Jan DeGaetani, and Richard Frisch. A word, too, for the poised comedy of Gordon Gottlieb, the percussionist, when his big moment came and he smashed a trayload of dishes to the ground. Afterward, the captivating Miss DeGaetani took the stand and answered our questions with refreshing candor and charm. A repeat performance of the *Nouvelles Aventures* then showed all too clearly that Boulez had been right, some years ago, to call Ligeti's work "musically thin." Boulez himself, at last, almost seemed relaxed, at ease, and unforbidding in his master-of-ceremonies role. A little more unbending still on his part, a slightly cozier ambience than the antiseptic Loeb Center, and he may yet find himself on Pierre terms with his public.

April 14, 1973

Haydn's L'incontro improviso *is published in two volumes (Series XXV, Volumes 6 ^I and ^{II}) of the Joseph Haydn Werke (G. Henle Verlag, Munich-Duisburg). Ligeti's* Aventures *and* Nouvelles Aventures *are recorded on Candide 31009.*

May Day

Through a spring blizzard to Brooklyn, on Sunday last week—and reward at the end of the journey in the form of a brand-new opera worth hearing, done with a dapper efficiency that recalled Liebermann's Hamburg troupe at its best. Robert Starer, born in Vienna in 1924, is best known to the world as the composer of Martha Graham's *Phaedra*. *Pantagleize*, his first full-length opera, is a work that one need not hesitate to recommend to Intendants in quest of something effective and new. Mr Starer is a member of the Brooklyn College music faculty; *Pantagleize* was put on by the Brooklyn College Opera Theatre. Students and faculty members of the college's Departments of Music, Speech and Theatre, and Dance were involved in this large, ambitious opera, which has three acts, each of about forty minutes, and requires a cast of fourteen, a chorus, and dancers. The composer drew his libretto from Michel de Ghelderode's play of the same title; in effect, he has simply abridged George Hauger's English translation. The result works well as an opera text. It might not have done so had Mr Starer not boldly imposed his own tempi on the piece. Ghelderode was much possessed by music. He said that his first play was written under the influence of a barrel-organ tune: "It was sufficient for me . . . to hear this orchestrion which painfully awoke, yawned, then suddenly burst out like a catastrophe, submerging the neighborhood, for me to be hurled roughly, headfirst, into the suspended play." He spoke of the "eternal music . . . that I want to find again in the best theatre, welling up hidden in the dramatic prose, and running beneath it, murmuring and invisible." *Fastes d'enfer* (which made Ghelderode famous when, in 1949, Barrault produced it in Paris) Ghelderode had planned in the form of a "spoken symphony." The trial scene of his *Pantagleize* is framed in a song, and through the play there runs, like a leitmotiv, the titular hero's phrase "Quelle belle journée!" The lovely day in question is at once the first of May, his fortieth birthday (on which, his horoscope declares, his destiny will suddenly flare, and as suddenly become extinct), the day of a total eclipse, and the day of a violent, bloody revolution for which Pantagleize unwittingly gives the signal. Ghelderode called his drama, written in 1929, a *vaudeville attristant.* His hero "passes through catastrophes in all artlessness." Like Chaplin, he is "bound to Parsifal by purity, and to Don Quixote by courage and holy madness." The author said that he saw his hero once in real life, in 1919, crossing a square raked by machine-gun fire, deep in a book. In the play, Pantagleize is surrounded by the stock figures of popular theater: a stage black, Bamboola (he talk simple, call himself word we don't say now); a black-bearded stage anarchist; a stage Jewess, Rachel Silberschatz; a stage waiter; a stage poetaster; a stage cop; a stage general, MacBoom. But these cardboard creatures can suddenly become dangerous, intelligent, pathetic, or romantic. Amid the scenes of broad buffoonery and the scenes of horror, while others are losing their heads—or keeping them—Pantagleize keeps his heart. At the end, the stupidity and the cruelty of the world conspire to destroy him, "and the farce to make you sad is finished."

Starer has done more than set a good and unusual play to music. Rather as two of Brueghel's paintings, and one of Ensor's, inspired plays by Ghelderode ("I had only transposed the vision of a painter"), Ghelderode's *Pantagleize* now seems to have been reshaped by Starer in musical form. The spirit and the matter are both apt for musical treatment. Even more precisely than words, music can handle transformations, contrasts, and cross-references; it can transmute a boisterous dance into a *valse macabre*, refashion a popular melody as a love theme, or convey a fleeting thought by an instrumental reference even when it is not uttered in words. Starer has a happy knack for scherzo inventions that match the farce, for pregnant snatches of melodic motif that can assume many tempers while keeping their audible identity, and for music in which grotesquerie and sadness are mingled. He has retained the nine scenes and the epilogue of the play. He has found a "music . . . running beneath" and brought it to the surface. This music, however, does not run at the speed the spoken drama would, but determines its own tempi, and at times even takes its own course. When other companies stage the work (the Flanders Festival might be a good place to introduce a Ghelderode opera to Europe; Pantagleize could just as easily have set off his revolution there, in the days of Philip II), producers are likely to want to make cuts. The composer must resist them. His scenes are well shaped. His varied pacings are effective. If anything, he might even expand the first lyrical scene in Rachel's room, and also risk some extension of his hero's final monologue.

How can one describe the musical idiom? *Wozzeck* is probably the handiest comparison—especially its first tavern scene. But Starer's music is leaner than Berg's, and more thinly scored. The orchestra is double woodwind, pairs of horns and trumpets, trombone, tuba, strings, piano, and percussion. In Brooklyn College's Whitman Hall, the words came through with perfect clarity—which was astonishing, considering the size of the auditorium, and was a tribute to the composer's skill. The performance, prepared and conducted by Károly Köpe, was splendidly confident. Wilson Lehr's staging was crisp and skillful, to be faulted, perhaps, only for the understatement of the caricature aspects of the revolutionaries at their first appearances. Tiny parts—such as those of the two sentries who guard the state treasure—were played with verve and precision. Eldon Elder's scenery, economical and striking, worked deftly, both in its mechanics and as apt settings for the drama. I heard the second of two differing casts. Harold Mason projected Pantagleize's music strongly, but sometimes tended to sing notes separately rather than connect them in a lyrical line. He did wrong to sport a black beard; it made him look like one of the revolutionaries. Edward Pierson's Bamboola should have been blacker and bouncier, less superfly. Rachel needed a warmer, fuller mezzo than Delphine Beauchamps's. Outstanding among the principals was Harlan Foss, as Innocenti, the waiter, the most intelligent and self-aware of the gang; he is a young baritone of presence and clear projection.

I had better find something to say against the opera, lest I be accused of indiscriminate enthusiasm. Well, it seems to me a mistake to have turned Ghelderode's epicene poet into a trousered poetess; the composer gained thereby a coloratura soprano in his predominantly male cast, but dramatically the role is spoiled. And I think that to enjoy *Pantagleize* consistently one needs to have read the whole play in advance, for some of what happens in the opera, both verbally and musically, is otherwise not altogether self-explicatory. (The play, however, is readily available, in several languages, so this will not be too much of an obstacle, provided audiences are ready to take a little trouble.)

The presentation of Humperdinck's *Königskinder* by the Preparatory Division of the Manhattan School of Music, in the school's Borden Auditorium, was fine as far as the contribution of the nonroyal children—more than a hundred of them—went. Cynthia Auerbach, producer, conductor, and translator of the piece, had individualized their roles in the busy town scene that forms Act II. Some of her invented characters specified in the immense cast—Hustler, Call Girl, Call Girl's Daughter—suggested the era of the current rather than of the earlier Engelbert Humperdinck, but the combination of medieval and mod that ran through the costuming and played through Miss Auerbach's treatment of the plot—the Witch's simples were "sunshine pills"—was easy, unforced, entertaining, and unexceptionable. William Schroder's costumes looked good. The children were bright and confident, and sang sweetly. The geese acted with aplomb but honked insistently through the first act. The Witch, Celesta Magnone, was a promising young mezzo; the Royal Children themselves and their friend the Fiddler needed stronger singing. A trio of principals comparable to Geraldine Farrar, Hermann Jadlowker, and Otto Goritz, who created the opera, at the Metropolitan, in 1910, could probably conceal the weaknesses, which are partly of plot and partly of melody, and make us aware only of the charm, which is considerable. The tale is too slight and too kitschy for the weight of moral symbolism—"the tragedy of human folly and blindness which judges by externals"— that it is expected to bear, and too scrappy to work simply on a nursery level. The best numbers are two the phonograph has made familiar: "Lieber Spielmann" (recorded by Farrar) and "O du liebheilige Einfalt du!" (recorded by

Goritz), both of them square-cut and sentimentally pretty. In his masterpiece, *Hänsel und Gretel*, Humperdinck drew on a rich font of folk tune. *Königskinder* is worked with the same care and craft; it succeeds where it follows the poetic formulas of the earlier piece, but loses us during its more Maeterlinckian flights.

Handel's *Saul* is the grandest of English music dramas, and Stephen Simon, conducting the Handel Society of New York's chorus and orchestra, was moved by it to give, in Carnegie Hall, the most impressive performance I have yet heard from him. The casting was good. Donald Gramm, though taxed by the passages of "A serpent, in my bosom warm'd," made a noble protagonist. Maureen Forrester, as David, was firm, ardent, and affecting. She rose to "O Lord, whose mercies numberless," Irene Jordan rose to Merab's "Author of peace," and John Stewart rose to Jonathan's "Sin not, o king"—each singer capturing the sense that here was a knockout number to be made the most of, phrase by phrase, but one that also had its part to play in the dramatic progress. Miss Jordan's narrow, powerful timbre was not unsuited to the character of the proud beauty. Mr Stewart's tone was excellently smooth and even, and he commands an art often neglected today—that of closing off a sostenuto note with delicate precision. Patricia Wise's Michal was neat but rather colorless. David Clenny was a colorful, pungent, and powerful Witch of Endor; there must be few male mezzos who can produce so fearless and secure a high trill. The best recitative singing of all came from Henry Price—at once rhythmical, forthright, and vivid in his use of the words; doubling in the small roles of Abner and the Amalekite, he was so good that when he turned up again in the Elegy to sing "Ye men of Judah" one regretted that the short setting and not the full aria was used. Elaine Comparone's harpsichord continuo was well judged, not fidgety and self-attracting. By the end of the evening, organ and orchestra had got slightly but not disastrously out of tune. A libretto was provided free of charge.

April 2, 1973

Miscellany

Carnegie Recital Hall has become a shabby, depressing little room that does nothing to lift the hearts of its audiences. We have to go there, since it is where a fair amount of new music is played, but going there isn't much fun. Peter Lieberson's Concerto for Four Groups of Instruments, played in the Recital Hall by the Speculum Musicae ensemble, did, however, successfully dispel the encircling gloom and leave the bright, exhilarant impression of a young mind that is lively, intelligent, exuberant in invention, and disciplined in utterance. The concert was broadcast by WNYC; I managed to borrow a tape, and each time I hear the piece I like it more. What was played was in fact only the first part, some eight minutes long, of a work to be done in full at Tanglewood this summer. It is a concerto for a broken consort of eleven instruments, grouped as flute, oboe, and clarinet; two violins and viola; bassoon, cello, and double bass; harp and piano. One group seizes on another's idea, refashions it to a new sound, a new pitch, a new tone color, varying and developing the dialogue. The effect is not pointillist or scrappy; a line of progress runs through the

composition. One can hear at what speed and in what
directions the music is moving. The periods are cogently
shaped. The control of timbres and of textures is confident.
A description of musical procedures cannot convey quality;
let me just say that I enjoyed the first encounter with a piece
that struck me as ambitious, fresh, and confident, and that
further acquaintance showed it to have plenty of good
things to say as well as a winning manner of saying them.
Music by Stravinsky, Webern, and Schoenberg completed
the Speculum Musicae program. This band of expert young
players should flash even more brightly when it appears in
the less dusty frame of Alice Tully Hall next month.

Three members of the Composers String Quartet accompanied Gloria Agostini in the first performance, again in
Carnegie Recital Hall, of Charles Wuorinen's Variations
for harp with trio accompaniment. This struck me as a
slightly arid, schematic work in which the composer concen-
trates on the harp's ability to define single notes and is
determined to avoid the voluptuous swirls and the tinkling
melodic prettiness usually associated with the instrument.
The program opened with Gunther Schuller's First Quartet—a New York première, though the piece dates from
1957. It is unassertive, even reticent, and finely and
thoughtfully worked. I should like to say more about it, but
I have heard it only once, and though the score has long
been in print, it proved impossible to buy a copy in New
York—even from Schuller's publishers. The recital, which
formed part of the "Pleasures of Modern Music" series,
included Elliott Carter's Second Quartet, something the
Composers String Quartet plays superbly. The program
ended with Bartók's Fourth, but I went home instead, to
hear the Carter again, this time with score in hand and
light to read it by, from the Composers' fine Nonesuch
record. Incidentally, Ruth Crawford Seeger's String Quartet (1931), that remarkable, arresting, and beautiful compo-

sition that I wrote about after the Composers String
Quartet's previous recital in the "Pleasures" series, has just
appeared on a Nonesuch record, together with George
Perle's Fifth, (1960, revised 1967) and Milton Babbitt's
Second (1952). The Perle is engaging; the Babbitt is a
thirteen-minute span of lucid, sustained discourse that
proves enthralling to follow. Discovering the American
string-quartet repertory, with the Composers, the Concord,
and the Juilliard Quartets as companions, has been a major
pleasure of the season.

Half of the latest Evening for New Music, brought to
Carnegie Recital Hall by the Center of the Creative and
Performing Arts of the State University of New York at
Buffalo, proved rewarding. This half was a performance of
George Crumb's *Songs, Drones and Refrains of Death* (1962–
1968), García Lorca poems set for baritone, for amplified
guitar, double bass, piano, and harpsichord, and for two
percussionists. Crumb is at once unafraid of the obvious,
where it is obviously called for, and a master inventor of
strange, thrilling sounds to enhance the stark, dark tragedy
evoked by Lorca's imagery. This early piece of Crumb's is
less exquisite than his *Ancient Voices of Children* but not less
powerful. With small strokes the composer makes great
effects. The work was pungently performed; Spyros Sakkas
was an able soloist. A text sheet with translations was
supplied, but, since the lights were turned out during the
performance, it was not as useful as it might have been. The
three works that made up the second half received New
York premières. Richard Trythall's *Second Round* (1972) was
a mess. The idea of the piece looked promising on paper:
scraps of Scarlatti live on the harpsichord, surrounded by
manipulated Scarlatti on tape; in practice, what emerged
from the loud-speakers was mere confusion. Theodore
Antoniou's *Parodies* (1970) was a protracted and ham-fisted
joke. Jani Christou's *Anaparastasis III* (1969), for mime,

instrumental noise, and tape background, is a composition very far from performance-proof (the score was put together, following Christou's death, after sketches, and memories of those who took part in early versions), and on this occasion it was just tedious.

There was more Crumb this month, in Alice Tully Hall, when the New York Camerata, who commissioned the piece, played *Vox Balaenae* ("Voice of the Whale") of 1971. I described this quiet, subtly enchanting composition when the Aeolian Chamber Players introduced it to New York, last year. It reveals Crumb's discoveries of new instrumental resource at their most lyrical; this second hearing confirmed that it is not a mere assemblage of sound effects but a sustained and beautiful dream vision of the deep. Richard Rodney Bennett's *Commedia II*, another Camerata commission, which received its first performance at this concert, is a fluent, competently made little piece, expertly tailored to show off the points of the three instruments involved (flute, cello, piano), solo and in all combinations—but thin stuff that goes in one ear and out the other. The three Camerata players are cultivated musicians. In a Haydn trio and a Hummel set of variations, they were elegant, poised, and stylish. Paula Hatcher's clear, unwobbly flute tone and Glenn Jacobson's smoothly rippling keyboard runs were an unfailing pleasure. Nothing was rough, but nothing was fiery. Jeannette Walters joined them as soloist in Ravel's *Chansons madécasses*. Her French pronunciation was not forward enough. The central "Aoua! Méfiez-vous des blancs," a song of racial hate, should have been much fiercer. But her soft-grained, sensuous timbre was well suited to the outer songs.

This has been the season for Monteverdi's *L'incoronazione di Poppea* and Kurt Weill's *Der Aufstieg und Fall der Stadt*

Mahagonny up and down the East Coast. Hard on the heels of *Poppea* productions at Yale and in the New York State Theater came a version by the Opera Society of Washington. Meanwhile, Washington's *Mahagonny* has been followed by the Opera Company of Boston's production of the piece, and a "Little *Mahagonny*" in the Manhattan Theatre Club. The Washington *Poppea* was done in an edition by Nikolaus Harnoncourt. He scores Monteverdi's music no less freely but far less lushly than does Raymond Leppard in the version chosen by both Yale and the New York City Opera. In one respect, Harnoncourt goes further than Leppard— by using woodwinds as well as strings, but (except at a moment like Otho's "Ho Poppea nel core," which he decks with soft string chords and a trickling harp) he accompanies in a more limber fashion, with fewer tricksy continuo effects and fewer invented countermelodies. The main focus is kept where Monteverdi meant it to be, on the stage. This is good. Moreover, the scenes are not marred by the interior snicks and sudden transpositions of the other version. In Washington, however, this edition was adapted under the influence of Leppard's: exactly the same scenes were omitted (among them Octavia with her Nurse, Otho's Act II monologue, the penultimate Nero/Poppaea duet); the same displacement of the Maidservant/Page scene was made; Busenello's three-act structure was similarly altered, and weakened, by a division into two acts with the break coming after the death of Seneca; and Nero, Otho, and the Page were similarly transposed down an octave.

The show was rather well sung. It was more gripping than the fancified City Opera presentation. It moved swiftly, in a striking unit set by Neil Peter Jampolis. Kristine Haugan's costumes—in the scenes where the characters wore any—were splendid. But, alas, Frank Corsaro, who directed, had adopted all those vulgar old clichés apparently designed to reassure audiences who might fear that *Poppea* was just a seventeenth-century historical curiosity that it can be as sexily "modern" as—well, say, *The Devil in Miss Jones* and *Bijou.* And so it can. The sensuality of many scenes is not in question. But the point of the drama—the interaction of amorous and political destinies—is obscured when it is played as little more than a series of sex scenes. Objections to Mr Corsaro's handling can be made on several grounds. On the simplest level, it was hard for Drusilla to sing sweetly while she was flat on her back with Otho thrashing about on top of her. When the hero was naked to a golden pouch and the heroine remained more or less modestly robed, the stress was wrong; though Alan Titus strips handsomely and had a good line of leers and steamy slouches, Poppaea, not Nero, is supposed to be the sex object. When an ecstatic madrigal in praise of Poppaea's beauty was presented in terms of a Park-Miller featurette, I finally lost my temper, for this staging was plainly the work of a man who cared nothing for the sense of the words or the sense of the music.

Well, I won't go on; Mr Corsaro has not touched bottom. At least Seneca was played straight. The process of vulgarizing *Poppea*, which began a decade ago, when Günther Rennert decided that the madrigal just mentioned should be done as a drunk scene, can still continue. The next director can have Seneca open his veins in a steam bath, petting his pretty disciples the while. In time, one might just leave the music out altogether. Paul Callaway, who conducted in Washington, had evidently not had time to rehearse his forces to the point where a conductor becomes unnecessary and players respond directly to the singers, and that is what Monteverdi needs. But Mr Callaway showed a good sense of pacing. Noël Rogers as Poppaea, Mr Titus as Nero, Brent Ellis as Otho, Mary Cross Leuders as a glittering Octavia, Thomas Paul as Seneca—all were in good voice. And let me, before leaving Washington, praise the incidental pleasures of attending a show at Kennedy Center. In Prague, it is agreeable, during intervals at the National Theatre, to stroll on the terrace above the Vltava, and in Stratford, Warwickshire—or, for that matter, in Stratford, Ontario—to watch swans on the Avon. But I doubt whether, until Sydney opens its Opera House later this year, any other theater can rival the setting of Kennedy Center's promenades above the Potomac.

Sarah Caldwell's production of *Mahagonny*, in Boston's Orpheum, was chaste, orthodox, and faithful to the directions of Brecht's libretto. There was no attempt to illustrate modern morals; no such attempt is needed. The show was conceived in the justified belief that audiences see the point of such a work most clearly when it is presented in the way that its creators conceived it. Helen Pond and Herbert Senn provided textbook scenery; Gilbert Hemsley's lighting was white and clear. A Brechtian stage director insensitive to Weill can wreck the opera if he considers only the libretto; I have seen this happen, in Hamburg. But Miss Caldwell is musical and stage director in one, and her perfectly balanced conduct of the piece gave one a marvelously clear idea of its greatness. Though great, *Mahagonny* is not unflawed; Weill's constant adjustments, in each successive production of the 1930s, show that he knew something was wrong, and there is no definitive edition of the score. *Mahagonny* the opera has its origins in the "Little *Mahagonny*," a "Songspiel" with six numbers and no plot; these numbers, reworked, were incorporated into the opera, but only three of them fit easily into the narrative. A further difficulty arose when Weill's publisher proposed that the brothel scene should be "softened" by the insertion of a love duet, and the composer provided the tender but unsentimental Crane Duet. Miss Caldwell tackled the difficulties boldly. She omitted the duet and gave the brothel scene in its original, fierce form. Good. She moved the Benares song—which drops the tension wherever it is placed—to a point between the announcement of the typhoon that threatens the city of Mahagonny and the first finale. A mistake: momentum was lost; a producer must either (for the sake of the music) accept a slack before the final, shattering funeral march or scrap Benares altogether. She took into the first act the first number of Act II. Ineffective —but forgivable in a theater not equipped for the quick scene change that would otherwise be involved. She made only one of the numerous cuts within numbers which Weill at one time or another indicated. I was glad to hear the numbers complete, for once, but I think that the cuts tighten things.

The whole presentation was marked by the enthusiasm, dedication, and vitality that radiate from this remarkable woman. But neither the Jenny nor the Jimmy sang the music beautifully enough. Leonore Morvaya's timbre became edgy and unsteady at the top. Richard Kness tended to shout lines that should be lyrical and smooth. The orchestra played very well. The Weinstein-Symonette English translation, as I noted after hearing it in Washington, fits the score less well than the Geliot-Drew version.

The "Little *Mahagonny*" is a powerful, punchy piece in its own right, and superbly scored. At the Manhattan Theatre Club, it was given a zesty, if somewhat rudely balanced, performance, with very bright orchestral playing, under Jeff Labes.

April 28, 1973

The Nonesuch record of string quartets by Ruth Crawford Seeger, George Perle, and Milton Babbitt is H 71280.

The Nureyev Version

In ballet history, the usual order is reversed; the Romantic works come first, then the Classical. And the Petipa-Tchaikovsky *Sleeping Beauty*, first performed, in St Petersburg, in 1890, is the grandest, fullest, and finest achievement of Classical ballet—its "definitive statement" and an enduring inspiration to later choreographers. Balanchine, Ashton, and Kenneth MacMillan all proclaim their debt to the inventions of Petipa. Brought from Leningrad to London by Nicholas Sergeyev, *The Sleeping Beauty* became, in 1939, the foundation of the Royal Ballet's work, and the dancers, directors, ballet masters, and teachers who have gone out from Covent Garden to play leading roles in ballet across six continents have all been brought up on *Sleeping Beauty* as ballet's Bible. Meanwhile, in Leningrad itself, *The Sleeping Beauty* remains the work that shows Maryinsky-Kirov dancing at its purest and most poetic. The Kirov company brought its *Sleeping Beauty* to London twelve years ago, and left a new mark on all subsequent Western productions. The influence was continued, in a highly personalized variant, by the participation of the ex-Kirov

248

dancer Rudolf Nureyev in the Royal Ballet performances and then by his own stagings of the work—at La Scala, in 1969, and now for the National Ballet of Canada. With a *Sleeping Beauty* "produced, staged, and with additional choreography by Rudolf Nureyev after Marius Petipa," the Canadian company made its Metropolitan début last week. It offered an exceedingly grand presentation of the piece— from a scenic point of view the grandest, in fact, that I have ever seen.

When August Bournonville, that great Romantic choreographer (whose *La Sylphide* is another work in the Canadian repertory), visited Petersburg in 1874, he was distressed by what he saw: "Much as I wanted to, I could not discover action, dramatic interest, logical continuity, something that would even remotely remind one of common sense. And if, on occasion, I did succeed in finding a trace of something like it (as, for example, in Petipa's *Don Quixote*), the impression was immediately obscured by an endless number of monotonous bravura appearances." Ivan Alexandrovich Vsevolozhsky, appointed Director of the Imperial Theatres in 1881, changed all that. He instituted production councils in which scenarist, choreographer, composer, and designer got together to plan a new work. Of *The Sleeping Beauty* he was both scenarist and costume designer; Tchaikovsky, "in large letters," dedicated the published score to him. Composer and choreographer worked closely together. Petipa told Tchaikovsky exactly how many measures he wanted for each episode, and specified the tempo, the style, even the scoring. Princess Aurora's first variation should be accompanied by violins and cellos pizzicato, and harps; at Carabosse's unmasking, at the end of Act I, "a chromatic scale must sound in the whole orchestra"; the Sapphire of Act III, being of pentahedral cut, required an accompaniment in 5/4 time. When, during rehearsals, the Panorama music of Act II came to an end before the great panorama of painted canvas had rolled its full course, Tchaikovsky composed extra music, whose length was determined, literally, by the yard. The three collaborators played each his different role in giving unity to the elaborate *féerie*. Vsevolozhsky had his conception of a glittering dance pageant mounting to its climax in an apotheosis-paean to imperial splendor (a paean in the precise sense, since the ending would show Apollo costumed as Louis XIV). Petipa had his sharp-cut scheme for a balanced and well-varied sequence of dances. And Tchaikovsky? He always delighted in the evocation of past centuries. Petipa's blueprint checked his tendency to sprawly form. And he poured out his heart. It is Tchaikovsky's music that gives character to the heroine and expresses the "inner theme" which raises *The Sleeping Beauty* above the level of a pretty divertissement.

Most of the fairy tales that adults go to the theater to see again and again—*Swan Lake, Cinderella, Hansel and Gretel, The Ring*—symbolically enshrine truths about human experience and human behavior to make their pleasures more than incidental. *Swan Lake*, for example, is a drama involving conflict and character; it gives scope for dramatic expression, for acting, and for diverse striking interpretations. By comparison with Prince Siegfried in *Swan Lake*, Prince Florimund of *The Sleeping Beauty* is a cipher. What does he do to deserve his princess? The briar thicket surrounding his bride is no dangerous Magic Fire through which only the dauntless can pass. And similarly, by comparison with the brave, pathetic Odette and the formidable temptress Odile, Princess Aurora is a passive heroine played upon by circumstance. Can we find a moral in *The Sleeping Beauty* beyond that guest lists should be kept up-to-date lest awkwardness result? Perrault, who wrote the fairy tale on which the ballet is based, suggested, "What girl would not forgo her marriage vows, at least for a while, to gain a husband who is handsome, rich, courteous, and kind?" Not enough! In a preface to the Penguin edition of Perrault, Geoffrey Brereton remarks that it is "tempting to adopt the nature-myth interpretation and see the tale as an allegory of the long winter sleep of the earth"—but adds that "the allegory, if it is one, is obscure." Tchaikovsky's interpretation was simpler. His *Sleeping Beauty* is a struggle between good and evil, between forces of light and forces of darkness, represented by the benevolent Lilac Fairy and the wicked fairy Carabosse. The prelude, a straightforward exposition of the music associated with the two characters, suggests it; the consistent employment of melodies related to or derived from these themes—the Lilac Fairy's transformation of the Carabosse music at the close of Act I, the Carabosse figuration that propels Aurora's dance with the spindle, the opposition of the two themes in the symphonic entr'acte that precedes the Awakening—makes it clear. These two forces shape Aurora's destiny, and although she initiates nothing, with just a little stretching of the imagination we can accept the declaration of the Russian composer and critic Boris Assafiev that the heroine's three adagios (the Rose Adagio, in E-flat; the Vision Scene appearance, in F; the Grand Pas de Deux, in C) tell "the story of a whole life—the growth and development of a playful and carefree child into a young woman who learns, through tribulations, to know great love." It is in this sense that Margot Fonteyn, since 1939 our leading Aurora, dances the role.

That question "Can we find a moral?" prompts others. Is it right to look for one? Does the "meaning" of *The Sleeping Beauty* not lie simply in its patterns of movement, as does that of, say, *Ballet Imperial*, Balanchine's homage to Petipa and Tchaikovsky? While spectacle, pure dance, expressive dance, narrative, and symbolism must mix in any presentation of the work, what importance should be given to any single ingredient? Different productions have provided different answers. The Kirov's has modest décor; the dances shine as rich, perfectly cut jewels in a quiet, rather dowdy setting; this Leningrad *Beauty* is not a drama but a long, lyrical poem in varied meters, spun on a thread of radiant narrative. Kenneth MacMillan's presentation, at the German Opera in Berlin, in 1967, was very grand indeed to look at (the epochs were moved forward, so that Aurora fell asleep in the reign of Catherine the Great and woke a century later, under Alexander II) and also rather dramatic—yet the main emphasis was again not on the story but on the dances, both Petipa's and those that MacMillan added in brilliant emulation. The famous old Covent Garden version, which did more than twenty years' hard service (and in 1949 introduced the company to New York), balanced all the ingredients listed above, but toward the end it fell apart; though the central Petipa episodes were lovingly preserved, around them was a ragged patchwork. The 1968 replacement was softly romantic, lavishly sentimental in appearance, and did not last long; I have not seen its successor, which opened at Covent Garden in March.

Nureyev's production for the National Ballet of Canada is different again. The décor, by Nicholas Georgiadis, is even more sumptuous than Barry Kay's in Berlin, though it does not sparkle so brightly. Mr Kay produced a jeweled effect, of diamonds, rubies, sapphires, with the softer gleam of pearl and opal in the Vision Scene; Mr Georgiadis prefers an impression of old gold, with touches of rich colors that are muted as if by a layer of fine dust; in the final scene the dominant tone becomes rust red. David Hersey's subtly elaborate lighting subdues the colors still further and blurs distinctions between them; a prevailing amber glow neutralizes all shades in the Vision Scene except when follow-spots fall on the principals, or the attendant fairies enter pools of white light stage-front. Blackness at the back strikes an unsuitably somber note at the christening party of the Prologue; Aurora's wedding, I think, also calls for a more splendid general blaze. All the same, the lighting is carefully and imaginatively wrought. There are some excellent stage effects: a streamer of red ribbon flies across the stage, to shape itself as Carabosse and her retinue; a boat for Florimund and the Lilac Fairy glides magically through the obstacles on the way to the palace. The tableau of sleeping courtiers through which the prince, marveling, picks his way is a triumph for designer, producer, and lighter at once. Mr Georgiadis's architecture, substantial and imposing, leaves plenty of space for the dance. His multitudinous costumes are beautiful both in detail and in massed effect. Only the cut of the tutus, which are large, floppy, and thus line-obscuring, is unhappy.

Nureyev's handling of the piece is extremely elaborate, from the first moment of the fairies' entrée; they come on four at a time, *bourrée*ing hand-in-hand, each group with an attendant cavalier, who then lifts the leader while she draws her companions through the mazes of a most un-Petipalike procession. The second fairy variation is danced in duplicate, which is unusual, but in the score the variation does bear the names of two characters (Coulante, Farine). Nureyev's main innovation in the Prologue is to divide the role of the Lilac Fairy into two: a "Principal Fairy," who does the dancing, and a Lilac Fairy "proper," who turns up at the party, last guest to arrive, only after Carabosse has spoken her curse. Crinolined and heavily draped, an ambulant tea cozy, this fairy can do little more than glide about and wave her wand. Carabosse is played by a woman, as she was by Natalia Dudinskaya in Leningrad a decade or so ago, and she is played by Celia Franca in terms of offended dignity rather than evil malice. Her retinue roughs up the good fairies in a rather infelicitous sequence. Amid all this complication, and with the roles of good and evil genii reduced, the point of the Prologue is not clearly made. The fact that the fairies are endowing young Aurora with the gifts characterized in their variations is unstated, and a newcomer might watch the scene without even becoming aware that a royal infant is the focus of the festivities. The knitting bee, at the start of Act I, becomes another production number, involving slatterns, cat's-paws, halberdiers, hangmen, and a good deal of fussy activity. At the close of the act, the four minor princes, lunging at Carabosse, run one another through. But Petipa's lovely inventions for Aurora are respected, even if eight minstrel girls figure too prominently in parts of the Rose Adagio. Veronica Tennant, Aurora at both performances I saw, places the choreography precisely, apart from a tendency to push forcefully into arabesque. She does not convey much sense of a developing character, and her dancing lacks, above all, legato—that feeling for a flowing line which links one image to the next. It is stop and start again—sequences chopped into short phrases. And this is a general company fault, observable in most of the solo dancing. The musical director, George Crum, has it, too; Tchaikovsky's long melodies do not flow smoothly enough. The anonymous orchestra is proficent but a bit short on strings. Some of Mr Crum's rhythms are sludgy and undramatic.

When, in Act II, Prince Florimund arrives, in the person of Rudolf Nureyev (who dances fourteen of the sixteen New York performances), he gives a splendid demonstration of that phrasing command which, so to speak, keeps the line going through the rests. In Petipa's original the Prince was not a large dancing role (the brilliant male technician of the Petersburg company, Enrico Cecchetti, created not the Prince but the Bluebird—and also Carabosse); Nureyev has enlarged it. He has given himself three variations in Act II, the second of them done to Panorama music shifted to an earlier point in the act. Aurora's second solo has been rewritten, without the alternating *relevés*, and not improved. The voyage to the palace and the Prince's entry are, as I said, strikingly achieved. After the Awakening, the climax of the story, there is a letdown. It is mainly Petipa's fault; here, surely, there should be a pas de deux for the Princess "whose radiant beauty" (in Perrault's words) "seemed to glow with a kind of heavenly light" and the Prince "who hardly knew how to express his joy and gratitude"—but, instead, the curtain drops after a few bars. In the old Covent Garden version the difficulty was solved by moving straight into the wedding celebrations, and for the 1968 production Ashton composed a tender new pas de deux to the music of the entr'acte. In the Canadian version, on the opening night, Miss Tennant and Nureyev made things worse by expressing no great interest in one another. Reactions in this production were often inadequate. Earlier in Act II, the Prince showed little surprise when the Lilac Fairy joined him but behaved as if fairy apparitions were an everyday occurrence. Act III in the Canadian *Beauty* opens not brilliantly but quietly, with the Sarabande, originally the penultimate dance, brought forward. Then things follow much their usual course. The pas de quatre of Jewels becomes a pas de cinq, with the Diamonds a twin set. (The male Diamond is allotted Sapphire's 5/4 solo variation.) Bluebirds are placed before Cats; Red Ridinghood, Hop-o'-My-Thumb, and Cinderella are omitted; so, unfortunately, is the apotheosis. Again, the plot point—that all the characters of fairyland have assembled to pay homage to the royal couple—is not potently made, but again there is a display of dense dance patterns around the solos, with much rich "doubling at the octave" in Nureyev's favored manner.

The National Ballet of Canada was conceived when the Sadler's Wells/Royal Ballet, after its New York triumphs in 1949, went on to appear in Toronto. The official début was late in 1951; the company comes of age with a *Sleeping*

Beauty that shows it need yield nothing in scale of presentation to the London company. Of course, a warning note must be sounded: the well-trained dancers will not mature until the company has a choreographer of its own who composes for them. Being brought up on the Bible— whether Petipa's Authorized or Nureyev's Revised Version —is good, but the dancers must also learn to sing their own songs if they are to live and grow.

May 5, 1973

Petipa's scenario and detailed "musical recipe" for The Sleeping Beauty *was published, in an English translation by Joan Lawson, in four issues of* The Dancing Times, *December 1942 and January, February, and March 1943.*

Grandeur

The opening night, last week, of the Martha Graham Dance Company's season at the Alvin Theatre was an affecting occasion. Not just because the ballet was a revival of *Clytemnestra*, Miss Graham's largest and grandest composition, created in 1958 and overwhelming still, but also because this is the company's first full season in which Miss Graham herself is not dancing. Even without that tremendous presence on the stage, her work is to continue—and it is something we cannot afford to lose. There is nothing like it—no other theater, whether sung, spoken, or danced, that thrills so keenly through muscles and mind at once. Miss Graham's long series of works have been to me like the cantos of a Divine Comedy. She has guided me through Hell, Purgatory, and Paradise; in her mind I have met again and marveled at the larger-than-life figures that people any Westerner's imaginative world. I write as an enthusiast, and my reactions are not pure but mingle, while I watch *Clytemnestra*, with memories of moonlit nights in silver-walled Mycenae; in *Phaedra*, with memories from a dawn when, as I walked to Theseus's palace of Troezen, I met women beside the swift torrent, enacting the first chorus of Euripides' *Hippolytus*, "rinsing rich-colored clothes in the rill-water,/ And laying them to dry on the sun-baked rock." Her *Cortege of Eagles* plays not only in Noguchi's set but in a compound of the imagined Troy I read of as a boy and the real Troy where once I stood and dreamed. *Deaths and Entrances* recalls at once *Wuthering Heights*, the emotions stirred by that novel, the fierce Yorkshire fell underfoot, and the high, wide sky. Miss Graham has given physical presence to the great dreams that shape the landscape of the heart. She has brought to tragedy the sense of touch—the different feelings of warm earth, and rock, and soft covering beneath the feet, the chill of steel to the palm, the surge or shudder of body pressed against body. Her dances are alive in every limb, and the spectator apprehends them in his own body. The scenery is not décor around the dance but part of it. No distinction between the costume and the body within, the throne and the priestess enthroned, the ground and the queen pressed close to it in anguish—they make one living image. Poetry and music also play their parts in this theater of mind and tingling muscle. The dance seems to embrace the music (and even transfigure some of the weaker, more conventional scores) and to embrace any words that may be spoken or sung, until we do not know whether we are watching and hearing, or dreaming.

In this age when Oedipus is more familiar as a complex than as a king, every schoolboy knows that the great actions of myth and history, by heroes and saints, emperors and artists, can be sexually explained. In Miss Graham's ballets, something of the opposite occurs. Through sexual statement she can lead us to feel the tragic magnitude of the actions. For example, in *Night Journey*, her work about Oedipus and Jocasta, the idiom is brutally explicit, from the moment when Oedipus plants his heel in Jocasta's groin, through the thickening and swelling of his limbs, to the fatal incestuous impregnation—but what stirs us is the sense of tragic destiny, not the physical events. Her *Phaedra* is a study of Aphrodite triumphant—"Vénus toute entière à sa proie attachée." Where D'Annunzio, treating the same theme (in his libretto for Pizzetti's opera *Fedra*), turned his heroine into a kind of super-Isolde proclaiming in empurpled torrents that love is a law unto itself, Miss Graham shows us Phaedra at the moment she yields, active and fevered, to her destiny—a moment of crisis that includes both what has shaped her (her mother's monstrous lust) and led her to this point and a vision of what will ensue from her yielding. Miss Graham's tragic ballets are made from emotion recollected not in tranquillity but in crisis. Usually they are centered on a single woman. In *Clytemnestra*, the protagonist is at the gates of Hades. In visions and memories she relives her life—that strange birth with her sister Helen from divine eggs, Helen's abduction, Iphigenia's sacrifice, Troy, Aegisthus, Agamemnon's return, the chain of murders that has led to her own by Orestes—and tries to order the tangled skein of bloodshed. Meanwhile, on earth, the curse on the house of Atreus continues, and Orestes is pursued by furious hellhounds his mother has loosed on him. The Prologue is a whirl of action. In Act I, Clytemnestra's meditations begin to find a pattern in the tragic sequence, reflected in the formal sequence of pas de deux. In Act II, at the moment when, in Athens, Orestes is freed of the curse and the Furies become Eumenides, Clytemnestra, in Hades, achieves a kind of peace.

Only a bold creator would tackle such a theme, and only a genius could have expressed it in a long work where the images are of such unfailing power and distinction. *Clytemnestra* is not a neat theorem but a threaded maze—an enactment of the agony that brings tragic understanding. Miss Graham can call on the resonances that are part of our heritage—that tremendous moment, for example, when

Agamemnon sets his foot on the red carpet (and, in her
ballet, the King of Death appears behind him to stalk his
blasphemous steps). She uses them not complacently, nor
with self-conscious reverence, but in unaffected grandeur.
When Miss Graham herself portrayed Clytemnestra, it was
hard to take one's eyes off her; the dance patterns seemed to
emanate, like lines of force around a magnetic pole, from
that burning, brooding presence. In the revival, it becomes
easier to discover how fully and vividly all the roles have
been composed. This season, there have been two Clytem-
nestras. Pearl Lang dances the part eloquently but limits
her range of facial expression to looks of bland indignation
and mild distress. Mary Hinkson's interpretation is more
fully intense. Both of them copy Miss Graham closely, and
both are very impressive. Bertram Ross's Orestes is as
trenchant as ever, but in miming Agamemnon's complacent
pride he now comes dangerously close to suggesting fatuity.
In his three pas de deux, Ross Parkes as Aegisthus gives a
lustrous, powerful, and subtle display of male ambition and
animal confidence. Yuriko Kimura as Electra, Takako
Asakawa as Iphigenia, Phyllis Gutelius as Cassandra must
all be praised, and it was exciting to discover how swiftly, in
successive performances, the new members of the company
increased their command of the style. A word, too, for the
instrumentalists' playing, under Stanley Sussman, of the
very effective, incantatory, obsessive yet undomineering
score by Halim El-Dabh.

There are two new works by Miss Graham in the
repertory. *Myth of a Voyage*, like *Circe* of 1963, deals with
Ulysses, and is one of her few ballets with a male
protagonist. Circe's animals reappear. Bertram Ross is once
again Ulysses. The music is again by Alan Hovhaness. But
where *Circe* explored one episode, of perilous, graceful
seductions, the new work includes Calypso and Nausicaä as
well. Ulysses is accompanied on his wanderings by the

Goddess of Change and by a steady Gray-Eyed One who represents both Athene and the dream of Penelope which lies beneath the luring idylls of his voyage; the adventures end in Ithaca, where Penelope and Ulysses sit quietly beside the loom. The work is an allegory of restlessness ("always roaming with a hungry heart"), of subtle enchantments, and of wisdom won. Ming Cho Lee's set, too fussy for my taste, is dominated by the loom and the bow. Matt Turney, grave and serene, plays Athene-Penelope; Miss Asakawa is the incentive goddess; Miss Kimura, Miss Gutelius, and Miss Hinkson play Calypso, Circe, and Nausicaä. All give memorable performances, as do Mr Ross and the corps of sirens, sailors, and suitors.

Back in 1936, Miss Graham presented a dance suite called *Chronicle*. Her new *Mendicants of Evening* is based on St-John Perse's *Chronique*, sections of which (in Robert Fitzgerald's translation) are recited during the ballet and are shaped in plastic imagery the while by the reciter herself (Marian Seldes), a robed Guide (Matt Turney), and a robed Poet (Bertram Ross), who give a quiet, slow continuity to the sweep of the work. Simultaneously, a series of dancers in kaleidoscopic pas de deux pattern the highly colored surface of the individual lines. *Chronique* is a poem that I find at once confusing and exalting; Miss Graham has not ordered it for me, but she has enhanced the sense of heady exhilaration that comes from Perse's contemplation of the whirl of civilizations and centuries in a moment of mystic stillness—his apostrophe of the Great Age, ending with a throb of acceptance at once passionate and calm. There is a simple, beautiful set by Fangor. David Walker's score is a gentle electronic musing.

In 1967, when last I saw the Graham company, I felt that I was watching a troupe, and an art, in sunset splendor; that a kind of settled, monumental quality had lessened the sharp, quick impact of the tragedies; and that, for example, the Adam and the Stranger of *Embattled Garden* had become slower, fleshier embodiments of the fulgent figures they once were. But any obituary sentiments were felt too soon. The current season is a new dawn, and the company, part veteran, part new, is in gleaming form. So much Graham movement has passed into the lingua franca of contemporary dance that there is a danger that newcomers trained outside her school may flip through her inventions without feeling the motivation behind them. The danger has not altogether been avoided. In *Diversion of Angels* and *Secular Games*, there were moments of fleet, overeasy lyricism that seemed to belong to the Joffrey rather than to the Graham company style—episodes that brought Gerald Arpino's *Sacred Grove on Mount Tamalpais* to mind. Merce Cunningham, Glen Tetley, and Paul Taylor have, in their different ways, eased her idiom while developing it into their own; but Miss Graham's utterances, even in joy, even when she celebrates without shadows the grace and energy of her divine acrobats, are extreme. The tensions and the tautness will surely come, for in the muscles of her dancers, as in those of her audiences, Miss Graham begins to wake ancestral memories; movement becomes thought and emotion in action.

Sir Georg Solti's performance of Act III of *Götterdämmerung*, with the Chicago Symphony, in Carnegie Hall last Wednesday, was greeted with extravagant rapture. The performance had the Solti virtues—vitality, excitement, flawlessly executed and imposing detail—and also what seem to me the Solti failings in Wagner: no long grand line, no lilt in the 9/8 music of the Rhinemaidens, no broad conception of the whole music drama to which all the tremendous passing effects are related. Chicago has a great orchestra, but it did not produce the characteristic Wagner sound (as heard in Dresden, Berlin, or Vienna)—that long-breathed, massive sound which generates its power slowly and then swells out to flood the auditorium. Solti prefers something more resiliently athletic, and in the climaxes of the Funeral March he encouraged his brass to jet forth and cover the strings. His Siegfried and Brünnhilde were Jess Thomas and Helga Dernesch—singers whom nature meant for a Walther and Eva, or Siegmund and Sieglinde, but who have ambitiously tackled the heavily heroic roles. They manage these roles ably enough, but Mr Thomas has paid the price of lyrical freshness and variety of timbre; his Siegfried, like his Tristan, easily becomes monotonous and unresourceful. Miss Dernesch's clear and excellently schooled soprano rang out more freely at the close of this single act than it does when she has the whole long opera to cope with; even so, the warmth and expansiveness of a true Brünnhilde voice were not there. Karen Altman and Donald Gramm sang truly and firmly as the Gibichung siblings. Martti Talvela was a terrific Hagen.

Mahler's Tenth Symphony, left incomplete at his death, in 1911, lay for nearly half a century largely undisturbed. In 1924 the sketches were published in facsimile, and just two movements—the opening Adagio and the "Purgatorio" that starts the second part—were performed; the full awakening came only when Deryck Cooke penetrated the thickets of an autograph difficult to read, prepared a fair copy, and discovered that "what I had deciphered was not a 'might-have-been,' but an 'almost-is,' five full-length movements in various stages of textural completion, but all sufficiently coherent to add up to a magnificent Symphony in F Sharp." Mr Cooke's first "performing version of the sketch" (he has been scrupulous not to call it a "completion" of the symphony), in which a few apparently intractable episodes were omitted, was performed in 1960; four years later, helped by some extra pages of sketch that Alma Mahler had produced, he filled in the missing episodes; the revised score was heard at the London Proms and later recorded by Eugene Ormandy and the Philadelphia Orchestra. "Continued rehearings of the record convinced me that the texture and the orchestration could still be greatly improved"; for five years Mr Cooke has worked at yet a new version, which had its première in London last October. His principal change has been to use fourfold woodwinds (with a fifth clarinet) instead of triple. It is true that Mahler's sketches, insofar as they show instrumentation, show triple woodwinds most of the time, but there are six measures in the Adagio (on the seventh folio of sketch pages, measures 203–208) in which the wind chords are clearly four-part. I looked forward to hearing this new version at the Philadelphia Orchestra's last Philharmonic Hall concert of the season, but was disappointed; the program-book was slipped with a "message to our audiences" in which Mr Ormandy announced that Wyn Morris, who conducted the first performance of the new score, holds the performing rights to it for two years, and that therefore the 1964 version would once again be used.

The Philadelphia performance was flawed by some uncharacteristically out-of-tune wind intonation. (The players may have been disturbed—as was the audience—by a high-pitched whistle, presumably from a light on the blink, that filled the silences of the *Parsifal* Prelude, which opened the concert, and was not fixed during the interval.) In episodes of the first Scherzo the "effect of a rehearsal for the violins and brass alone," which Mr Cooke sought to right in his revision, was again noticeable. Nevertheless, it was moving to experience again this last outpouring of the composer. The despair and horror are keener than in any of his earlier works, but the close is a tenderly passionate affirmative gesture. The construction of the long piece is magnificent. It is a noble work. Good news that the score is to be published.

May 12, 1973

A perceptive—if distinctly severe—account of Solti as a Wagner conductor emerges from Robin Holloway's four articles, "The Problems of Music Drama," in Music and Musicians, April to July 1973 *(Nos. 248–251). On the performing version of Mahler's Tenth Symphony, see Deryck Cooke's article "Mahler's Tenth Symphony" in* The Musical Times, June 1961 *(Volume 102, No. 1420). Mr Cooke's revised edition is to be published by Faber Music; the Ormandy recording of his earlier version is on Columbia M2S 735.*

'Bold and 'Resolute

A history of opera—one that would take in Purcell, Rossini and Bellini, Berlioz, Wagner and Verdi, Benjamin Britten and Samuel Barber, and many lesser men—could be based on the pieces whose plots derive from Shakespeare. In the approaches to the plays, in the kinds of compression and distortion deemed necessary to fit them for the lyric stage, in the proportions of recitative and aria and the shifting balance of monologue, dialogue, and ensemble, and in the increasing importance given to the orchestra the development of opera can be traced. Such a history is, in fact, implicit in the long chapter on Shakespearean opera that Winton Dean contributed to *Shakespeare in Music* (St Martin's Press); during the course of his survey Mr Dean observes that "of all little-known Shakespeare operas Bloch's *Macbeth* most deserves professional revival." Ernest Bloch's *Macbeth* has had several champions, especially in Italy, but few performances since its première, at the Opéra-Comique in 1910. Last week it reached New York, in a production by the Juilliard American Opera Center. Seeing the opera on the stage for the first time confirmed the impression, left by broadcasts, of an ambitious and well-wrought score in which poetic sensibility is wedded to sterling musical craft, but also suggested that the theatrical gait of the drama is too even to catch the fancy of a big public. Seeing it thrice placed me among its champions, for at each successive performance I found it more impressive and interesting.

Bloch was only twenty-four when he began it. *Pelléas* was new, and so was *Tosca*. Although *Boris Godunov* reached the Paris stage after most of *Macbeth* was written, Bloch seems to have known Mussorgsky's score. His Frankfurt and Munich training had also taught him about Wagner; his opera is based on a handful of related leitmotivs that interact and are transformed in a way to show lessons from *The Ring* thoroughly learned. Those are the main influences on the work of an original young musician whose fluctuating meters and disturbed harmonies are without obvious precedent. No system but, rather, a spontaneous musical response to the tensions of any situation seems to prompt his innovations. In the first finale—after the discovery of Duncan's murder—a hundredfold alternation between the notes B-flat and B pounds relentlessly through ever-shifting meters, harmonies, and vocal textures. Dissonances result from traditional harmony not so much enriched, Puccini fashion, as rent by opposed forces; then dramatic and harmonic resolutions coincide. The vocal lines are declamatory, not patterned into lyrical periods. Words are not repeated. There are dialogues, but no duets in which characters sing together; the Witches and the crowds provide the only ensembles. Edmond Fleg's libretto reshapes the play in a prologue and then three acts of two scenes each. Almost all Shakespeare's events are here, but Macbeth's visit to the cavern, with its warning of "Beware Macduff," follows the murder of Macduff's family instead of prompting it, and the Second Apparition's equivocal reas-

surance, "None of woman born shall harm Macbeth," is
omitted. Each act ends with a chorus, though to the first
finale there is appended a brief, quiet solo coda, the Old
Man's "Threescore and ten I can remember well . . . but
this sore night hath trifled former knowings." (The effect
recalls that of the Simpleton's song in *Boris*.) "In *Macbeth*,"
wrote Bloch, "the essential thing is the psychology of the
characters; I based my work passionately on this in my
musical conception." His drama is an exploration of
motives, in both senses of that word. The musical images for
ambition (the "imperial theme"), remorse, innate nobility,
evil, and the rest of it (but labeling them oversimplifies the
composer's subtle, unschematic procedures) weave through
the numerous monologues, and form the substance of three
imposing orchestral interludes that are far more than mere
scene-changing music.

It is very surprising that, after so resolute and masterly a
start, Bloch wrote no more operas. Was he, perhaps,
dissatisfied with the circumstances in which operas get
done? (The Paris première, according to his daughter,
involved "all sorts of upheavals and intrigues," while over
the tardy second production, in Naples in 1938, Hitler's
impending visit to Italy cast an anti-Semitic shadow.) Did
he despair of touching audiences that, as he noted bitterly,
"wanted pretty melodies!!!"? Or was he dissatisfied with his
command of the medium? If so, needlessly; there is nothing
wrong with this *Macbeth* that experience would not have put
right; moreover, some of the faults observable at the
Juilliard presentation were introduced by the particular
execution. To reach a just assessment, it was necessary to see
and hear "through" that production to the work as Bloch
wrote it and fill in what was missing. For one thing, the long
opera was reduced to less than two hours of music, and its
three acts were collapsed into two. We lost, as did the
Neapolitans in 1938, Act II, Scene 2—the murder of

Macduff's family, his grief, and the rallying of the forces
against Macbeth. A new, alternative bridge passage in the
second edition of the vocal score may suggest that Bloch
sanctioned the cut, but it is not a happy one: the episode for
Lady Macduff and her prattling son is of great beauty, and
a brief and necessary idyll amid the terrors; besides, the
scene as a whole is the only one in the opera not dominated
by Macbeth. The extra weight thrown on the protagonist by
its removal may have dictated other cuts, yet more grievous:
Macbeth's "Now o'er the one half-world Nature seems
dead" (the second part of his "Is this a dagger?" speech); his
"Light thickens"; his "But let the frame of things disjoint
. . . Duncan is in his grave; After life's fitful fever he sleeps
well" (Bloch divided Shakespeare's Act III, Scene 2, into a
monologue before the banquet and a dialogue with Lady
Macbeth after it); and the Show of Kings, with Macbeth's
awed commentary. Thus the recurrent sleep/death imagery, stressed by Bloch as it was by Shakespeare, was
diminished; the reflective aspect of the hero was underrep-
resented; and the careful preparation, both musical and
theatrical, for the final monologue, "Life's but a walking
shadow," which Bloch marked to be sung "as though here
were embodied the philosophic essence of the drama," was
largely removed. This was a pity. Abridgment of long works
is common enough in the full-time professional houses; of a
school performance one expects integrity that puts such
expedient surgery to shame—especially when an unfamiliar
piece is being introduced.

Peter Herman Adler's musical direction was accomplished. The Juilliard Orchestra played well. The young
cast was secure. By the second performance, Macbeth and
his Lady, Lenus Carlson and Hedy Barnsley, were singing
their difficult roles with considerable authority. The acoustics of the Juilliard Theatre are overrated; though it seats
but a thousand, when the pit is open even large voices do

not set the place ringing. The sound is perfectly clear, but a powerful, resonant, and truly focused bass-baritone like Mr Carlson's does not arouse the almost physical enthusiasm that is its due—and such a reaction simply to the sound of a splendid voice is one of the things that an operatic composer quite legitimately counts on. Not one of the operas I have heard at the Juilliard, from Virgil Thomson's *Lord Byron*, last year, onward, has come over quite as strongly as it deserved; acoustics must be in part responsible for the prevalently temperate response to the Center's work, and they should be borne in mind when assessing either singers or the general effect of an opera. Mr Carlson's tone was beautiful. Miss Barnsley's was not, but her utterance was incisive. Both singers pronounced the words distinctly, and did not pull back the tongue and throttle the timbre (as many Americans do when singing in English) on the "r"s of a line like "Reti*r*e we to ou*r* chambe*r*; A little wate*r* clea*r*s us of this deed." The English raised other problems. Bloch composed his opera in French—a clear French naturally declaimed and easily followed on the contours and rhythmic stresses of his vocal line. On this line he and Alex Cohen (first chairman of the Ernest Bloch Society) later sought to reimpose Shakespeare, adjusting sometimes the notes, sometimes the Bard. A few examples will show what happened. First, misaccentuation: the Third Witch's "Un jour tu seras *Roi!*" (my italics indicate musical emphasis), for which fitting English would be "One day thou shalt be *King!*," becomes "Thou shalt be King here*after!*" Second, lines hard to follow: the measures to which Lady Macbeth sang "les deux chambellans qui veillent auprès de lui" now carry the words "[so convince] his two chamberlains, that the receipt of reason shall *be* a limbeck only"—a difficult line to follow at the best of times, doubly so as here set. Third, jarring little repetitions: "And yet are *on't, and* yet are on't" (for Banquo's "Et qui pour*tant fou*lent la terre") or

Macbeth's "Out *out*, out *out*, brief candle!" As these quotations show, the result is not quite Shakespeare (anyone who knows the play is jarred by the run of very palpable near misses); and it is not good to perform. What's the answer? To do *Macbeth* in French, I guess, or else boldly translate Fleg's libretto into an unaffected English that sings naturally.

Robert Yodice's big, brooding set and the rich costumes, supervised by Timothy Miller, were handsome. It was a swagger show. (Some company should take over the décor and use it for an *Aroldo*, a *Puritani*, Verdi's or Bloch's *Macbeth*—any opera set in a castle; wasteful if it were to be scrapped after just three showings.) John Houseman's stage direction was plain, decent, not especially sensitive, and in some respects diminishing to the work. The acting lacked intensity. The problem of getting choristers both to sing and to act was evaded by leaving them offstage, electrically amplified, while others mimed. The Witches' voices were similarly piped in by loud-speaker while three mute hags mopped and mowed; and the Apparitions failed to appear. So the supernatural confrontations were tame, not tremendous. (Some admirable singing, though, particularly from the Third Apparition of Lorna Myers—a role created in 1910 by the great Alice Raveau.) The staging, like the cutting, reduced contrasts, and emphasized that evenness of gait noted above. All the same, the production was a signal achievement. If Bloch's *Macbeth* did not come at us with full force, we could easily deduce what that full force might be.

Of the Philharmonic concerts I heard this season, the last—devoted to that Victorian favorite Dvořák's *Stabat Mater*—was, in point of execution, the most rewarding. For Rafael Kubelik the orchestra played with its closest approach to warmth and beauty of tone and passionate

intensity of phrasing. Kubelik, while retaining his freshness
and vitality, has matured into a conductor whose command
is broad and serene. The combination of free, flowing, and
stylishly ample rubato with vigilant attention to finesses—
the dotted rhythms were keenly articulated—removed any
staleness from a work whose sequences sound too comfort-
ably dolorous if the detail grows blunt. The Camerata
Singers were in good voice; the ladies' ethereal murmurs of
"Sancta mater," refrain to the solo bass's "Fac ut ardeat,"
floated out delicate and true, and in the difficultly poised
D-major chords of the close it was the woodwinds, not the
choir, whose intonation had become impure after some
ninety minutes of performance without an interval. In the
solo quartet, Judith Blegen's soprano was flexible, Peter
Schreier's tenor excellently smooth, and Paul Plishka's bass
commanding while also precise. The Inflammatus, however,
calls for a real contralto, both weighty and wieldy, and
Brigitte Fassbaender, a mezzo, was not suited by it.

May 19, 1973

Shakespeare without Words

There can be little dispute that Prokofiev's *Romeo and Juliet* is the most successful full-length ballet score written since Tchaikovsky's. I have seen it set to movement in six different versions, and only one of them—Serge Lifar's, for the Paris Opera—was without marked merit. John Cranko's, created for the Stuttgart Ballet in 1962, and chosen for the opening night, last week, of the company's current Metropolitan season, is a very successful dance drama that has worn well. It continues to display the special virtues and strongly individual character of the troupe for whom it was made, and provides extended, uncommonly telling roles for the major stars—Marcia Haydée, Egon Madsen, and Richard Cragun—that shine in the splendid ensemble. The Royal Ballet, they say, dances best in New York; perhaps the Stuttgarters do so too. I was bowled over on the first night by the power and eloquence of their presentation, and certainly Jürgen Rose's *Romeo* scenery and costumes never look as handsome and striking as they do on the Metropolitan stage. Dramatic force, potent projection, is a mark of German dancing; in Stuttgart, with his international team

of dancers, Mr Cranko has combined this force with Royal
Ballet "school," developed his artists by composing new
works for and "on" them, and created one of the world's
leading companies.

Approaches to a Shakespeare ballet are almost as diverse
as those to a Shakespeare opera. Prokofiev in his *Romeo* score
devised appropriate melodies and motifs for the characters
and their attributes (Juliet as a girl, Juliet as a woman,
Romeo's ardor, Mercutio's wit), wrote movements that
mount to passionate climaxes in the right places, supplied
the necessary (and some unnecessary) ensemble dances, and
achieved all this with his wonted flair for theater music.
Leonid Lavrovsky did the original choreography; his version was first performed, in Leningrad, in 1940. He worked
on the piece with Prokofiev (and once told me how tiresome
and silly the composer had been—wanting, for a while, a
happy ending, not wanting to lose a Dance of Carpet Sellers
that he had somehow managed to bring in). While Prokofiev's "libretto" was, so to speak, the plot, the characters,
and their emotions, the choreographer added a more
detailed attention to Shakespeare; in his version specific
lines from the play seem often to ring out from the motion of
the dancers: Romeo's "O! she doth teach the torches to
burn bright" when first he sees Juliet, his "I do protest I
never injur'd thee" to Tybalt, and then, after Mercutio's
death, "Fire-ey'd fury be my conduct now," Juliet's "My
only love sprung from my only hate," her "Is there no pity
sitting in the clouds?," and many others. By comparison,
Ashton's version for the Royal Danish Ballet, in 1955, to the
same score, was a Lamb's Tale that became lyric poetry in
the duets for the lovers. Kenneth MacMillan's *Romeo* for
Covent Garden, ten years later, borrowed Cranko's solutions to the structural problems set by Prokofiev's ensembles, and acquired its special character from the detailed
concentration on Juliet's development. In the monologues

and duologues of MacMillan's version there is the same sense found in Lavrovsky's of words just below the surface of the dance. The successive quatrains and couplets of the antiphonal sonnet spoken by Romeo and Juliet when first they meet ("If I profane with my unworthiest hand") are transmuted into plastic imagery. Cranko's *Romeo* is more generalized, less intense in its close-ups. We do not follow the balcony and bedroom scenes "line by line"; his approach, like Prokofiev's, is less literary. But the dances do not lack emotion, and they flow effectively. Cranko's presentation of the world around the tragedy—the street scenes, the assembly of Capulet's guests, the ball—is the most successful of all; a theater flair kin to Prokofiev's is apparent in his handling. I miss Juliet's pas de deux with Paris on the wedding morning, a poignant moment in both the Lavrovsky and the MacMillan version; the Friar Laurence scenes are rather skimpy, and Act III passes too swiftly. (Lavrovsky did well to insert a solo for Romeo in Mantua, corresponding to "Is it even so? then I defy you, stars!") Comparisons are helpful in description; in its own right, Cranko's *Romeo* is an excellently vigorous, youthful, unrhetorical yet affecting work, couched in a fluent, eclectic choreography that I suppose could be called free-Fokin with modern ingredients, and very skillful in its theatrical shaping.

The first night presented the nonpareil cast of Miss Haydée and Mr Cragun in the title roles and Mr Madsen as Mercutio. The second brought a new Juliet, the young Joyce Cuoco, touching and vulnerable, a promising actress and fleet technician—prone, in fact, to phrase some of the lyrical choreography too crisply. The Romeo and Mercutio swapped roles: Mr Madsen now made a courteous, romantic Romeo, rather less boldly ardent than Mr Cragun had been, while as Mercutio Mr Cragun lacked only the twinkling beats with which Mr Madsen had tripped

through the Queen Mab solo. Jan Stripling's cold, strong
Tybalt, the contrasted interpretations of Paris from Reid
Anderson (a formal wooer) and Vladimir Klos (more
tender), and Andrew Oxenham's bright Benvolio deserve
mention; so do the unforced buoyancy, verve, and warmth
with which the whole company took the stage.

The first of the four Composers' Showcase concerts at the
Whitney Museum was made of three works for large
ensemble (or small orchestra; thirty-nine of New York's
crack free-lance players had been assembled to cover the
varying instrumental requirements) which had been commissioned to celebrate the twentieth anniversary, last year,
of the Fromm Music Foundation. Good planning brought
together three worthwhile pieces similar in scale yet distinct
in character, and—since these were not first performances—
reflected the Foundation's concern that a composer so often
goes now from première to première lacking not commissions but the deuxièmes and troisièmes to establish his work.
In Mr Fromm's words, "New York knows one piece,
Tanglewood another, and maybe Chicago or Los Angeles
still another. . . . In a reversal of our former policy, we are
now planning to support additional performances of already
existing scores rather than devoting ourselves exclusively to
commissioning." Two of the pieces, Bruno Maderna's
Giardino religioso and Gunther Schuller's *Tre invenzioni*, were
first played at the Berkshire Music Festival, last year; Roger
Sessions' Concertino was first done in Chicago.

For the Maderna the players are set out in a symmetrical
pattern—pianos and percussions scrummed at the center,
horns as halfbacks, and trumpets on the wings. The
conductor is a kind of referee, who directs play not only
with his baton but also with signals on bongo and triangle.
Giardino religioso is one of those pieces built from sounds

rather than themes—wave of timbre lapping upon wave, a
pitter-patter scurrying from place to place, soft-shimmering
webs of indistinct tone, and tiny fanfares from muted
trumpets which recall the sound-world of Debussy's *Fêtes*.
Presumably the piece has a "program," but none was
disclosed on a program-sheet limited to bare titles. Schuller's *Inventions* also involve a spatial disposition of the players
as an element in the music. The ensemble for this work
consists of five quintets: high woodwinds to the conductor's
left; trumpets and trombones to his right; behind those,
respectively, low woodwinds and a mellow quintet of two
horns, flügelhorn, baritone (the instrument, not the voice),
and tuba; and then, center-back, a cluster of keyboards
(glockenspiel, celesta, harpsichord, and piano) and harp.
They should be "as widely separated as possible without
losing contact and jeopardizing ensemble"; in the resonant
Whitney room not much separation, either physical or
acoustic, was possible, but enough to give the idea. The first
Invention is largely an interplay of lines and notes tossed from
quintet to quintet. The second is a densely scored, somber
chorale that rises from the depths to a shrill scream on the
piccolo, and then subsides. The third is a toccata in varied
tempos, including reminiscences of the other movements
and "breaks" for various soloists. Set between these two
works, which are based, in large part, on the exploration of
timbres in space, Sessions' Concertino, for twenty players,
made a positively neoclassic effect. Its three movements are
cast in the traditional, and satisfying, pattern of an allegro,
a lyrical slow movement (*lento molto*), and a scherzo-finale
(*molto vivo*). It is concerned with themes and their developments. There are long-breathed melodies. (The start of the
slow movement, balanced poetic periods for contrabassoon
and alto flute, is particularly memorable.) The outer
movements, energetic and purposive, contain many lively,
engaging solo utterances, as the concertino role passes from

one department to another. On paper the piece looks complicated, with its frequent metrical shifts; the ear accepts it without question as a cogent, distinguished, and finely wrought stretch of musical discourse. This Concertino is a work that may well deserve a place in the staple small-orchestra repertory; its almost Haydnesque compound of science and wit should bear repeated hearing.

Gunther Schuller conducted, and his direction of the three pieces was very sure. As far as the music and its execution were concerned, this was a concert on a high level. It did not offer the added attractions to be found at a museum concert in, say, the Phillips Collection, in Washington, where there is food to be had and there are pictures to be seen. The Whitney Museum was less hospitable; its restaurant was closed, and so were the galleries (no chance to peek at the Winslow Homer show during the intermission). But then, once off Lincoln Center Plaza or away from Carnegie Hall, New Yorkers accept Spartan conditions of concertgoing, and do not even expect that there should be somewhere to meet, drink, and eat, somewhere agreeable to walk and talk. Hunter College, the McMillin Auditorium of Columbia University, Whitman Hall at Brooklyn College, Carnegie Recital Hall, the Juilliard Theatre, the Guggenheim and Cultural Center auditoriums—all have their various rigors, surprising to a foreigner and unhelpful, surely, in attracting audiences.

Town Hall, in its six-o'clock Encore series, contrives a jollier ambience, with a fake-French décor rigged up in the foyer (the concerts are presented jointly by the Hall and Dubonnet) and a busy bar. The programs are planned frankly for pleasure. Patricia Brooks and Alan Titus, who gave the second recital in the series, drew on the repertoires of Lotte Lehmann and John Charles Thomas. Mme

Lehmann in her treatise on *More Than Singing* limned the arts of winning an audience by deportment, gesture, and glance; Miss Brooks commands them. On a less relaxed occasion, one might have found her wreathed smiles or—to set the mood for *Gretchen am Spinnrade*—her eyes' sad, leaden downward cast a bit much; I remembered a wicked imitation that Elena Gerhardt, the greatest of lieder stylists, used to give of the comic and tragic masks that the features of Lula Mysz-Gmeiner, another great lieder singer, would assume in rapid succession during the first line of Schubert's *Lachen und Weinen.* But Miss Brooks proved thoroughly beguiling, not dull for an instant. Her timbre in soft middle ranges is attractive, and she threaded it, with gentle, subtle care and expert breath control, through Schubert, Schumann, and Marietta's Lute Song from Korngold's *Tote Stadt.* In climaxes the sound was less agreeable. Mr Titus is a charmer, and knows it. He sang Ravel, Poulenc, Warlock, and Rossini with a bonny beam—yet also with a delicacy and refined attention to word, accent, and tone which suggest he may mature into a very considerable artist. English text epitomes were provided, and—a sign that someone had thought about presentation—lights that were dipped during the purely instrumental items (there was a third artist sharing the bill, the pianist Abbey Simon) were brought up to reading level during the songs. After the intermission, there was Wolf, and operetta duets; I wanted to stay—but that would have meant missing Virgil Thomson's brilliant, acute, and salutary address on music criticism, up at the Manhattan School of Music. Mr Thomson was well worth hearing; he remains the master of us all.

Renata Scotto is a singer who has pleased me ever since she came to London, unheralded, in 1956 and, with an Italian tour troupe, sang in quick succession Mimì, Violetta,

Adina, Lucia, and Donna Elvira. The voice was fresh, true, and flexible; all her musical instincts were right, and the personality was winning. Nine years later, a bewitching Butterfly, she reached the Metropolitan. In the later 1960s, she entered a period of affectations, when onto the dear little Miss Muffet appearance there was grafted a set of absurdly regal gestures, when pianissimi were finespun into inaudibility, and when, in quest of "expression," rhythms were distorted to the point of dismemberment. But she has come out of it. As Miss Scotto puts it, "I mature in the head and in my studying"—and she has emerged as an artist with very definite convictions about what she can and should do. Her Carnegie Hall recital, last week, was devoted to Rossini: his *Soirées musicales* complete, with good supporting artists for the duets; that captivating little cycle *La regata veneziana*; and arias from *Armida* and *Le Siège de Corinthe*. Delectable music. Miss Scotto has devised a platform manner all her own, which involves raising now one dimpled finger to emphasize a point, and now arms and eyes to heaven. It would not do for Wolf, but it serves well for Rossini, and was all of a piece with interpretations that had been carefully considered. By classical standards, Miss Scotto's technique is faulty: her trill is indistinct; sustained notes diminished from forte to piano are apt to crack on the way; most serious, F-sharp and G at the top of the staff, at mezzo-forte and above, can be scorchers, and on this occasion they generally were. But who, except a few record collectors who listen to Melba and know what perfect vocal equipment can be, gives a hang for such standards today? Once Miss Scotto had got through the first few numbers, which were flawed by coarse, violent, and tonally strident accents, fully seven-eighths of her singing was beautiful— and that is much. Soft phrases were supply molded. Merry phrases were bouncy and accurate. Anzoleta's excitement during the central *Regata* song was irresistibly appealing. John Wustman accompanied; in some of Rossini's trickier passages he sounded as if he had not practiced quite hard enough.

May 26, 1973

Proper Bostonian

When I want to hear good opera," said Maria Theresa
after Haydn's troupe had put on *L'infedeltà delusa* and
Philemon und Baucis in her honor, "I go to Esterház." New
Yorkers can be heard declaring that when they want to
hear good opera they go to Boston—where Sarah Caldwell
directs performances uncommonly satisfying to anyone who
believes that opera should be more than a vocal display
amid lavish scenery. Verdi's grand opera *Don Carlos*—of
which the Opera Company of Boston has just given, in a
sense to be defined below, the world première—is a piece
that calls for the Caldwell approach. The composer himself
said that the best singers and players in the world could not
do it justice unless there was also first-rate direction, and
"an ensemble, a whole." "One superior intelligence," he
declared, "must be in charge of the costumes, the scenery,
the props, the staging, etc.—quite apart from the exceptional musical interpretation that is required." He had been
reading Wagner; he believed, with some justice, that in *Don
Carlos* he, too, had created a new kind of opera that should
be performed as a *Gesamtkunstwerk*. Or as Giuseppina Verdi

put it, "A magnificent voice, a sublime artist are not enough to make a contemporary *opera-poema* understood in all its aspects. You need an ensemble. The singing, the playing, the acting, the costumes, the staging—all these are elements in the ensemble."

Now, Boston is not Bayreuth. For one thing, it has no fit theater for opera. (The famous Opera House was torn down, to make way for a parking lot, in 1957; and the Back Bay Theatre, which housed Miss Caldwell's company for four seasons and saw the American premières of Schoenberg's *Moses und Aron* and Luigi Nono's *Intolleranza*, and Mussorgsky's *Boris Godunov* without Rimsky-Korsakov's revisions, was demolished in 1968.) The Opera Company of Boston at present perches in the Orpheum, which is an ingeniously designed and pretty building but has only a small stage, little wing space, and no real pit for the full orchestra, which must spill out into the house. So not all the elements of the *Carlos* ensemble could be provided. The opera was commissioned to be the great glittering showpiece at the Paris Opera in 1867, the year of Napoleon III's Universal Exhibition. Verdi himself, when he received the commission and a prose outline of the libretto, suggested that the spectacular content should be increased, and it was. *Carlos* calls for elaborate processions, multiple choruses, stage bands on the grandest possible scale. Verdi's intention was plain: to give a new nobility and purpose to grand opera; to unite what was best about the Meyerbeer manner, with its enormous sonic and visual paraphernalia, and his own ideas about character and dramatic impact and what he called warmth. Even the obligatory Paris ballet played a necessary, not an irrelevant, role. "It's a long opera, I know," Verdi wrote. "But it has to be. It's not a question of showing off the voices, or allowing time for a ballerina to display her legs." For St Petersburg, Verdi had written *La forza del destino*, on a very large scale. Now he set out to show

Paris—where Meyerbeer's *L'Africaine* had been the previous
"spectacular"—what elevated grand opera could be. A
libretto drawn from Schiller's play *Don Carlos* provided an
ideal subject. It proclaimed themes dear to the composer:
his love of individual and national liberty, his detestation of
political and ecclesiastical tyranny. And it was "warmed"
by the individual predicaments of five interesting and
contrasted characters, enmeshed in a web of Church and
State, where their actions affect not only one another but
also the fates of three nations. Public and personal destinies
interact, and the titular hero is the common point of three
emotional triangles: Elisabeth and Eboli both love Carlos;
Philip and Carlos both love Elisabeth; and Philip and
Carlos both love Posa.

In a program-note for the Boston performance, Miss
Caldwell observed that while "it would be ridiculous to
pretend to match the scope of the spectacle for which the
Paris Opera was so famous . . . we believe we can produce
the work with musical and dramatic integrity." Her scenery
was borrowed from San Antonio; designed, by Donald
Oenslager, for a much larger stage, it looked coarse in the
Orpheum. The costumes, borrowed from San Francisco,
looked handsome. With her wonted genius, Miss Caldwell
made the most of her resources. In any case, spectacle,
though important to *Carlos*, is not what matters most. In
Paris in 1867 no expense was spared, and the rehearsals
lasted six months, but Verdi found the results cold, and he
was soon contrasting spirited, fiery Italian productions,
achieved after only a few weeks' preparation, with that
lackluster première on which so much time and so many
thousands of francs had been lavished. The Boston *Carlos*
bore signs of inadequate rehearsal time and of last-minute
improvisation, and the massive effects could only be suggested, but the presentation was spirited, fiery, and sensitive,
and it was directed by "one superior intelligence"—Miss

Caldwell was both producer and conductor—which insured a vivid, stirring, and very beautiful interpretation of the opera.

It was also the first production of the opera that Verdi originally conceived and composed—so long and so ambitious a work that it had to be shortened before the Paris première. Three whole numbers—the prelude and opening chorus, a duet for Elisabeth and Eboli (before "O don fatal"), and a duet for Carlos and Philip (after the death of Posa)—and three substantial mid-scene episodes were removed. The relevant pages were cut bodily from the autograph and also (apart from one passage) from the conducting copy of *Carlos* used at the première. They remained unpublished and, until 1969, unknown. Now, at this point I should, as they say, "declare an interest"— scholarly if not financial. At a Verdi congress in Verona, the musicologist David Rosen produced the missing section of the Philip-Posa duet, which he had found folded down in the conducting copy. Spurred by his revelation, when I was next in Paris I examined the 1867 performance material, still in the Opera Library, and discovered that, line by line, it was possible to reconstruct the rest of the "lost" music, for in the individual parts the unperformed passages had been not cut away but merely pasted, pinned, or stitched down. It was exciting to see page after page of music by the mature Verdi taking shape as I copied. It was exciting, in Boston, to hear this music in the theater. Some excerpts had previously been given in concert form, and the BBC has prepared a full recording, due to be broadcast soon, but Miss Caldwell is the first to put the "complete" opera to the test of a theater performance. (Well, very nearly complete. Though Boston restored what Paris had cut, the ballet *La Pérégrina* was omitted. A pity; it plays its part in the formal scheme of things. Perhaps next time? As it was, a show that began soon after seven ran until a quarter to twelve. There were

just two short intervals.) Lest a critic be thought to be
reviewing his own work, let me add quickly that Miss
Caldwell and her colleague Osbourne McConathy prepared their own edition afresh from the Paris materials. To
be precise, just twelve measures of my contriving (a missing
harp accompaniment in the Elisabeth-Eboli duet) found
their way into the Boston text—and very timid and feeble
they sounded!

Quite apart from the "new" passages, this was an
unfamiliar version of *Don Carlos*. What we usually hear is a
revised and abridged four-act score that Verdi (still working
in French) made in 1882-83—sometimes prefaced, and
sometimes not, by the original, unrevised Act I, set in
Fontainebleau—and we generally hear it sung in a poor
Italian translation. As far as I know, the 1867 Paris score,
even as cut before the première, has not previously been
revived in our century. And, of course, the "unknown"
passages can be restored only to this earlier Paris score; they
do not fit the revision—one of whose purposes, in fact, was
to reinstate, in the form of dramatic dialogue, vital theatrical points that had disappeared when the pages were cut
from the autograph. I apologize for all these textual notes.
But *Don Carlos* is a long, complicated opera with a long,
complicated history, and before discussing any performance
of it one must at least establish what was performed. So, to
sum up, the Boston company gave, in the original French,
and uncut (except for the ballet), the first performance,
ever, of the immense opera that Verdi prepared in 1867;
and in doing so it opened a new chapter in the stage history
of the piece.

Miss Caldwell's direction showed a masterly command of
the long, linked themes running through this expansive
drama. She held it together, while illumining the passing
moments of emotion with many vivid touches, both dramatic and musical. On the first night, though the details

were vivid from the start, it took her a little time to find that sense of "basic pulse" which seems to keep all the individual tempi in just relationship. It arrived in Act III, when the great ensemble launched by the plea of Flemish deputies proved overwhelming, despite the relatively small forces at hand. And thereafter everything was magnificently done. In Act III, Carlos's public life reaches its climax; the following scene, the only one in which Carlos does not appear, and the only one without chorus, is a series of private crises. In superb fashion, Miss Caldwell handled the long sequence of Philip's monologue, his tremendous interview with the Grand Inquisitor; his confrontation with Elisabeth; the quartet; the duet between the women, alternately tense and tender; and, finally, "O don fatal." The full shape of Act IV, Scene 2, was likewise revealed for the first time: after the death of Posa, a long, elegiac duet (Verdi reused the theme later for the "Lacrimosa" of his Requiem), in which Philip mourns his only friend and Carlos prays for strength, and then the popular rising, with Eboli at the head of the insurgents, quelled by the appearance of the Grand Inquisitor. The action at the very end of the opera—the Emperor Charles V (alive? dead?) emerges from the gates of his tomb and draws his grandson Carlos into the cloister—presents a problem that Verdi himself never solved to his own satisfaction. There is one simple way of making "sense" of the scene without alteration to the music: assume that Charles V is alive (in history, he did retire into a monastery, after celebrating his own obsequies), and that Carlos dies. In a working draft of the libretto, preserved in Verdi's villa of Sant'Agata, the composer actually penciled in the line "L'Infant Carlos est mort! Priez pour lui!" though he did not set it to music. Miss Caldwell's solution was an on-the-spot execution of Carlos by the Inquisition soldiers— an impossible proceeding in so sacred a place.

There was a good cast. Best of all was the Philip of

Donald Gramm—a marvelously intelligent, subtle, and powerful interpretation, never just boomed out but vocally imposing where necessary, profoundly affecting in the monologue, and always quick to convey the nuances of text and musical phrase. The Elisabeth and Eboli, Édith Tremblay and Michèle Vilma, were making American débuts. Miss Tremblay is a young Canadian lyric soprano of exquisite, delicate timbre. Though her voice does not have the weight and richness of tone usually associated with the role, its purity, freshness, and steadiness insure that it carries effortlessly, while her feeling for attack and portamento, her sensitive, instinctively graceful shaping of the phrases, suggest that she was trained in an older and more refined school than most Elisabeths of our day. Her singing represented the nearest thing I have heard in life to the kind of art represented on records by Graziella Pareto and Eidé Noréna. As an actress, Miss Tremblay lacks passion, as yet, but she is beautiful, both dignified and touching in demeanor; her features lit into joy in the duets of Act I. Miss Vilma is a very accomplished, very "professional" French mezzo, with a flash in the personality that made her an uncommonly vivacious, sparkly, spunky Eboli. The Veil Song was brilliantly achieved—the voices of King Achmet and of the veiled beauty wittily characterized, the "Moorish" cadenzas bubbling out of the situation. Her *lionne blessée* of Act III was formidable. And with a passionate "O don fatal" Miss Vilma brought the house down. It is not a great voice, but her expert use of it, her big, lively eyes, and her general air of chic assurance carried the day. At the Paris première, Verdi risked a young, untried tenor, Morère, in the title role. Miss Caldwell played safe by engaging John Alexander, who was absolutely reliable but a bit of a stick. William Dooley's baritone has the right sort of thrust for Posa, that ardent young idealist, but it was not in good shape—uneven and sometimes untrue of pitch—on the first night; he had been fighting a cold.

And the effect of the whole? I thought it was tremendous. When Verdi revised *Don Carlos*, in 1882, *Otello* was already germinant; in fact, the recomposed episodes can be viewed as preparatory studies in his terse, taut-muscled *Otello* style. So the revised, abridged score, part new and part old, is inconsistent. Moreover, when Verdi "stripped the first section of the Carlos-Posa duet of everything that is purely musical, and kept just what is necessary for the action," he did not improve the number; what he left needs to be balanced by what was lost. He declared that the four-act version was "more practicable and, I guess, maybe also better from an artistic point of view." And, I guess, maybe we should agree with him. But the extensive, abundant five-act *Carlos* of 1867, before surgery, is a masterpiece of its kind and also well worth performing from time to time. When Verdi reworked the scene between Philip and Posa, he made it still more powerful—but the original version is in its own right very strong and very beautiful. The two "lost" duets deepen the character-drawing of the two women and of the King. In the revised *Carlos*, sentiments are less generously expressed; the lyrical appeal to our emotions is less open. Posa's unrestrained, almost effusive death scene, which was not altered, is characteristic of the earlier manner—and who would not listen gladly to more music in that vein? There was no reason to conclude that any of the composer's preperformance cuts had been prompted by artistic considerations, or for any purpose other than the need to shorten the running time.

Lastly, on the question of language I see little room for argument. Fine musical points and fine dramatic points are blunted by the Italian translation, and there is no good reason, outside Italy, for ever using it again; *Don Carlo*—

and, for that matter, *I vespri siciliani*—should go the way of *Il flauto magico*, *I maestri cantori*, and *Gli Ugonotti*. No one hearing this Boston *Don Carlos* could doubt that the opera sounds keener and more beautiful in the original tongue.

June 2, 1973

An account of the Don Carlos *"discoveries" appears in my "The Making of* Don Carlos*" in* Proceedings of the Royal Musical Association *98 (1971–72), and in Ursula Günther's "La Genèse de* Don Carlos*" in* Revue de musicologie *Volume 58, No. 1 (1972). For the problems of staging the final scene, see my "*Don Carlos *and the Monk-Emperor" in* Musical Newsletter *Volume 2, No. 4 (October 1972).*

Swan Upping

There is no closed season on Swan Lake. Because few people can read Stepanov's ballet notation; because the choreographic text by Marius Petipa and Lev Ivanov, the third attempt at making a stage success of Tchaikovsky's score, involved musical alterations to the original and the participation of Riccardo Drigo; and because, as Brendan Gill was saying the other day, man is a meddler who feels irresistibly tempted to tamper with things, the Tchaikovsky-Petipa-Ivanov *Swan Lake* has long been regarded as fair game by ambitious choreographers. Last month, the Metropolitan housed two different productions of the work, by the National Ballet of Canada and the Stuttgart Ballet, in which the poor birds were harried unmannerly through unfamiliar paces. The familiar, beautiful paces were set by Petipa and Ivanov in St Petersburg in 1895; Nicholas Sergeyev brought them to London in 1934, and although Londoners meddled with them, they are restored in the Royal Ballet's latest production. They survive, too, in the American Ballet Theatre's presentation of the piece, and survive in black-and-white in the Harvard Theatre Collection, where Sergeyev's choreographic scores in Stepanov notation have come to rest.

The first two shots at *Swan Lake*—Julius Reisinger's in 1877 and Emil Hansen's in 1880, both for Moscow's Bolshoy Theatre—missed the mark. Then, for the Maryinsky Theatre, in St Petersburg, Petipa devised the carefree dance suite of Act I and the glittering formal ceremonies and national divertissements of Act III, while Ivanov, his assistant, composed the more lyrical, "symphonic" Acts II and IV. The contrasted styles reflected a drama concerned with a romantic dream and a glittering delusion—and on another level they compounded a great role for the ballerina who is the heroine of both. Petipa's contribution passes in daylight and then beneath the blaze of chandeliers; Ivanov's elegiac acts are soft-lit by the moon. Why should anyone wish to alter what they made so well? Some answers are suggested above, and for another we must consider the story.

Swan Lake is about a prince, Siegfried, who falls in love with a maiden, Odette, whom the sorcerer Rothbart has transformed to swan shape during the hours of day. His spell can be broken only by a vow of faithful love. On the moonlit lakeshore, Siegfried swears to be true; day dawns, and Odette becomes a swan again. At a ball that evening, the Prince rejects all the suitable matches his mother parades before him, and plights his troth to Odile, the sorcerer's daughter, who is indistinguishable in appearance from Odette. He has broken his vow. Back by the lake, he joins Odette in a suicide by drowning; in a final tableau, we see them reunited in a Kingdom Beneath the Waves. This German romantic tale, with its echoes of *The Flying Dutchman* and of *Lohengrin*, can obviously be made to yield many kinds of allegorical meaning. One might imagine a version in which Siegfried is a fundamentally good fellow caught up in a society with a false sense of values. In Act II,

he finds in Odette a symbol of higher ideals struggling to
escape from Rothbart's oppression. In Act III, by clever
distortion, the ideals are made for a while to seem reconcil-
able with the corrupt materialism of the court, until
Siegfried discovers the fraud, comes to self-knowledge, and,
in Act IV, joins his Odette in the fight for truth and a better
world—leaders together of an underground resistance. This
was not exactly the version danced by the Bolshoy Ballet
when first it came West from Moscow, in 1956, but the
company did charge *Swan Lake* with its special qualities of
fierce emotional projection, passionate involvement in the
action, and very clear definition of character. The Moscow
way with the classics is to galvanize them into life by a bold,
gleaming, flamboyantly dramatic approach to the dance.
Petipa-Ivanov was hotted up in Act III by the revisions of
Alexander Gorsky and emotionalized in Act IV by the new
choreography of Asaf Messerer. At the close, Siegfried
fought the sorcerer and triumphed. The Bolshoy *Swan Lake*
was a heroic drama in which courageous youth overthrew
the old tyranny. Meanwhile, in Leningrad, the Kirov
company adopted a very different approach. Giving but a
token nod now and again to the narrative, and performing
in neutral, unemphatic décor, the dancers ignored acting,
ignored blazing dramatics, ignored spectacle, and concentrated on lyrical dancing purely executed in all its glory.
They preserved what Fokin had revolted against, and what
Balanchine has also preserved—classical dance-in-itself, in
which the plastic imagery carries all the "expression," as
opposed to the more openly vivid emotionalism of dance
drama. Another influential production of *Swan Lake* was
Vladimir Bourmeister's, first seen at the Stanislavsky and
Nemirovich-Danchenko Lyric Theatre, in Moscow, in 1953.
Bourmeister went back to Tchaikovsky's original score,
before Petipa and Ivanov had adapted it, and he concentrated on telling the story in as theatrical a way as possible.

From these varied versions, all of which have traveled widely, and from their derivatives depend the numerous modern workings and reworkings of the piece.

The Canadian *Swan Lake* is by Erik Bruhn, and is about a young man whose sex life is in a muddle, chiefly because he cannot decide whether his mother is a kindly, maternal body, just a little tiresome in her insistence that he should settle down and get married (something he has no taste for), or whether she is really a dazzling, glamorous creature who can bring him every kind of happiness if only he will obey her wishes. In this production, Rothbart is replaced by a Black Queen, an alternate image of the White Queen who is Siegfried's official mother. At the end, Pseudo-Mother turns nasty, the swan maidens become maenads, and Siegfried, Orpheus-like, meets his death. It is all a bit of a muddle, in fact, made more so by the scraps of original choreography, the dances borrowed from the Bolshoy, and the two pas de deux by Nureyev that have gone into it. When the ballet was first done, in Toronto, there was a certain odd fascination in watching the Freudian plight threaded through the familiar tale; it was perverse but curious. Now, played less boldly, in calmer, more conventional accents, it seems merely wrongheaded. Mr Bruhn's ensemble inventions, especially the waltz of Act I, are neat and clearly laid out; his opening sequence left a fresh, clean, "Danish" impression; he is a decent but unremarkable choreographer with an honest sense of style.

John Cranko's version of *Swan Lake*, for the Stuttgart company, rouses stronger but contradictory feelings. On one hand, Mr Cranko must be praised for having devised a production that shows off his dancers at their most spirited and, as only choreography done "on" particular artists can, inspires them to new achievement. The show opens buoyantly and maintains a pretty flashing level. In tone, it follows the Moscow line, and aims at limning characters and telling a story—one, however, that ends unhappily, with the Siegfried drowned and the Swan awaiting the arrival of the next prince. There are some ingenious innovations: the national dances of Act III are assigned to the four prospective brides; Siegfried is no princeling but heir to an obviously important throne, perhaps that of Bavaria (there is sumptuous décor by Jürgen Rose), and much depends on his marriage. So far so good—apart from schoolboy larks like a first entrance for Siegfried cribbed from Rossini's *Comte Ory* and a dreadful stage-comic of a tutor. On the other hand, there is the choreography to consider. Mr Cranko notes that "I have tried to base my own work on the classic/romantic style of Petipa, working freely and in my own manner." For much but not all of Act II, Ivanov has been retained. Elsewhere, the classical style has been not enriched but sullied by cheap additives suggestive of ballroom adagio dancing or of ice-skating. Mr Cranko shows no sure command of Petipa grammar or Petipa geometry; he commits solecisms in almost every sentence. He becomes a choreographic Mrs Malaprop whose derangement of etiquettes is far from nice. This is flashy "classicism" for the masses, and on that level it is effective—and preferable to correct but lifeless classical pastiche. The company danced with verve. Both Marcia Haydée and Birgit Keil gave expert performances of Odette and Odile. On the first night, Egon Madsen, as Siegfried, showed surprising technical weaknesses in inventions that need a "Russian back" to carry them through; Richard Cragun in the role proved stronger. In the pas de six that Mr Cranko has composed for Act I, and as the Princess of Naples in Act III, Joyce Cuoco's virtuoso balance while turning drew gasps of astonishment. During the Black Swan pas de deux of Act III, Odile dances her variation to Siegfried's traditional music. The spatchcocking in of other music for Siegfried and the latching together of Odile's

entrance music and the pas de deux produce some horrid
wrenches of key; and the waltz of this act is barbarously
broken up into sixteen-measure periods by intrusive fanfares. Tchaikovsky's Elegy for Strings, composed in 1884
and later incorporated into his *Hamlet* music, has been
added to the score of the last act, where it lies uneasily
among numbers more regularly patterned for dance.

Mr Cranko's *Eugene Onegin* raises fewer questions. It is a
fluent, successful dance drama, freely choreographed in the
Soviet manner and consistent in idiom, and it exhibits his
flairs for telling a story in dance, for communicating
emotions, and for pacing numbers and placing climaxes to
maximum theatrical effect. The personal tensions that run
through the social dances at Tatiana's birthday ball are
clearly and effectively portrayed. Pushkin, not Tchaikovsky,
is given as the source, but in fact the dramatization of
Pushkin's verse novel leans heavily on the opera: a similar
organization into scenes (two of Tchaikovsky's are ingeniously made into one) and a similar conversion of the
elegant, gentle satire into lyrical sentiment. Mr Cranko, like
Tchaikovsky, omits the nightmare of Chapter 5, which
could have provided a striking dance episode. The score,
assembled and orchestrated by Kurt-Heinz Stolze, is a
Tchaikovsky anthology (nothing from the opera *Onegin*) of
pieces passionate and pieces decorative that accompany the
drama fitly and, unlike Tchaikovsky's carefully architected
ballet scores, make no style demands of their own. The
lovely Miss Haydée was direct, affecting, and eloquent in
every line as Tatiana; Miss Keil was charmingly merry,
then sad, as Olga; Mr Madsen made a romantically
vulnerable Lensky. Heinz Clauss's Onegin was suitably
moody and stern—it was Mr Cranko's lapse into under-
lining that made him, at the country ball, not merely bored
and haughty but positively boorish, in a way Pushkin's hero
could never have been.

To see what classical choreography can and should be, one had only to cross the plaza to the State Theater, where in the new *Cortège hongrois* Balanchine paid his latest tribute to Petipa's *Raymonda* and at the same time honored Melissa Hayden on her retirement from the New York City Ballet. The score of *Cortège* is drawn mainly from the Hungarian divertissements that end the Petipa-Glazunov ballet, but the Grande Valse from Act I is also included. There are sixteen "national" and sixteen "classical" dancers, plus two leading couples, similarly distinct. They are smartly dressed by Rouben Ter-Arutunian in dashing green-and-white costumes (which swear at the blue flanking columns unhappily inherited from *Ballet Imperial*), and Balanchine gives them dashing things to do. He is one of the three choreographers of our day—and the most masterly of them—who command what I called the grammar and geometry of the language that Petipa perfected. On occasion, in *Cortège*, he quotes Petipa verbatim; mainly, he creates his own compositions in that elegant, exacting, and precise tongue. Its rules are strict, but within them there is limitless opportunity for individual utterance, achieved by new combinations of timing and texture, accent and placing. One can, of course, bend, amend, and break those rules to achieve a new vocabulary and syntax for a new work—as Balanchine has often done. His works are so satisfying partly because implicit in each is a code that sets bounds to what movement is possible, and what would be uncouth. In *Cortège* he composes purely, and perfectly, within the canon of Maryinsky academic-cum-national steps. The final Apothéose centers on Miss Hayden, ringed by the company and applauded for all she has achieved.

The City Ballet's other new work is *An Evening's Waltzes*, by Jerome Robbins, set to five of the six numbers (lifted from *Cinderella*, *War and Peace*, and the score to the film *Lermontov*) that make up Prokofiev's Suite of Waltzes, opus

110. An elegant wisp of a set by Mr Ter-Arutunian. A swirl of light, attractive costumes in very subtle shades. Three solo couples and sixteen other dancers. Waltzes neither noble nor sentimental. No more than a fleeting hint, on occasion, of that sense of doom which flecked the revelry by night in both Balanchine's and Ashton's *La Valse*. Rather, a distillation, in fluent, arresting imagery, of diverse three-four movements and the diverse three-four emotions that go with them. "Seductive Waltz! . . . Voluptuous Waltz!" as Byron wrote, and also a rather sneaky, sinister waltz danced to "diabolic" strains from *Lermontov*. Everything cunningly understated, so that we seem to be looking on at a series of waltz dreams. As nearly always, Mr Robbins's work leaves me with mixed feelings: ready, unstinted admiration for the skill, the mastery, with which it is all done, but also a disquieting suspicion, difficult to define, that there is something slick and a shade opportunist about it.

After much exposure, this season, to modern dance in close, uncomfortable Village quarters, accompanied by music emerging from loud-speakers with varying degrees of distortion, it was a pleasure to watch the work of the Juilliard Dance Ensemble show to advantage in the well-equipped Juilliard Theatre, accompanied "live" by excellent players. I did not see all the program. Kazuko Hirabayashi's *Black Angels* is set to George Crumb's score of the same title, for amplified string quartet—which is music so arresting and was (by Martin Foster, Laurie Carney, Robert Becker, and Daven Jenkins) so arrestingly played that it was hard to give due attention to Miss Hirabayashi's elaborate, proliferous inventions. Many choreographers have been drawn to Crumb, and it is easy to hear why, for his "gestures" are graphic and rich in emotional evocation. Miss Hirabayashi's dances—skillful, shapely compilations, for a large ensemble, of what might be termed academic-modern movement—had plenty of atmosphere but not the terse economy or singularity of the score. In this piece and in Daniel Lewis's *Irving the Terrific*—an elaborate production number built around a small central idea—the Juilliard dancers appeared to be excellently trained, assured, and fluent modern movers.

Squatting on the floor of the American Theatre Laboratory listening to canned Mendelssohn and watching Lar Lubovitch's *Clear Lake* at very close range, I wondered what impression this "scattered fantasy" might make when provided with décor, costumes, and a pleasing musical accompaniment. Proximity threw all attention on the quality of the movement—and, frankly, I found it hard to understand from that why Mr Lubovitch's work has drawn so much notice. There were nice feelings perceptible in *Clear Lake*, which seems to explore emotional bonds that sprang up between the members of the company while they lived, one summer, beside a New England lake. The piece has a fresh, honest tone to it. But the choreography is neither polished nor interestingly rough. It looked rather amateurish. Mr Lubovitch's *Joy of Man's Desiring* is a set of dances laboriously set, phrase by phrase, to a Bach anthology, and made more than mildly interesting only by the tense lyricism of Jeanne Solan's performance in the Air from the Third Suite. And the first part of *Scherzo for Massah Jack* (the work that Mr Lubovitch wrote this season for the American Ballet Theatre), reduced here to pure dance, amounted to little.

The happiest "studio hours" of the season were those I spent in Merce Cunningham's spacious, airy, and very agreeable Westbeth studio, attending both the open rehearsals for his Dance Company's Brooklyn season and the studio "events" in their own right. Mr Cunningham deserves a whole essay. Since there is not room for that, let me at least record that he has been composing with a beauty and a precision of line and form that surpass anything he has done before. New York, they often tell us, is the dance capital of the world. Sometimes, in the field of modern dance, it seems more like a high-heaped junk yard of good intentions and rude execution—until something like this comes along. No need here of décor, costumes, or music. Indeed, I enjoyed Mr Cunningham's pure, warm, personal, nobly danced plastic poems in the unadorned bareness of the studio even more intensely than when they were decked with sound and settings in the Brooklyn Academy of Music.

This is also the time when the music schools give their end-of-year concerts. One at the Manhattan School was dull: no bright new minds among the composers represented by their graduation compositions—only competence in orchestral handling, and able playing from the student orchestra under student conductors. Juilliard students, under Richard Dufallo, gave a rewarding concert that included shiny, dapper, alert performances of works by Hall Overton, Gunther Schuller, Yannis Xenakis, and Luciano Berio, and ended with the sexiest piece of music I have ever heard. Heard and seen, I should say, since Jacob Druckman's *Animus II* is a piece of music theater enacted through the hall while it is sung and played by mezzo-soprano and two percussionists. (There is a CRI recording, with Jan DeGaetani in the lead, but a record can capture only part of the experience.) The singer leads, lures, stimulates, cajoles the two instrumentalists, who respond to her siren song with trembling, quivering, pattering, shimmering, excitable eruptions of fierce or flickering sound and sometimes a low vocal moan of desire. At one point, the two attack the vast gong and the palisade of tubular chimes that bar their way to her while she teases them from beyond it.

Electronic music adds its provocative commentary on the progress of the drama. Mr Druckman calls the piece "the celebration of a sybaritic ritual." Perhaps it is all rather shameless; it is also delicately and subtly constructed in its musical and dramaturgical incidents. And, lustrously, voluptuously, wittily performed by Barbara Martin, with Barry Jekowsky and Joseph Kuhn as her rapt accompanists, it proved immensely exciting.

June 9, 1973

George Crumb's Black Angels *is recorded on Nonesuch H 71255. The recording of Jacob Druckman's* Animus II *is CRI S 255.*

Index

Passing references to people or works not directly under review have generally not been indexed. Compositions appear under their composers but titles are included only when there is some extended discussion of the pieces in question, or in order to distinguish between several page references. Performing organizations outside New York are entered with the place name first (e.g. "Boston, Opera Company of"). Halls and theatres are indexed only when there is some comment on their acoustics or appearance.